OUR RICHES
IN CHRIST

OUR RICHES
IN CHRIST

Discovering *the* Believer's Inheritance *in* Ephesians

RAY C. STEDMAN

DISCOVERY HOUSE
PUBLISHERS®

Our Riches in Christ:
Discovering the Believer's Inheritance in Ephesians
Copyright © 1998 by Elaine Stedman
All rights reserved.

Discovery House Publishers is affiliated with RBC Ministries,
Grand Rapids, Michigan.

Requests for permission to quote from this book should
be directed to: Permissions Department, Discovery House
Publishers, P.O. Box 3566, Grand Rapids, MI 49501, or contact
us by e-mail at permissionsdept@dhp.org

Library of Congress Cataloging-in-Publication Data
Stedman, Ray C.
   Our riches in Christ : discovering the believer's inheritance
in Ephesians / by Ray C. Stedman with James D. Denney.
    p. cm.

ISBN 1-57293-033-0

1. Bible. N.T. Ephesians—Commentaries. I. Denney, James
D. II. Bible. N.T. Ephesians. English. New International.
1998. III. Title.
BS2695.3.S65   1998   227'.5077—dc21   98-7250
                                      CIP

Printed in the United States of America
Sixth printing in 2012

Contents

PART TWO: THE MINISTRY OF THE SAINTS

Ephesians 4:1–16

Introduction

The book of Ephesians has changed my life again and again.

In fact, of all of Paul's writings, the two letters that have affected me most profoundly are Romans and Ephesians. Both set forth a clear, concise explanation of the entire Christian view of life and the world. While Paul's other letters deal with specific situations and problems, Romans and Ephesians deal with the panoramic sweep of God's truth.

How has Ephesians changed my life? In several ways:

This letter taught me to recognize and combat the spiritual attacks of the enemy so that I could effectively deal with doubt, temptation, fear, anxiety, and depression. Ephesians is the believer's guidebook to spiritual, mental, and emotional wellbeing.

As a young man, I learned from Ephesians how to handle the sex drive God had given me and how to live an upright life in a sex-saturated society. America today is amazingly similar to Ephesian society in Paul's day—both are highly immoral and sex-obsessed cultures. Both then and now, it is a difficult challenge to stand for Christ and for Christian morality. But this practical letter teaches us how to come to grips with life as it is.

Ephesians taught me profound truths about marriage and family life. I can't imagine any married man or woman trying to live out God's ideal for marriage without being immersed in Paul's letter to the Ephesians.

Ephesians taught me how the body of Christ functions. The truth of Ephesians 4 blazed in my heart when I was a young pastor-in-the-making, fresh out of seminary. I began to pastor a small group of people meeting together in Palo Alto, California, and I was convinced that ministry is the function of *all* believers, not just the so-called "minister." The pastor's function, I believed, was to help people find their ministries and to prepare them to exercise their spiritual gifts. Ephesians 4 was our foundation during those formative days at the beginning of Peninsula Bible Church—and it remained so throughout my years there.

As you begin your study in Ephesians, I hope you are eager and excited about the tremendous truth that is so densely packed into this letter by the apostle Paul. I would encourage you to take at least an entire month to live in Ephesians, immerse yourself in it, revel in its sparkling riches. I suggest that as you read this commentary, you also take time to read the letter to the Ephesians from start to finish at least once a week.

The first week, clear a couple hours on Sunday afternoon and read the entire letter in a single sitting. The next week, read a chapter a day for six days. After that, read Ephesians in two or more contemporary paraphrases or translations, such as the J. B. Phillips version or Eugene Peterson's *The Message.* Let the truth of Paul's letter come to you afresh in a new way. I guarantee that if you will faithfully, daily bathe your thoughts and emotions in this powerful, practical letter to Christians, you will never be the same again!

One thing you are sure to notice is that this letter builds toward a crescendo in chapter 6, where Paul deals with spiritual warfare—the struggle between good and evil, between the prince of peace and the prince of darkness, a battle that stretches from one end of history to the other, a battle that rages across the planet and within every human heart. Since it is a battle none of us can escape, we should make sure we are on the winning side! In Ephesians, we learn how to be effective soldiers under our Lord and commander, Jesus Christ—and we learn the secret of ultimate victory in this epic struggle.

So come explore with me. Come search for riches beyond your wildest dreams and discover adventure and glory beyond anything else this world has to offer. Turn the page—and set foot on the pathway to courageous, confident, victorious Christian living.

PART ONE

Our Riches in Christ

Ephesians 1–3

CHAPTER ONE

God at Work

Ephesians 1:1–2

Billy Graham tells a true story told him by a pastor he met in Glasgow, Scotland. There was a woman in this pastor's parish who was in financial difficulty and behind in her rent. So the pastor took up a collection for this poor woman at church, then went to her home to give her the money. He knocked and knocked at the door, but there was no answer. Finally, he went away.

The next day he encountered the poor woman at the market. "Why, Mrs. Green," he said, "I stopped by your house yesterday, and I was disappointed that there was no answer."

The woman's eyes widened as she said, "Oh, was that you? I thought it was the landlord and I was afraid to open the door!"

The riches of God have been made available to us in Christ, yet most of us shrink back from receiving all that God eagerly wishes to place in our hands. The riches of God cannot help us until we open the door of our hearts, until we open the pages of Ephesians, and reach out with both hands to receive from Him. The first three chapters of Ephesians reveal to us the riches of God in Christ and tell us how to lay hold of those riches for our lives.

PAUL'S CIRCULAR LETTER

This letter was written about A.D. 61 from Rome during Paul's first imprisonment there. The recipients of the letter were the Christians in the Roman province of Asia (which is Turkey in the modern world). While this letter is commonly called the Epistle to the Ephesians, many ancient manuscripts do not mention any specific city as the destination of the letter. Many scholars believe this is a "circular letter," intended to be circulated among many churches in the region around Ephesus.

Some Bible scholars suggest that it may have been addressed to the very churches addressed by the Lord at the beginning of Revelation, beginning with Ephesus and ending with Laodicea. In his letter to the Colossians, Paul writes, "After this letter has been read to you, see that it is also read in the church of the Laodiceans and that you in turn read the letter from Laodicea" (Colossians 4:16). Some Bible scholars believe the letter from Laodicea to be this letter to the Ephesians.

The letter to the Ephesians was dictated by Paul to Tychicus and hand-delivered by Tychicus. It may well be that it was circulated from church to church and read in each one, and that it finally ended up in Ephesus where it was labeled, "The Letter of Paul to the Ephesians." As Paul says in his concluding footnote, this letter is truly addressed to all Christians everywhere. Ephesians 1:1–2 begins:

> Paul, an apostle of Christ Jesus by the will of God, To the saints in Ephesus, the faithful in Christ Jesus: Grace and peace to you from God our Father and the Lord Jesus Christ.

That is the briefest salutation in any of Paul's letters, composed of three components:

1. Paul's credentials. Paul describes himself as "an apostle . . . by the will of God." An apostle was a messenger from God, a spokesman for God. Paul gloried in the fact that he was an apostle of Jesus Christ. As he tells us in Galatians 1:11–16, the Lord Jesus appeared to him directly. Paul did not learn what he knew about the gospel by discussing it with the other apostles, but by receiving it directly from Jesus Christ. That is his authority. So when you read Paul, you are reading an authorized spokesman for the Lord Jesus.

Notice that Paul offers no other credentials. He doesn't refer to his elite training at the feet of Gamaliel nor to his privileged Hebrew background (see Acts 22:3 and Phil. 3:4–6). He simply says, in effect, "I'm an apostle by the will of God. That is the foundation for everything I say in this letter."

2. An affirmation of the saints. Paul describes these Christians as "the saints . . . the faithful in Christ Jesus." That word *saints* makes us shudder a little, doesn't it? We don't like to be called "saints" because we have such a plaster-icon image of what a saint is. We think of "saints" as being unreal—so beatific, so holier-than-we, so unlike ordinary human beings. But the saints of the New Testament are not that way. They are people like us. Saints are people who struggle with problems in their families, problems at work, even emotional and spiritual problems. They're normal people like you and me.

But one thing is remarkable about them: They are *different* in that they are set apart for God. That is what *saint* means: someone who is set apart. In the Greek, the word for "saint" comes from the word for "holy." And *holy* means distinct, different, whole, set apart for God. A saint is just like other people, except that he or she is expected to live differently—to live for God. That is the mark of the saint. He has problems like everyone else, but he approaches them differently. He has a different lifestyle. That is what Paul is talking about here.

The essential characteristic of a saint is *faithfulness*—saints don't quit. They just can't quit being Christians! A young man once called me in his discouragement, telling me he had lost his confidence in prayer because he felt no answer was coming. "I feel like quitting," he said. I replied, "Well, why don't you quit, then? Just stop being a Christian." Surprised, he said, "But I *can't* quit!" And I said, "That's right, you can't quit. You're a saint, and saints don't quit." Christians—saints—are sealed by the Holy Spirit, so we can't quit! The Holy Spirit keeps us faithful to God. That faithfulness is the mark of a believer in Christ.

3. A greeting of grace and peace. Then comes the invariable greeting of Paul to the believers: "Grace and peace to you from God our Father and the Lord Jesus Christ." The two great heritages of the Christian are grace and peace. These are two things you can always have, no matter what your circumstances.

Grace is all God's power and all His love and all His favor made available to you. The Greek word for "grace" comes from the same root word from which we get our English word *charm*. Grace is charming, lovely, and pleasant.

Peace is freedom from anxiety, fear, and worry. Together, these two characteristics should mark the life of every Christian, all the time. Grace is the sign that God is at work in our lives. Peace is the sense of security and trust in God.

A man once said to me, "I've learned something new about trust. Trust is not knowing—yet still being at rest and at peace." That's true. A baby doesn't need to know how Mom and Dad are going to pay the mortgage and buy the food and meet all the bills. A baby simply trusts her needs will be met without knowing all the whys and wherefores. A baby simply trusts that Mom and Dad have matters under control. If you have to know everything, you aren't trusting. Trust is not knowing, and still being at peace.

THE BLESSINGS OF GOD

Following the salutation, the letter follows the usual structure of Paul's letters. First comes doctrine—the great spiritual principles that God wants to set before us. Next comes the practical application, the working out of those principles in the trenches of our daily lives. The practical application is our everyday response to the fundamental spiritual principles of the doctrines of God.

Many people think of doctrine as just as much theological double-talk. No! Doctrine is truth, it is reality. The doctrinal section of Ephesians is not merely academic theory—it is truth that we are to base our lives and our everyday actions on. That is why Paul always starts his letters by setting forth the radical facts of life—God's doctrines—exactly as he has received them from Jesus Christ.

Paul begins with a great doctrinal statement that gathers up the great themes of Ephesians. He will return to this theme again and again in Ephesians: The theme of blessing.

> Praise be the God and Father of our Lord Jesus Christ, who has blessed us in the heavenly realms with every spiritual blessing in Christ.

This is Paul's summary of the themes of Ephesians, and there are four elements in this summary in Ephesians 1:3 that we will explore in the rest of this chapter:

1. The One who is the source of all blessing.
2. The aim of God's blessing.
3. All blessing is "in Christ."
4. The place of all blessing is in "the heavenly realms."

Let's look at each of these four elements in turn.

1. The One who is the source of all blessing. Paul begins in Ephesians 1:3 with the One who is behind all blessing, the God and Father of our Lord Jesus Christ. That is his starting point. Is that your starting point and mine? Our problem, all too often, is that we don't start our thinking with God. Instead we tend to start with ourselves and our experience, which is only a partial view of truth. We narrow the range of our vision to what we are going through and what is happening to us, and we don't see this in relationship to the entire span of reality around us. So we end up with a distorted idea of what God is doing in the world.

The only way to view truth and understand truth is to start with God. Only He is great enough to encompass all truth.

That's the difference between what the Bible calls "natural" thinking of "the natural man" versus the "spiritual" thinking of "the spiritual man." Natural thinking is limited and myopic. Spiritual thinking is God-centered, expansive, and eternal. We need to learn to be spiritual thinkers about ourselves and about life. We need to begin where Paul begins: with God, the Source of all blessing.

2. The aim of God's blessing. The second element in Ephesians 1:3 is the aim of the work of God. Paul says God "has blessed us in the heavenly realms with every spiritual blessing." That is what God intends to do. His goal is to bring about a world, a universe, filled with blessing. Throughout Ephesians we find that everything occurs "to the praise of God's glory"—that is, in order that God be praised. He wants His people to be so struck by the wonder of what has happened to them that their hearts will automatically reflect praise, glory, and blessing back to God.

This is not because God needs his ego to be massaged. Rather, praise and glory to God is simply a natural consequence arising from the true nature of God's awesome power, character, and deeds—once the true, shining reality of God breaks through upon our dull intellects! Once we truly, accurately see the blessing of God upon our lives, what can we do but stand in abject awe and amazement, saying, "My God, how great Thou art!"

That is what God is after—a sense of awe and amazement that mirrors the reality of His greatness, and that causes us to stop and give thanks and praise to the great and glorious God who has given us every spiritual blessing. Paul goes on to list these spiritual blessings for us. First:

> For he chose us in him before the creation of the world to
> be holy and blameless in his sight (1:4).

That is blessing number one. It goes back before the beginning of time, before the foundation of the universe: He chose us even before the world existed to be His holy children. The second spiritual blessing:

> In love he predestined us to be adopted as his sons through
> Jesus Christ, in accordance with his pleasure and will—to
> the praise of his glorious grace, which he has freely given
> us in the One he loves (1:5–6).

21

What an immense, awe-inspiring blessing that is—to be members of the family of God, partakers of His divine nature! Third spiritual blessing:

> In him we have redemption through his blood, the forgiveness of sins, in accordance with the riches of God's grace that he lavished on us with all wisdom and understanding (1:7–8).

Think of it! All our guilt is removed, utterly gone—an incalculable blessing from God. The fourth spiritual blessing:

> And he made known to us the mystery of his will according to his good pleasure, which he purposed in Christ to be put into effect when the times will have reached their fulfillment—to bring all things in heaven and on earth together under one head, even Christ (1:9–10).

We have been taken into the secret councils of the Almighty. He has unfolded to us what he plans to do, what he is going to accomplish in the future. Fifth spiritual blessing:

> In him we were also chosen, having been predestined according to the plan of him who works out everything in conformity with the purpose of his will, in order that we, who were the first to hope in Christ, might be for the praise of his glory (1:11–12).

God has appointed us to demonstrate His great truths, and to live our lives so that He might receive praise and glory. Sixth spiritual blessing:

> And you also were included in Christ when you heard the
> word of truth, the gospel of your salvation (1:13).

God has blessed us with His truth, the straight scoop on all real-ity—and when we heard His truth and responded by turning our lives over to Him, we were included in Christ and His salvation. Seventh and final spiritual blessing:

> Having believed, you were marked in him with a seal, the
> promised Holy Spirit, who is a deposit guaranteeing our
> inheritance until the redemption of those who are God's
> possession—to the praise of his glory (1:14).

These blessings make life worth living. Without them, life is deso-late, dull, and ultimately unbearable. We cannot produce these bless-ings on our own; we can only receive them from God. These are the blessings, the gifts of God.

3. All blessing is "in Christ." The third element of Ephesians 1:3 is that the apostle points out that all of this blessing is "in Christ." All this comes to us in Christ—in the Person and work of the Lord Jesus himself. This fact is stressed again and again throughout the letter to the Ephesians. No two words appear in it more frequently than "in Christ," or "in him."

We cannot claim to have God's blessing in our lives without ac-knowledging the centrality of Christ in our lives. The only spiritual blessing that can ever come to you from God is that which comes in Christ. There is no other way we can receive God's spiritual blessing.

If you are involved with a group that sets aside the Lord Jesus Christ and tries to go "directly to God" to claim the great spiritual promises of the New Testament, you are being led into a realm of spiritual fraud. God only accomplishes spiritual blessing in Christ. Material blessings are available to "the righteous and the unrighteous" alike (Matthew 5:45), but the inner spirit of man can be healed and cured only in Christ. There is no other way.

4. The place of all blessing is in "the heavenly realms." Finally, notice the locale where all spiritual blessing occurs—"in the heavenly realms." Now, that doesn't mean heaven, as we usually conceive it. Paul is talking here about the *present* experience of those blessings. We are involved with the "heavenly realms" right now. These heavenly realms, which are mentioned throughout Ephesians and other passages of Scripture, are really the realm of invisible reality, of things that are real and true about life in our universe, but which we can't see or touch right now.

The heavenly realms are intensely real, and they play an important part in our lives right now. This is what Paul refers to in another letter: "So we fix our eyes not on what is seen, but on what is unseen. For what is seen is temporary, but what is unseen is eternal" (2 Corinthians 4:18).

We see a powerful illustration of the heavenly realms in the Old Testament story of Elisha and his servant. They were in a small city, surrounded by the armies of Syria, as we read in 2 Kings 6:15–17:

> When the servant of the man of God got up and went out early the next morning, an army with horses and chariots had surrounded the city. "Oh, my lord, what shall we do?" the servant asked.
>
> "Don't be afraid," the prophet answered. "Those who are with us are more than those who are with them."

> And Elisha prayed, "O LORD, open his eyes so he may see." Then the LORD opened the servant's eyes, and he looked and saw the hills full of horses and chariots of fire all around Elisha.

If only we could see the horses and chariots of fire who are arrayed about us, and the angels God has placed in charge of our circumstances. The real spiritual battle takes place there, in the heavenly realms—not somewhere in the clouds or in outer space, but right here, within and around each of us. We need to ask God to open our eyes so that we may see His reality.

Paul's starting principle in this passage regarding the blessing of God is that His blessing is something that has already been accomplished. It is not a promise to be fulfilled, but a present gift to be grasped. It is not based on human activity, but on God's love and grace. God's blessing is something only God can do, something He has already done. All progress in the spiritual life comes by understanding a truth that is already true. It is available to us the moment we open our hands to receive it.

WHAT GOD IS DOING

Ours is a busy world of busy people. Our newspapers, magazines, and airwaves are filled with the latest stories of what our leaders and trendsetters are doing around the world. We easily forget that the only activity which truly, eternally affects lives, hearts, and human events is the activity of God. His activity, though profound, often goes unseen and unnoticed by the world. Yet that is where we need to focus our thoughts: on what God is doing.

It might be useful for you to take a pen and underline all the verbs of this passage. You will notice that they all refer to God, to the work

He has done: "blessed," "chose," "predestined," "has freely given," "loves," "in Him we have redemption," "He has made known to us his will," and on and on. As you go through this passage, you will see that every verb you highlight is a sign of God at work.

Man's glory shall fade. All the accomplishments of our present day will someday be little more than footnotes in some future history—if that much. Only the work of God will endure. Rudyard Kipling once wrote about the British Empire:

> Far flung, our navies melt away,
> on dune and headland sinks the fire.
> Lo, all our pomp of yesterday
> is one with Nineveh and Tyre.

The glory of Rome is a distant memory. In our own lifetime, imperial England has been eclipsed. The greatness of the Soviet Union has collapsed. America's greatness too will fade, as will the greatness of all the nations of the earth. Only what God is doing endures. If we want our lives to have eternal meaning, then we must give our attention to these great thoughts that God planned before the foundation of the world. Most of all, we must give our attention to the one Person who, in all the span of history, is able to accomplish what no other man could do, Jesus Christ.

That is what Ephesians is all about.

As we move through the rest of this great letter of the apostle Paul, given to him by inspiration from God himself, let us ask Him to remove the dimness from our vision and the dullness from our understanding, so that we can see the grand and blazing spiritual reality that is all around us in the heavenly realms in which we live from day to day. Let us ask Him to help us to think deeply and seriously about these incalculable spiritual blessings he has given us, so that our lives would better reflect the awesome reality of who God truly is and what He is doing in our world.

CHAPTER TWO

The Work and Blessings of the Father

Ephesians 1:3–6

A rich man was in the habit of giving his wife an expensive piece of jewelry every year on her birthday. One year he might phone the jeweler and say, "Send me your finest pearl necklace, along with your bill." Or, "Send me your finest diamond pendant, along with your bill." Or the finest emerald bracelet or ruby ring. Each time, the jeweler did as the rich man asked, dispatching a messenger to the rich man's mansion to deliver the jewelry piece in a box along with his bill.

But every year the rich man would play a game with the jeweler. He would send the messenger back to the jeweler along with the original box, a note, and a check. The check was always written in the amount of several thousand dollars less than the price of the jeweler's bill. The note would say, "Sir, I like the jewelry piece, but I do not like the price. If you will accept the enclosed check for a reduced amount, then please return the jewelry box with the seal unbroken."

For years the jeweler put up with the rich man's game, accepting the reduced check, and returning the box with the seal unbroken. He still made a profit on the jewelry, even if it was a lower profit than he liked—and at least he was able to keep the rich man's trade year after year. In time, however, the jeweler began to tire of this charade.

Finally the day came when the rich man placed an order for a lavish diamond necklace, and the jeweler decided he would not get clipped again. As usual, the jeweler sent the necklace in a box, along with his bill. Again, as usual, the box was returned with a reduced check for payment and a note.

Enough was enough! The jeweler refused the check, kept the box, and sent the messenger away in disgust. When he opened the box to reclaim the necklace, he found that the necklace had been removed. In its place was a check for the entire amount of the jeweler's bill.

For years, the rich man had been sending the entire asking price of each jewelry piece—hidden inside the sealed jewelry box. In all that time, the jeweler had accepted thousands of dollars less than he could have received—because he didn't open the box and look inside.

The hidden riches of Christ are available to you and me—but to find them, we have to open the letter of Ephesians. It is here, in this letter, that we find the description of the riches we have in Jesus Christ.

Paul speaks passionately and extensively about these riches—and with good reason. Having traveled throughout the Roman empire, he had seen the spiritual and material poverty of the Roman world. He had spoken to rulers, soldiers, business leaders, merchants, laborers, farmers, and slaves. He saw that all of them, regardless of material wealth or status, suffered from the same spiritual deprivation. All were depressed, discouraged, beset with fears and anxieties, jealousies and hostilities. They were under the grip of superstition and filled with the dread of the future. They had no hope of life beyond death.

Paul's great joy and mission in life was to unfold to us the riches available to us in Jesus Christ—riches which liberate and transform us, bringing us into a new experience of joy, love, and radiant faith. He gloried in the vast riches of God in Jesus Christ.

THE STRUCTURE OF EPHESIANS 1

In the previous chapter, we examined the summary statement with which Paul gathers up the great themes of this letter, Ephesians 1:3:

> Praise be to the God and Father of our Lord Jesus Christ, who has blessed us in the heavenly realms with every spiritual blessing in Christ.

There is an unusual sentence structure in this passage which is apparent in the original Greek New Testament, but which cannot be seen in the English translation. Verses 3 through 14 were actually composed as a single unbroken sentence filled with many adjectives to amplify and enrich our understanding of God's blessings in Christ. If you want to get the full effect of it, take a deep breath and read those verses together without pausing. You'll gain a real appreciation for just how much meaning Paul crams into that one great sentence!

It is easy to imagine that Paul is dressed in khakis and pith helmet, looking like Indiana Jones, taking us on a guided tour through a treasure chamber like those of the Egyptian Pharaohs, describing what he sees. He starts out describing the most immediate and evident facts—then something else comes into view and he shines his lantern on it. Then comes some new glorious object or artifact, and glory flashes upon glory until he has compiled a dazzlingly complex sentence describing the vast and nearly indescribable riches of the chamber.

That is how Paul shows us that all of God's truth is interwoven and interconnected—you can never touch upon one great theme without finding that it leads to others, and that those lead to still others. All of God's truth is like that—His spiritual truth, and also His truth in nature. You can't study one subject in nature without touching upon a great many others.

But though these verses are presented to us in a single complex sentence, there is actually a very natural, simple division within Ephesians 1:3–14. It divides into three parts around the three Persons of the Trinity, because that is how the spiritual blessings are divided. These blessings gather about the three Persons of the Trinity—the work of the Father, the work of the Son, and the work of the Holy Spirit. In verses 3 through 6 you have the work and blessings of the Father:

> Praise be to the God and Father of our Lord Jesus Christ, who has blessed us in the heavenly realms with every spiritual blessing in Christ. For he chose us in him before the creation of the world to be holy and blameless in his sight. In love he predestined us to be adopted as his sons through Jesus Christ, in accordance with his pleasure and will—to the praise of his glorious grace, which he has freely given us in the One he loves.

Then, in verses 7 through 12, you have the work and blessings of the Son. Notice the rich and exalted language Paul uses to describe the Son and our relationship to Him:

> In him we have redemption through his blood, the forgiveness of sins, in accordance with the riches of God's grace that he lavished on us with all wisdom and understanding. And he made known to us the mystery of his

will according to his good pleasure, which he purposed in Christ, to be put into effect when the times will have reached their fulfillment—to bring all things in heaven and on earth together under one head, even Christ. In him we were also chosen, having been predestined according to the plan of him who works out everything in conformity with the purpose of his will, in order that we, who were the first to hope in Christ, might be for the praise of his glory.

Then in verses 13 and 14, you have the work and blessings of the Holy Spirit:

And you also were included in Christ when you heard the word of truth, the gospel of your salvation. Having believed, you were marked in him with a seal, the promised Holy Spirit, who is a deposit guaranteeing our inheritance until the redemption of those who are God's possession—to the praise of his glory.

All of these blessings take place, remember, not in some future time and place, not in the afterlife, but in the here and now, in an unseen but utterly real dimension that Paul calls "the heavenly realms"—the invisible realities of our lives today. Yes, "the heavenly realms" do extend on into eternity—but this dimension of life is also something to be experienced now, in our daily lives.

That is what Paul is talking about—your thought-life, your attitudes, your inner life, your behavior—the place where you experience conflict, pressure, struggle, temptation, disaster, and triumph. It is the place where we are exposed to the attack of the principalities and powers mentioned later, in Ephesians 6—those dark spirits in high places who get to us, depress us, frighten us, and fill us with dread, anxiety, rage, and hostility. "The heavenly realms" are a place of conflict—but also a place where God can release us and deliver us, where the Spirit of God touches us at the seat of our intellect, emotions, and will.

These principles are not mere doctrinal or theological ambiguities, they are the rock-solid foundational truths that sustain us through every moment and every trial of the Christian life. They are as reliable as the laws of nature, and they function regardless of how we feel.

Once, while I was doing some amateur electrical repairs in my home, I discovered that electricity follows a pattern of its own and takes no notice of how I feel at the moment. While I understood this fact in theory, it was quite a shocking experience to encounter this fact experientially. The electrical current I came in contact with was not in the slightest degree impressed with my position as a Bible teacher, pastor, or author. When I closed the electric circuit with my own body, that current didn't hesitate to flow through me as if I were an insulated copper wire.

Spiritual principles operate with the same impartiality as electrical principles. We respect spiritual truth to our own benefit, and we violate it at our own risk. Spiritual principles are not respecters of persons. For our own good, we must come to understand spiritual truth, respect it, and align our lives according to its principles.

THE WORK OF THE FATHER

In the rest of this chapter and the two chapters that follow, we will take a closer look at the three natural divisions of Ephesians 1:3–14, the work and blessing of the three Persons of the Trinity. We will begin in this chapter with the work and blessings of the Father, and examine the work and blessings of the Son and the Holy Spirit in the next two chapters.

Look at the first statement:

> For he chose us in him before the creation of the world to
> be holy and blameless in his sight. (1:4).

This is an expression of what theologians call "the doctrine of election," or predestination—the fact that God chose us to be in Christ even before the creation of time and space. If you try to encompass that truth with your finite mind, you will experience a mental overload! It is an astounding truth, and we struggle with it, we question it, and I would submit to you that we really don't believe it, because so often our actions just don't show it. We wonder, "How could God choose us, and yet still offer a choice that we must make?" We struggle over the seeming conflict between our human free will and the sovereign election of God.

Many try to explain away this paradox. "Well," they say, "God can foresee the future, so He looks ahead in time, sees we are going to make a choice, and 'elects' us on the basis of a decision He knows we will someday make." But that is not what the Scriptures say. Others say, "Well, God sees what kind of people we will be, and recognizing our value to His plan, He chooses us on that basis." Nothing could be more unscriptural. God doesn't need our help to carry out His eternal plan. To think that we, by our own effort, can make ourselves useful to God is pure human arrogance. We can accomplish nothing for God apart from His choosing, empowering, and will.

As hard as it is for us to understand and accept, the fact is that we are chosen by God. Jesus said so himself: "No one can come to me unless the Father who sent me draws him" (John 6:44). That's putting it plainly, isn't it? You can't come to Christ unless you are drawn by the Father. God has to initiate the activity.

Then why does God appeal to our individual human will? For in Matthew 11:28, we also read, "Come to me, all you who are weary and burdened, and I will give you rest." That means it's up to us as individuals to make a choice. You cannot become a Christian until you choose to come—yet it is equally true that you cannot become a Christian unless God has chosen you. Both facts are true. We can't reconcile them in our puny intellects, but we can accept them by faith.

Think of it: Before the creation of the world—uncounted millions and billions and trillions of years in the past—God chose you to belong to Him. Let that sink into your mind for a moment! Drop to your knees in awe and humility before this loving eternal Being who is not confined by past or future, by years of time or light-years of space; who knows the future as certainly as He knows the past; who determines all things by the counsel of His will.

Do you see how this fact elevates your identity as a child of God? We are not afterthoughts in God's plan. There are no second-class citizens in the body of Christ. We are all chosen of the Father, selected as members of His forever family. He has chosen us to be holy and blameless. These truths are so revolutionary we are *afraid* to believe them! We can scarcely believe that these truths literally apply to us!

The reason we find it hard to believe is that our understanding of the word *holiness* is so distorted. We think holiness is sanctimoniousness, when the truth is that *holiness* actually means "wholeness"— being restored to the useful function for which we were originally created. Physical wholeness prevails when the body works the way it was intended to work, and spiritual wholeness results when our entire being functions as God designed it to function. When we are spiritually whole, we are holy.

And what does it mean to be "blameless" before God? It doesn't mean to be sinless, because (as Romans 3:23 tells us) *all* have sinned. But thanks be to God, though we are sinful, we can still be blameless. While it is not in our power to go back in time and undo the sins we have done, we can still accept the righteousness of Jesus and the forgiveness of the Father as a covering and cleansing for our sin. When God lifts the blame and shame of sin from us, we become blameless.

Verse 5 records a second great aspect of the work of the Father, which is related to the first:

> He predestined us to be adopted as his sons through Jesus Christ . . . .

Here is a partial explanation of how God takes care of all the past failures and the shame of our lives, to produce a Christian who is holy and blameless for His use. God accomplishes this change in us by means of a new family relationship. He destined us to be sons, to be adopted as His own children.

Adoption means leaving one family and joining another, leaving behind all that was involved in the first family and assuming the name, identity, resources, and history of another. This is how Paul describes this new relationship. We all were born to the family of Adam. We have left that family to belong to a new family, the family of Jesus Christ. That doesn't mean that we are not human; it means that we are no longer identified with the sinfulness of Adam. Though we are human and subject to the temptations of Adam's race, we are no longer enslaved by death and sin. We've been transferred into a new family, and we have received a new identity.

As adopted sons of the living God, we have the only begotten Son of God as our forerunner and example. We learn how to live from

Him—and we are to copy His life. Our aim is to live exactly as Jesus lived. We are to derive our way of life from Jesus, just as Jesus derived His life from the Father. In John 6:57, He said, "Just as the living Father sent me and I live because of the Father, so the one who feeds on me will live because of me." God the Father was His resource, wisdom, strength, and power. Everything Jesus did was in reality the life of God the Father being lived out through the Son. In the same way, we are to derive our life from Christ, to become a channel through which God can work. As adopted children of the Father, we are to share the life of God's only begotten Son. That is what pleases the Father.

IT'S ALL GOD

The rest of verse 5 and verse 6 tell us why the infinite God of the universe should stoop to choose weak, failure-prone, sin-ridden creatures like you and me as part of his ultimate plan:

> . . . in accordance with his pleasure and will—to the praise of his glorious grace, which he has freely given us in the One he loves.

That really makes it clear that we have no reason to feel important because we have been chosen by God. On the contrary—we are humbled by the truth. There is not anything in us that God needs to fulfill His plan. His choice is based not on our intrinsic merit, but on the kind of God He truly is. He chose us for adoption as His sons for two reasons:

> Reason 1: "In accordance with his pleasure and will."
> Reason 2: "To the praise of his glorious grace."

It is all God. None of it is us. It begins with God's pleasure and will. It gives him pleasure to save us for his use. And the final result of his choice is praise—all the universe responds with joy, praising God throughout creation.

The final phrase of verse 6 introduces the next theme—the work of the Son. Here Paul speaks of the grace, "which [God the Father] has freely given us in the One he loves," Jesus Christ. God "engraced" us (that is a good rendering of the original Greek); He poured out His grace upon us in Christ. Jesus was sent to us by the Father. That is the mark of His love. Jesus came to be poor, to be misunderstood, opposed, and hated, to be spat upon, beaten, and crucified—and why?

So that we might be rich!

Remember how Paul put it in 2 Corinthians 8:9: "For you know the grace of our Lord Jesus Christ, that though he was rich, yet for your sakes he became poor, so that you through his poverty might become rich." So my question to you is: Are you enjoying your inheritance?

Every morning, when the sunlight opens our eyes, our first thought should be, "I'm a child of the Father! I've been chosen by Him to be a member of His family! His peace, His joy, and His love are my legacy, my inheritance—and I can draw upon his riches every moment of every day, no matter what my circumstances may be." The letter to the Ephesians ought to be a treasure store to which we go whenever we feel discouraged.

I once read of an old Navajo Indian who became rich when oil was found on his property. He took all the money and put it in a bank. His banker became familiar with the habits of this old gentleman. Every so often, the Indian would show up at the bank and say to the banker, "Grass all gone, sheep all sick, water holes all dry." Without a word, the banker would take the old Indian into the vault, show him several bags of silver dollars, and say, "All this is yours." The old man would spend about an hour stacking up the dollars and counting them. Then he'd return the bags to their places, come out of the vault, and say "Grass all green, sheep all well, water holes all full."

It is amazing the change that comes over us when we simply review our resources and count our blessings. That is where true encouragement is found—in an honest accounting of the Father's limitless resources and blessings, made available to us in Christ.

CHAPTER THREE

The Work and Blessings of the Son

Ephesians 1:7–12

When I was a student at Dallas Theological Seminary, I spent my summers working at the Lincoln Avenue Presbyterian Church in Pasadena. My wife, Elaine, and I would drive to California at the end of the school year very short of cash, and it took all our pitiful savings just to buy gasoline for the trip. We slept in the car and arrived flat broke and hungry, having skipped the last few meals. There would be a week, sometimes two, until I received my first check, so I had to pawn something to make ends meet.

The only thing of pawnable value in my possession was my typewriter. So the first thing I did when I arrived in Pasadena was to hock my typewriter. The pawnbroker and I got very well acquainted over those summers. We would live on the money I got from pawning my typewriter, and when my first check came, I would redeem my typewriter from the pawn shop. During the time my typewriter was in hock, it was useless to anyone. I couldn't use it, the pawnbroker had no right to use it, nor could he sell it to anyone else. Only when it was redeemed could it be put to its proper use.

As we are about to see, this is the word-picture Paul uses to describe the work of Jesus the Son: He has redeemed us from being "in hock" or in bondage to sin. Have you ever thought of yourself that way? In your natural human condition, you were useless to God—unfit for the purpose He created you for. Only when you were redeemed could you achieve your true God-given purpose.

Redemption is the work and blessing of the Son. In verses 7 and 8, we see how the Son of God, the second Person of the Trinity, accomplishes what the Father has willed and decided. The act of deciding was the Father's; the act of accomplishing the Father's decision is the act of the Son:

> In him we have redemption through his blood, the forgiveness of sins, in accordance with the riches of God's grace that he lavished on us with all wisdom and understanding.

The key word in this section is *redemption*. Unfortunately, that term has largely lost its original meaning. It sounds vaguely theological to modern ears, but it is not a term we use much. Unless we visit a pawnbroker or use coupons regularly, few of us know what it means to redeem something. So I want to substitute a more common synonym in place of *redemption*. That word is *liberation*. In Christ the Son, we have liberation through His blood, and the forgiveness of sins. That is the work of the Son. That is the truth the apostle Paul wishes to bring home to us.

The picture the word *redemption* suggested to the original hearers of Paul's letter to the Ephesians was that of a slave market—a common sight in the Roman world. Human beings were offered as merchandise for sale. In Paul's imagery, we were bound as wretched slaves in a great slave market. Jesus came, paid a price, bought us, redeemed us, and liberated us for useful service. When we were slaves in the slave market of sin, God could not use us. Once our liberty was purchased by Jesus Christ, we were free to be useful and profitable to God.

LASTING FULFILLMENT

Our relationship with Christ, then, is the source of our purpose in life. But does that mean nonChristians cannot have a purpose in life, that they cannot achieve worthwhile things? Understand that we are not talking about a sense of achievement or feelings of fulfillment in human terms. We are talking about finding God's ultimate, eternal purpose for our lives. Many human activities and achievements can give us a temporary sense of well-being and happiness, but they do not eternally satisfy. Only the work God does through us gives lasting satisfaction and has eternal value. That is what Paul is talking about.

I once taught a home Bible class in Newport Beach. The host and hostess invited their neighbor from across the street—a brilliant engineer and a tough-minded agnostic. He announced to the group that he had no need of God or religion in his life, but he came to the Bible class as, in his words, "the Devil's Advocate." I replied, "Well, curl your tail around the chair, and sit down. We'll be glad to have you." He spent most of the evening challenging our statements and trying to disprove them. But it was obvious that, beneath his skepticism and intellectual arrogance, there was a hunger, almost a longing, to be proved wrong!

I maintained contact with him for a time afterward, and occasionally talked with him at length about the Bible. He continued to insist that he had no need for God. In time I learned that he had been stricken with terminal cancer. Many of his Christian friends prayed for him, hoping that he would turn to God in this ultimate hour of need. He had money, he had intellect, he had position in the community—all of which came to nothing, nothing at all, in the face of his spiritual poverty at the end of his span of years. Tragically, he made a heartbreaking choice to take his own life rather than turn to God for strength in his time of crisis.

This man's tragedy affirms what Paul is saying to us in Ephesians. A man can have all the achievements in the world—but that is not authentic fulfillment. True, lasting, satisfying fulfillment comes only in Christ. It is the result of our liberation by the saving work of Christ.

THE CROSS ARGUES FOR US

Jesus came into our slave pit, He struck off our fetters, and He set us free. He restored us to fruitful, eternally significant living. Paul goes on to tell us that in Christ, we have the forgiveness of sin. Those sins were once our slave-chains, binding us in our enslaved condition. Our guilty awareness of those sins makes us hide from God and from each other—and even from ourselves. Sin brings shame, withdrawal, and denial. The memory of our sins makes us feel unacceptable to ourselves and others. The shame of sin makes us reclusive, secretive, suspicious, lonely, and despairing.

When Jesus comes into our lives, His light dispels the darkness of our sin. As He said to the woman who was caught in the act of adultery, "Neither do I condemn you. . . . Go now and leave your life of sin" (John 8:11). By what right does this Man forgive the sins of others? How can He set our guilt aside and still remain just?

Paul's answer: "We have redemption *through his blood*, the forgiveness of sins" (Ephesians 1:7 emphasis added). That is how it happens. His blood paid the price for our redemption. His blood bought our liberation from enslavement to sin. His blood, spilled on a cross of shame, set our guilt aside. That was the work of the Son.

The cross is not a pleasant thing. Blood is a sticky, messy, even sickening subject for most people. There are many who faint at the sight of blood. So this whole business of a bloody Savior is offensive to people, because they do not understand why God insists upon blood before there is forgiveness. Yet there is no other way. Scripture is clear: "The law requires that nearly everything be cleansed with blood," says Hebrews 9:22, "and without the shedding of blood there is no forgiveness." Why? Because the blood underscores the reality of our guilt. Jesus died because we deserve to die. We deserve the judgment of God.

Jesus died in our place. His blood is the substitute for our blood, His cross the substitute for the cross you and I deserve. And He was not merely a substitute, a replacement for us on the cross—He was identified with us. He actually became us on the cross. "God made him who had no sin to be sin for us, so that in him we might become the righteousness of God" (2 Corinthians 5:21). When Jesus took our place and identified with us, God put Him to death—because that is what *we* deserve. It is a fact that Scripture will not allow us to escape.

Some people are offended by the blood of Christ. They don't want to hear about the cross, the blood, or the debt of sin and shame He died to repay. I don't think it is the blood itself that so offends them—it is what the blood means. It signifies the fact that we are guilty, we are to blame, we deserve the sentence of death—and many people deny the fact that God's judgment against sin is true, and that we all deserve His wrath. To such people, the cross is bad news—even unbearable news.

We need to understand that the cross is truly the best news of all. The blood of Christ tells us that God is just, and He deals with sin. When Christ died, God's integrity and justice were upheld. He is now free to love us to the utmost degree. No one can ever stand in the shadow of the cross and argue that God takes a light view of sin. This gory episode in human history speaks to the fact that God will never, ever put up with evil. All have sinned—you have and so have I—but the cross argues for us, the blood liberates us. Our account is stamped paid in full, and God now fully accepts us in Christ.

GOD'S LAVISH RICHES IN CHRIST

This marvelous truth is what Paul calls "the riches of his grace." God did it all. I did nothing, I didn't even add to it. I can't deserve it or merit it in any way. I owe everything to the riches of God's grace, as Paul goes on to say:

> . . . in accordance with the riches of God's grace that he lavished on us with all wisdom and understanding (1:7–8).

When Paul says that God has "lavished" His riches on us, he is drawing a word-picture of riches that are heaped, piled, and spilled onto us, beyond measure, beyond counting. This is a reference to the fact that God not only washed us clean at the moment of our conversion, but he continues to cleanse and liberate us throughout our lives. Though we are now God's adopted children, we are still prone to sin and fail—so God continues to lavish his riches of grace and forgiveness on us. When we stumble and cover ourselves with the filth and grime of sin, He picks us up, dusts us off, forgives us, and restores us to our proper service for Him.

God's forgiveness is ever-present, lavished upon us throughout each new day and throughout our lives. It is a magnificent sense of liberation that we receive anew and afresh on a daily basis. Again and again, as we walk with the Lord, we can experience the joy of being set free and restored to usefulness. God fully, lavishly accepts us. We are not second-class citizens of heaven, but full-fledged children of the living God. Because He freely accepts us, we are free to accept ourselves.

Some may say, "Well, if God is so lavishly forgiving, then I can sin all I want, knowing that God will always let bygones be bygones, right?" Wrong. If that is your attitude toward the grace of God, then it may well be that you've never truly experienced it! Those who truly know God's forgiveness would never take it so lightly. Grace is a thing to be accepted in awe and reverence—not exploited or trampled underfoot.

As Paul writes in Romans 6:1–2, "What shall we say, then? Shall we go on sinning so that grace may increase? By no means! We died to sin; how can we live in it any longer?"

There is no agony like the agony of guilt. Nothing haunts the soul like the shame of sin. At the same time, nothing liberates the soul like the knowledge of God's forgiveness and the experience of God's wholeness. Once we have been set free from sin, why would we ever want to go back into bondage and struggle under that awful, crushing load again?

Thank God we have been set free by the work of the Son upon the cross.

THE MYSTERY OF UNITY

Some years ago, I received a thick envelope from the city of Palo Alto. The envelope contained a letter and a petition signed by 114 neighbors living near the church. The petition asked the city government to revoke the use permit of Peninsula Bible Church and to restrict our church's operations. My immediate reaction was anger. *Who do these people think they are,* I seethed, *wanting to stop the work that God is doing in this church? Don't they understand that lives are being redirected, marriages are being saved, and people are coming to Christ because of this church?*

But then the Lord brought to my mind the fact that few of these people had even been inside our church—they had only been outside. They didn't see the wonderful things that were happening inside our church. They only saw that traffic in the neighborhood was snarled on Sunday mornings, and that exhaust fumes wafted into their yards from our crowded parking lot, and that the lights of our church shone into their homes during our evening services—and their annoyance was perfectly understandable!

I realized that this petition against our church might actually be God's opportunity to be a witness to our own neighborhood. So in the next few weeks our congregation made it a point not to fight the petition with legal action, but instead to demonstrate a genuine, loving spirit to our neighbors. We sent delegations from the church into the neighborhood with the message, "We are sorry for the inconvenience and irritation our church has inadvertently caused you, and we want to be good neighbors. Please tell us how we can help reduce this irritation in your life."

The neighbors responded positively to this outreach, and we made a number of changes that lessened the impact of our crowds on the neighborhood—and we made some new friends. We even began to see some of our neighbors joining us in Sunday worship!

God showed us how to break down the barriers that we had unwittingly erected in our own neighborhood, and He showed us new ways to build relationships with the people He loves. If only we could see all our problems this way—not as obstacles, but as opportunities to witness the miracle and mystery of unity in Christ.

In Ephesians 1:9–12, Paul tells us that this is the purpose of history, the reason for the existence of time and space: to unite all things in Christ. God wants to bring unity and wholeness to His creation, and that means there must be unity, not division, between the sacred realm and the earthly realm; between the church and the neighborhood, between those who have already received His good news and those who desperately need to hear it. In these verses, Paul writes:

> And he made known to us the mystery of his will according to his good pleasure, which he purposed in Christ, to be put into effect when the times will have reached their fulfillment—to bring all things in heaven and on earth together under one head, even Christ. In him we were also chosen, having been predestined according to the plan of him who works out everything in conformity with the purpose of his will, in order that we, who were the first to hope in Christ, might be for the praise of his glory.

If we will apply ourselves to truly understanding these powerful words, then we will begin to understand God's purpose in the world. We will begin to understand the world around us and the course of history as it rolls through time and space. But in order to understand the statement Paul makes in these verses, we must take this statement apart. There are four major divisions in this statement:

1. The mystery of God's will.
2. How the mystery of God's will was made manifest.
3. The time the mystery of God's will is to be manifested.
4. Our part in manifesting the mystery of God's will.

Let's look at each of these divisions in turn:

1. The mystery of God's will. Here, Paul tells us that God has a hidden purpose, which he calls a "mystery." A mystery is a secret God understands, and that people need to know, but which cannot be understood unless it is disclosed by God. The mysteries of God answer the great questions that throb in the human heart. No seminar, no university class, no scientific probe can reveal these answers. They can only be revealed by God himself. Once God reveals the mystery of His purpose in the world to us, then the swirling chaotic events that flicker on our TV screens and scream from our headlines begin to make sense in God's cosmic scheme. Only after we have read and understood God's revealed Word can we even begin to read a newspaper or watch CNN with any intelligence and comprehension—because only then can we see how our current events fit into the program and purpose of God.

We in the Christian church have the answers to the mysteries of God. He has made us the stewards or dispensers of those answers. Tragically, we have too often failed in the job God has given us. We do not speak clearly to the world about the mysteries of God, and that is why the world continues in its confusion and darkness. It is up to us to tell the world, loudly and clearly, the answers to God's mysteries.

In verse 10, Paul says that the great secret or mystery of God is that He plans "to bring all things in heaven and on earth together under one head, even Christ." That is what God is doing in history: uniting all things in Christ. You may wonder, "How can that be? I look around and it doesn't seem that the world is uniting in Christ, but falling apart and falling away from Christ! I don't see unity, I see division! I don't see Christ's unity—I see atheism, paganism, and immorality! There is even division within my own soul, as the good Christian person I want to be is constantly at odds with the desires of my old sin nature!" Paul has an answer for that objection, which we'll come to in a moment—but first he wants us to understand that God's ultimate plan is to bring all things together under the headship of His Son, Jesus.

When Paul says "all things," he means all things. In fact, he amplified it: "all things in heaven and on earth." He is saying that, ultimately, all things in both the invisible realm of reality, heaven, and the visible realm, earth, will be united under the lordship of Christ. Where we now see a struggle between good and evil, struggle among nations, and struggle among people, we will one day see unity. Christ will be the supreme administrator of all things, both in the heavenly realm and the earthly.

We see this principle in Philippians 2:5–11, where Paul writes that our Lord Jesus took the form of a servant and humbled himself, being obedient to death on the cross—and as a result, "God exalted [Jesus] to the highest place and gave him the name that is above every name, that at the name of Jesus every knee should bow, in heaven and on earth and under the earth, and every tongue confess that Jesus Christ is Lord, to the glory of God the Father." That is God's purpose in the world; that is where all of history is moving.

2. How the mystery of God's will was made manifest. In Ephesians 1:9 Paul tells us how the mystery will be revealed: "And he made known to us the mystery of his will according to his good pleasure, which he purposed *in Christ*." That is the clue: the revelation of the mystery of God's will and purpose in the world takes place *in Christ*.

The wisdom and plan of God has been manifested in the life and ministry of Christ. Look at the Lord's life and you will see what Paul means. Take, for example, the Lord's miracles. There is that beautiful passage in Isaiah 35:5–7 where the prophet predicts that God shall come to us, and that the result of his coming will be that the blind will see, the deaf will hear, the lame will leap, and the dumb will sing for joy. In other words, the coming of the Lord will be manifested by a great eruption of healing and gladness.

That is exactly what happened when Jesus came. He healed the blind, deaf, lame, and mute—and more! He mastered the forces of nature, stilled the storm, changed water into wine, released captives from bondage to Satan in the spiritual realm. This was the visible demonstration at the beginning of a work that is continuing today, and which will one day be completed when all things in heaven and on earth are united under the lordship of Jesus Christ.

The principles by which this healing manifestation would take place in men's spirits, as well as their bodies, are set forth in the words of Jesus. So it is important that we listen to His words, as recorded in the four Gospels. That is why we should heed the Beatitudes, the life-changing message in the Sermon on the Mount and the parables, His dialogues with His disciples, the clashes with His opponents, the rich words of His prayers, His final instructions in the Upper Room, the intense words He spoke from the cross, and the words of comfort He gave following His resurrection. These words reveal the mystery of God's purpose in the world, and in our individual lives.

3. The time the mystery of God's will is to be manifested. In verse 10, Paul says that God's purpose in history will be fully accomplished "when the times will have reached their fulfillment." He is talking here about the cycles of history. Historians tell us that history moves in cycles. There are times of peace and prosperity which lead to a time of apathy and lethargy; this foments calamity and uncertainty, producing a time of rebellion and revolution; these changes bring us back to peace and prosperity—and the cycle begins all over again. These cycles are called "seasons" in the Bible.

Paul is telling us that a time will come when the seasons have been completed and the cycles will be ended. At that point, God will have fulfilled His promise to tear down the old creation, destroying it utterly, while building up the new. This is hard for us to understand in the finiteness of our experience. To our way of thinking, it is necessary to tear down first, then rebuild. You must demolish the old, run-down, rat-infested, graffiti-scarred tenement before you can put up the brand-new high rise.

But God doesn't work that way. He tears down the old at the same time He is building up the new. In fact, the marvel of God is that He tears down the old and builds up the new at the same time, in the same process. When we look around us at the decay, misery, injustice, and sin around us, we only see the tearing-down of this world. We forget that God is also building a new creation at the same time, on the very same spot. By means of the hate and the hurt of this old creation, He is building His new creation. As the old is destroyed, the new emerges—finished, complete, and exactly as He planned. That is what Paul means when he says, "when the times will have reached their fulfillment."

4. Our part in manifesting the mystery of God's will. What is our part? Well, Paul has put it in one phrase in verse 12: "in order that we, who were the first to hope in Christ, might be for the praise of his glory." That is our part.

Unfortunately, this translation softens the cutting edge of Paul's statement in this verse. What Paul literally says is, "We have been made Christ's inheritance." As believers, we are the inheritance of Christ—His heritage. Later, in verse 18, Paul will expand on this theme, writing, "I pray also that the eyes of your heart may be enlightened in order that you may know the hope to which he has called you, the riches of his glorious inheritance in the saints."

So there is a double inheritance in the Christian life: We inherit Jesus and He inherits us. He is our inheritance and we are His. He is our resource, our power, our strength, our love, our wisdom, our truth, the precious One from whom we draw our life and our purpose for living—and we are His precious prize, which He himself has redeemed from the muck and mire of our sin, and it pleases Him to use us to glorify the Father.

Once we truly understand what that means, it puts an end to complaining about "our lot in life." It is God in Christ who has chosen us, allowed us to go through the situations we are in (many of which, if we are honest with ourselves, are of our own making), and it pleases Him to bring His blessings about and to weave His perfect plan out of our problems and hurts and failings. His riches of grace are manifested in our lives, and the life of Jesus is released in us as we learn to respond to trials and sufferings in the same way that He did. Day by day, moment by moment, God is destroying the old in us and creating the new, bringing us to wholeness and inner unity in Christ, conforming us to the likeness of the Son.

May God give us grace to play our part by faith, to cooperate with God and not resist, as the old self gradually collapses within us and a new and Christlike self—glorious, eternal, and pleasing to God—arises to take its place. The more we understand and allow this process to take place within us, the greater will be our joy as we see God's purpose fulfilled in our lives.

In this and the preceding chapter, we have examined the work of the first two Persons of the Trinity, as presented by Paul in Ephesians 1:3–14. In the next chapter, we will examine Ephesians 1:13–14—the work of the Holy Spirit.

CHAPTER FOUR

The Work and Blessings of the Spirit

Ephesians 1:13–14

The great American preacher, Dwight L. Moody, was scheduled to launch an evangelistic campaign in England. Hearing of Moody's plans, an elderly English pastor complained to a younger colleague, "Why do we need Mr. Moody to come here and preach to us? He's an uneducated former shoe-clerk—and he's an American, for goodness' sake! Who does Mr. Moody think he is, preaching to us? Does he fancy he has a monopoly on the Holy Spirit?"

"No," the younger pastor replied, "but the Holy Spirit seems to have a monopoly on Mr. Moody."

That was true. In fact, D. L. Moody himself once observed, "I believe that the moment our hearts are emptied of pride, selfishness, ambition, and everything that is contrary to God's law, the Holy Spirit will fill every corner of our hearts. But if we are full of pride, conceit, ambition, and the world, there is no room for the Spirit of God. We must be emptied before we can be filled."

Many people today miss this simple but profound truth about the Holy Spirit, as given to us in Ephesians 1. When we placed our trust in Jesus Christ, we were sealed by the Spirit of promise, and our inheritance of God's riches was guaranteed. We already have all there is of the Holy Spirit. The issue that confronts us is: Does the Spirit have all there is of us?

THE WORD AND THE SPIRIT

As we return to Ephesians 1, we should remind ourselves that verses 13 and 14, dealing with the work and blessings of the Holy Spirit, are actually the closing phrases of a single sentence that begins in verse 3 and doesn't stop for a breath until verse 14. This one unbroken sentence (in the original Greek language) gathers up in a single vast statement all the tremendous themes to which Paul will return again and again in his letter to the Ephesians.

This is the normal structure of Paul's apostolic letters—they usually begin with a summary and then that summary is broken down into detail, enabling us to focus keenly upon the truth presented. Paul wants us to see both the forest and the trees, the broad sweep and the minute details, of God's truth for our lives.

In the previous two chapters, we looked at the first and second aspects of God's threefold work—the work and blessings of the Father and the Son. The Father chose us and called us before the creation of the world to be part of His family. The Father made a decision about us before the foundation of the world. Then the Son accomplished the Father's decision. He took our place on the cross and liberated us from sin and death. Through Him, God's grace continues to be lavished upon us again and again. In Christ, God breaks down divisions, destroys the old, raises up the new, and brings all things into unity under the lordship of the Son.

Now we come to the work of the Holy Spirit, Ephesians 1:13–14:

> And you also were included in Christ when you heard
> the word of truth, the gospel of your salvation. Having

believed, you were marked in him with a seal, the promised Holy Spirit, who is a deposit guaranteeing our inheritance until the redemption of those who are God's
possession—to the praise of his glory.

Notice two areas of emphasis that are always found together in
Scripture—the Word and the Spirit. Both are absolutely essential.
There is no salvation without both of these instruments of God's eternal purpose. It is always a mistake to emphasize one to the exclusion
of the other.

Some groups and individuals emphasize the Spirit and ignore the
Word. They say, "We don't need the Word. All we need is the Spirit
within. All we need is to trust our feelings—the indwelling Spirit will
lead us." This is almost invariably a prescription for error and heresy
as people drift away from the revealed truth of the Bible and into
all sorts of confused, mystical, cultic views and practices, all in the
guise of "following the Spirit within." Many a cult has begun with
earnest, sincere believers who fell under the spell of a false messiah
who claimed to speak for the Spirit of God, even while contradicting
the clear teaching of the Word of God.

Yet, there is an equal danger in following the Word and rejecting the ministry of the Spirit. I have been in many churches that
have been orthodox in their adherence to the Word, but completely devoid of the freshness and vitality of the Spirit. In such
churches, worship has become mechanical and perfunctory—a
ritual that enshrines the form of the Word while denying its life-
changing power. Such churches are orthodox to the core, but
they are also sterile, dull, and lifeless. The result of emphasizing
the Word to the exclusion of the Spirit is a kind of clenched-teeth
piety in which the people resolve to do their "Christian duty"

while demonstrating no motivation, satisfaction, love, warmth, or joy.

In Scripture and in every faithful, dynamic fellowship of believers, you find the two together, the Word and the Spirit. The Spirit interprets the Word, and the Word becomes fresh and vital where the Spirit of God is present. Through the ministry of the Spirit, Jesus Christ steps out of the pages of the Bible and stands in our presence as a living, breathing, life-changing Man. By the light of the Spirit, we can see the Lord's face, we can touch His nail-pierced hands, we can hear His voice and sense His heartbeat. That is the job of the Spirit—to take the words of the pages of our Bible and make them come alive in our daily experience.

The Word of God identifies the Spirit and validates His voice within us. The Spirit of God would never urge us to violate the teaching of God's Word. So we can be assured that if some inner urging runs counter to God's Word, it does not come from the Holy Spirit. There are many spirits abroad today, many voices talking to us, many sources of information and ideas that bombard us daily. How do we know which of these voices and sources are true and which would lead us into error? The Word of God points to the true Holy Spirit, while detecting all false spirits. We must have together the Word and the Spirit for balance and sanity in our Christian lives.

THE THREE ESSENTIAL EXPERIENCES OF A BELIEVER

Next, notice in verse 13 that there are three experiences Paul says every Christian should have in the course of the Christian faith:

First, "you heard the word of truth";

Second, you "believed" in Christ; and

Third, you "were marked in Him with a seal, the promised Holy Spirit."

Let's examine each of these experiences in closer detail.

1. The "word of truth." Paul begins by saying, "You have heard the word of truth." The world in which Paul lived and wrote was a world like ours today—filled with all kinds of distorted ideas and godless philosophies. Then as now, there were many delusions and illusions abroad. The gospel is a return to reality, it is truth, it is the end of illusion. By hearing and receiving the Word of truth, we get back in touch with reality.

For example, the gospel describes the true condition of the human heart. It punctures our human denial, our false and self-deceptive desire to insist that there is nothing seriously wrong with the way we live, the sinful habits we tolerate, the wrongs we perpetrate. We all want to see ourselves as "good people," as being "okay." Sure, we sin and fail like everybody else, but we're really not so bad.

The gospel comes crashing into our denial, rubbing our noses in the fact that our condition is so bad, so desperate, that our sins literally nailed the Son of God to a cross! Our problem is so desperate that it is truly incurable, from a human perspective. We cannot save ourselves. Only God himself can save us.

Today, because of what Scripture calls "the wrath of God," human evil is allowed to run its course in the world—with devastating consequences. But the good news of the gospel is that God loves us, He hasn't forgotten us, and He has entered human life to share in our sorrow and pain. God, through the Son, has personally taken the penalty for our evil upon himself. It is a deep, dark, impenetrable mystery, far beyond our imagining and our reasoning—but even though we cannot grasp it, we can accept it and receive God's pardon, deliverance, and freedom from bondage as God's own adopted children. That is "the word of truth" that we have received, the first essential experience of a believer—the gospel of salvation.

2. Belief in Christ. The second essential experience of the Christian, says Paul, is that we believed in Christ, we placed our trust in Him. "And you also were included in Christ when you heard the word of truth, the gospel of your salvation," says verse 13. "*Having believed*, you were marked in him with a seal, the promised Holy Spirit."

Belief is an essential prerequisite to a relationship with Jesus Christ. Paul stresses this fact: We must not only *hear* the word of truth, but we must also *respond* to it in faith. We must believe it. And to believe it means to accept it as truth, and to act accordingly. You have never believed unless something is changed in your experience. If you say that you hold something to be true, but you go on living in the old, unbelieving way, then you haven't really believed it. You are only kidding yourself. Belief results in change, in conforming yourself to the reality of what you believe.

What's more, our belief must be focused in a Person—the Lord Jesus Christ. The apostle Paul never lets us forget this. In the first fourteen verses of Ephesians, he mentions the Lord Jesus Christ fifteen times. He is constantly bringing Him before us because God wants to drive home this great fact—that we cannot experience blessing in our lives apart from a personal relationship with the Lord Jesus Christ.

I once counseled a woman who was a highly respected medical doctor. For forty years she had been a member of a denominational church, but when she came to me for counseling, she said that her life was empty and filled with anxiety and fear. She took medication to quiet her nerves, but found her emotional problems growing worse, not better. Though doctors could find no cause for it, she had a perpetual pain in her stomach. By the time she came to see me, she was on the verge of a breakdown. When she talked to her own pastor about these problems, he told her, "You're just feeling sorry for yourself."

As we talked, it became obvious to me that, despite all her years of church attendance, she had never experienced a personal relationship with the Lord Jesus. I explained to her the simple invitation of Jesus: "Here I am! I stand at the door and knock. If anyone hears my voice and opens the door, I will come in and eat with him, and he with me" (Revelation 3:20). I asked, "What is your response to this invitation?"

Very quietly, without another word from me, she bowed her head and began to ask Jesus to take control of her life. She told Him quite honestly how empty her life was, and she asked Him to enter her life and be Lord of all her circumstances. The moment she finished praying, I could see the new radiance on her face. "Oh, thank you so much!" she said, "I can't tell you how much this means to me. Already things are different!"

Once she placed her trust in Christ, this woman's emotional and physical problems receded. The pain in her stomach left her immediately after she prayed. And she quit taking medications for her anxiety and depression. Her problem was not medical or emotional, but spiritual—and only a spiritual cure would work. The cure was to experience a personal relationship with Jesus Christ—not just believing *about* Him, as she had for many years in her church, but believing *in* Him, *trusting* in Him, and *knowing* Him in a personal way.

3. Sealed by the Spirit. The third essential experience of the believer is described by Paul with a rather strange phrase: "you were marked in him with a seal, the promised Holy Spirit." What does it mean to be sealed with the Spirit? This is undoubtedly a reference to the ancient practice of sealing letters or other official objects with sealing wax and impressing the wax with a raised seal worn on a ring, bearing an identifying image. The use of the seal always denotes two concepts: *ownership* and *preservation.*

The seal on the letter made it clear that the letter was owned by the individual who had sealed it. And the seal of the Holy Spirit makes it clear that the life that is sealed by Him belongs to God. As Paul says elsewhere in the New Testament, "Do you not know that your body is a temple of the Holy Spirit, who is in you, whom you have received from God? You are not your own; you were bought at a price" (1 Corinthians 6:19–20); and, "The Spirit himself testifies with our spirit that we are God's children" (Romans 8:16). The Spirit who seals you is God's mark of ownership upon you.

Just as the seal on a letter preserved it from tampering, the Spirit's presence speaks of God's preserving seal upon our lives. We find this concept richly described for us when Paul writes, "Having believed, you were marked in him with a seal, the promised Holy Spirit, who is a deposit guaranteeing our inheritance until the redemption of those who are God's possession—to the praise of his glory." As Paul puts it here, God has guaranteed our inheritance by means of the Holy Spirit.

The New International Version brings out this concept with clarity in rendering Paul's concept of the Holy Spirit as "a deposit guaranteeing our inheritance." In Greek, the word *deposit* is *arrhabon*, which means "a down payment." If you've ever bought a car, you know what *arrhabon* is all about. You sign a paper and pay a down payment, a deposit, and that is the *arrhabon*, the guarantee that there is more to come. The presence of the Spirit in your life—the joy and the peace He gives—is the guarantee that there is more yet to come from God. The Spirit is the down payment on a much greater, fuller, richer experience of God than you have ever known before. The Holy Spirit is just the beginning of the blessings you will receive in Christ.

Paul goes on to say that this deposit or down payment guarantees our inheritance "until the redemption of those who are God's possession," as the NIV puts it. In the original Greek, this phrase is literally "until the redemption of the walk-around." This sounds strange to our ears, but the first century readers of Ephesians instantly understood this phrase as a reference to the custom of buying a piece of ground and then going out and walking around it to symbolically establish your ownership rights to that ground. By walking around the property, you made it yours. It was a sign that the property was now in your name.

That is what Paul says God has done with us. It is not we who acquire God, but He who acquires us. He has made the down payment on our lives, the Holy Spirit, and that preserves us as His possession until He returns to claim his purchased possession—your life and mine, which is now in His name.

When Paul talks of the "promised" Holy Spirit, he refers to the promise made to Abraham. Some 4000 years ago—2000 years before Paul's day—God told Abraham, "I will surely bless you . . . and through your offspring all nations on earth will be blessed, because you have obeyed me" (Genesis 22:17–18). God was promising Abraham that all who would exercise the faith of Abraham would receive the Holy Spirit. And that promise has been fulfilled, because that is how you and I receive the Holy Spirit today—by faith. Paul makes this same point in Galatians 3:6–8 and 13–14 (emphasis added):

Consider Abraham: "He believed God, and it was credited to him as righteousness." Understand, then, that those who believe are children of Abraham. The Scripture foresaw that God would justify the Gentiles by faith, and announced the gospel in advance to Abraham: "All nations will be blessed through you." . . . Christ redeemed us from the curse of the law by becoming a curse for us, for it is written: "Cursed is everyone who is hung on a tree." He redeemed us in order that the blessing given to Abraham might come to the Gentiles through Christ Jesus, *so that by faith we might receive the promise of the Spirit.*

You don't have to plead with God to send the Holy Spirit. You don't have to wait and hope for a second experience after salvation. It is impossible to have salvation apart from the indwelling Spirit. The promised Spirit is received simply by faith in the Lord Jesus. The minute you believe in him, you receive all you will ever have of the Holy Spirit. As you grow and mature in your faith, becoming progressively more obedient in your walk with God, the Holy Spirit gains more and more of *you.*

TO THE PRAISE OF HIS GLORY

The Spirit is God's seal upon your life. He marks you and identifies you as His own. He guarantees that he will perform every word he has promised, until the moment you stand in God's presence, overwhelmed by all that God has done for you—to the praise of His glory.

That is a crucial phrase Paul uses at the end of verse 14—"to the praise of his glory"—and it is the third time Paul uses that phrase in the passage. Each Person of the Trinity—the Father, the Son, and the Holy Spirit—accomplishes His work so perfectly that it always produces praise and glory. When we see the work and the blessings that each of the Persons of the Trinity has performed in our lives, we can't help but sing and glorify God for all He has done.

We have been sealed by the Holy Spirit, who was promised to Abraham. Here is where we find our identity and our purpose in life. Here is where we find the power and resources to cope with the problems that come to us each day. This is not mere theological double-talk. These are practical truths that enable us to handle the difficulties, pressures, problems, stresses, uncertainties, and disappointments of living out our lives. Knowing that we are sealed and possessed by God is the greatest, most life-changing truth of our existence.

We should awake every morning and say to ourselves, "I am a child of God. I have been forgiven of my sins. I am accepted in God's family. He has marked me out as His own. He has put His Spirit within me, releasing in me the full life of the Lord Jesus Christ. All the power that Jesus himself relied upon is now mine through the promised Holy Spirit. I am equipped to handle whatever comes today. I can take whatever life throws at me because I have the Spirit, and all the fullness of His life."

That is our identity. That is the truth which transforms our lives.

CHAPTER FIVE

Praying with Power

Ephesians 1:15–18

Samuel Morse, the inventor of the telegraph, was once asked if, in the process of researching and experimenting with his invention, he ever came to a place where he didn't have a clue what to do next, "Oh, many times," Morse replied. "Whenever I was baffled and frustrated, I went to my knees and asked God for light and understanding. He showed me the way. I believe God wanted the telegraph to be invented because He knew what it would mean to mankind. After the invention of the telegraph, I received many honors—but I feel undeserving of honors. I have made a valuable application of electricity not because of superior gifts and abilities, but because God was pleased to answer my prayers and reveal to me a few of the wonderful secrets of His universe."

It is significant that the first message ever tapped over the telegraph key was the words of Samuel Morse himself: "What hath God wrought!" He believed the telegraph was not so much his invention as it was God's answer to his prayers. The prayers of Samuel Morse unleashed an enormous power in the world—the power to electrical communication. As we approach the end of Ephesians 1, the apostle Paul tells us how we are to pray with power.

PAUL PRAYS FOR THE SAINTS

With Ephesians 1:15 we leave the great doctrinal passage in which the apostle Paul teaches the fundamental principles of the Christian faith. We turn now to the issue of prayer and the crucial place of prayer in the Christian experience. Paul, having finished the great passage in which he set forth the work and blessings of our threefold God, now adds these words addressed to the Ephesian Christians:

> For this reason, ever since I heard about your faith in the Lord Jesus and your love for all the saints, I have not stopped giving thanks for you, remembering you in my prayers. I keep asking that the God of our Lord Jesus Christ, the glorious Father, may give you the Spirit of wisdom and revelation, so that you may know him better. I pray also that the eyes of your heart may be enlightened in order that you may know the hope to which he has called you, the riches of his glorious inheritance in the saints.

Paul starts with the words: "For this reason," then he goes on to list the evidence for his confidence in the genuineness of the faith of the Ephesian Christians. The phrase, "For this reason," looks back upon the great passage that we previously examined, Ephesians 1:3–14, in which the apostle outlined the fundamental truths of our faith—the fact that we were called by the Father, that we are destined to be His children, that redemption and forgiveness are available to us in the Son, that our eyes have been opened to the eternal plan of God, that we have been sealed by the Spirit, and that the Spirit has guaranteed our inheritance in Christ. It is for this reason, Paul says, that he prays for the saints at Ephesus and others who read this letter. It is because they need to understand these truths.

Paul is convinced that they are genuine Christians because of two things that have come to his attention—their faith and their love. The apostle has evidently heard in Rome of the faith of these Christians, many of whom he had never met. He has heard that they have confessed Christ and turned from their pagan idols. But the most convincing evidence of their faith was their love. Their genuine caring for each other proved that Jesus was actively at work in their lives.

That is crucial: If your faith has not made you a more loving person, it is not genuine faith. It is mere intellectual assent to an orthodoxy, which means nothing. That is the point the apostle James makes in his letter, where he says that authentic faith is revealed by a concern for the hungry, the homeless, the needy, and the oppressed. He said, in effect, "Show me your love, and I'll see your faith; but don't talk to me about faith unless love is present" (see James 2:18).

Paul notes that their love is demonstrated toward all the saints, not just toward some of them. The truth is that some saints are easy to love—and some are not so easy. True faith in Christ is demonstrated by a love for all the saints, not just the most beautiful or the most powerful or the most good-natured. The church is a family of faith. If we want harmony in our family, we must learn to love all our brothers and sisters. That is what the Ephesian Christians have demonstrated to Paul.

Assured of the genuineness of the believers in Ephesus, Paul tells them, "I have not stopped giving thanks for you, remembering you in my prayers. I keep asking that the God of our Lord Jesus Christ, the glorious Father, may give you the Spirit of wisdom and revelation, so that you may know him better." Notice, first, the two unusual names for God that Paul employs: "the God of our Lord Jesus Christ, the glorious Father." Why does Paul say that? It is interesting that Paul makes no mention here of the fact that the Son is truly the equal of the Father—God in human form. He is not praying directly to Christ; he is praying to the God of the Lord Jesus.

The reason Paul addresses his prayers in this way is that God the Father is the One to whom the Lord Jesus prayed. He is the One upon whom Jesus depended for the enlightenment of His own disciples. Jesus prayed for His disciples—sometimes spending whole nights in prayer on the mountainside—that the truth might grip their hearts, and that the truth would change their hearts. Paul wanted the Ephesian Christians to understand that the same God to whom Jesus prayed, and upon whom He depended, is the God to whom they were to pray, and upon whom they were to depend.

Paul's next name for God, "the glorious Father," is a beautiful name. It speaks of the One who originates and radiates glory. I recall attending a glorious wedding, followed by a glorious reception. The setting was resplendent, the food was lavish, the decorations were festive, the bride was beautiful, and the people were joyful. I found myself talking to a man in the corner, and discovered that he was the father of the bride. He was the one who would pay all the bills for the entire glorious occasion. He was, on that day, "the father of glory."

That is very much the idea Paul conveys when he calls God "the glorious Father," or as some translations render it, "the Father of glory." He is the source of all glory and beauty and delight in the universe. He is the one who has paid all the bills, the one who makes all this glory possible.

WHAT PAUL PRAYS FOR

Paul turns now and prays for these Christians. Notice what he prays for in verse 17: "I keep asking that the God of our Lord Jesus Christ, the glorious Father, may give you the Spirit of wisdom and revelation, so that you may know him better." Why does Paul say that? Aren't these Christians he is speaking to? Haven't they already received the Holy Spirit? Yes. Paul has already acknowledged that. He has said that they were sealed with the Holy Spirit of promise. So he is not praying that they will be given the Holy Spirit. He is praying for a special ministry of the Holy Spirit.

In the book of Isaiah, the prophet speaks of the seven spirits of God—the spirit of wisdom, the spirit of understanding, the spirit of counsel, the spirit of knowledge, and so forth. He doesn't mean that there are seven Holy Spirits, but that the one Holy Spirit has a sevenfold ministry of illuminating and enlightening the heart. That is what Paul is praying for here.

Paul doesn't take it for granted this ministry of wisdom and revelation will automatically take place—he goes to God and asks for it on behalf of his Ephesian brothers and sisters. If you want the Word of God to come alive in your life, you must ask for illumination. That is what this passage teaches us. And if you want it to come alive in the life of another, you must intercede in prayer for that person, asking that your friend be granted the Spirit's ministry of wisdom and revelation. As the apostle James tells us in James 4:2, all too often, the reason we fail to receive is that we fail to ask.

If the Bible seems dull and boring to you, perhaps it is because you have never asked God for a touch of the Spirit's wisdom and revelation. You hear the words, but the message falls flat because you have not asked God to open your heart to His message for your life.

We must also be aware that there is a spiritual war going on around us. Later in Ephesians, we will examine the issue of spiritual warfare, and we will see that we have a cunning enemy who seeks to rob us of the reality of God's Word for our lives. So some of the dullness or flatness we feel when we open God's Word may be due to the blinding, darkening work of the powers of darkness which want to wall us off from God's truth. To counteract the enemy's attacks, we must bathe ourselves in prayer, asking God for the wisdom and revelation that only the Spirit of God can provide.

Do you pray when you read your Bible? Do you open the pages and say, "Lord, show me yourself; make yourself real to me in these pages"? Remember, the Bible is not just a history book about the past or a prophecy book about the future. It isn't just a self-help book of ethical guidelines and life principles. It is, first and foremost, the revelation of the living God. He gave us His Word in order that we might see Him, know Him, feel His love, discover His wisdom, draw upon His strength, and rely upon His power. The purpose of the Bible is to introduce you in a personal way to the God of the universe, and His Son, Jesus Christ. So, if your Bible study time is dull and dreary, take that as a hint and pray that it would come alive, so that you may truly know Jesus Christ.

THE EYES OF YOUR HEART

Now let's look at Paul's final statement in his introduction to prayer in verse 18: "I pray also that the eyes of your heart may be enlightened in order that you may know the hope to which he has called you, the riches of his glorious inheritance in the saints." That's an odd expression, isn't it? "The eyes of your heart." What does Paul mean?

We know that the eyes are expressive. You can sometimes look at a face that seems dull and impassive—a "poker" face—but the eyes usually give an indication of what is going on inside. I have often visited people in the hospital whose faces and bodies have wasted away, but their eyes are full of life and vitality. So the eyes are extremely expressive, and the eyes of the heart express the feelings of the heart.

The eyes are also the instruments of perception, enabling us to see. The eyes of the heart, then, are also the instruments of the heart's perception. If you listen to truth, your heart is receiving and perceiving. You are absorbing reality at the innermost level of your being. The heart, which the Bible describes as the seat of human emotion, is an instrument of perceiving and understanding deep truth and deep reality.

Truth comes first to the mind, the seat of the intellect—but for truth to truly take hold of us, it must penetrate all the way to the heart, the seat of our emotions and motivations. The will is never properly energized and motivated until the heart has been moved as well.

In Luke 24 two disciples are walking on the road to Emmaus after the crucifixion of Christ. They don't know that the Lord has already risen. Suddenly He appears to them, but they are so defeated and discouraged over the crucifixion that they don't recognize Him. He walks along with them as a stranger, unfolding to them the passages of Old Testament Scripture which promise the coming of the Messiah, including His sufferings and His resurrection. Suddenly they recognize Him—and He vanishes from their sight. Remember what the disciples said to each other? Luke 24:32 records, "Were not our hearts burning within us while he talked with us on the road and opened the Scriptures to us?"

That "holy heartburn" represents the eyes of the heart being opened. Paul desires that our hearts—yours and mine—would burn within us in the same way. When the heart burns with truth, when God's truth becomes so vivid and real to you that your heart is captivated by it and begins to burn within you, then you know with certainty that God is real, that the hope of your calling is genuine, that the power of His presence is coursing through your life and the riches of His ministry have been poured out upon your being.

I remember one couple at Peninsula Bible Church who provide

a vivid illustration of the power of prayer to ignite a cold heart and make it burn for God. The husband had become a Christian and had married a young woman who grew up in PBC. At first this young man was on fire for God, but gradually his excitement and passion for God began to wane. He turned cold, lost his interest in the Scriptures, and quit coming to church. He avoided other Christians.

His wife was very alarmed over the decline in her husband's spiritual condition. She could have nagged him and begged him to come back to church, but she knew that it would probably have the opposite effect, driving him further away. So she asked a friend to pray with her for her husband every day. They met daily for a month, praying faithfully, and at first nothing happened. But they remembered that Jesus said in Luke 18:1 that we should pray persistently and not give up. So they kept praying.

In time, the wife noticed a gradual change in her husband's attitude. One day, she was astonished to come home and find him reading the Bible. She didn't say anything to him about it, and he didn't say anything to her—but her heart sang when she saw it. One Sunday, he said to her, "Honey, I'd like to go to church with you." She rejoiced inwardly, but avoided making a big deal over it. Finally he said to her, "You know, dear, I've really been way out of it! Somehow or other I lost all my interest in the Lord. But God has met me and brought me back." And he came alive again—without his wife saying a single word to him about the Lord. What a wonderful testimony to the power of prayer to open the eyes of the heart!

So let's be in prayer as we continue our study in Ephesians. Let's pray that God would give us the Spirit of wisdom and revelation as we study His Word, and that He would open the eyes of our hearts to the burning truth He has for our lives.

CHAPTER SIX

Hope, Riches, and Power

Ephesians 1:18–23

The issue in the closing verses of Ephesians 1 is *motivation.* The apostle Paul understood the Christians in the area of Ephesus. A veteran warrior of the cross, Paul had been a Christian for many years by the time he wrote this letter. He was well aware of the many moods and experiences a Christian is subject to. He knew the lukewarmness that often sets in—the lethargic, apathetic attitudes that can sometimes arise after a warm and hopeful beginning. He knew of the danger of losing one's motivation in the midst of the Christian struggle.

Perhaps you know that danger yourself. No Christian escapes it in his lifetime. At times, our passion for Christ cools and our spirits grow apathetic. The apostle understood that. So he turned to prayer, and his prayer reflects a deep understanding of the needs of those who would hear this letter. He prays in verses 18 and 19 (emphasis added):

. . . that you may know the *hope* to which he has called you, the *riches* of his glorious inheritance in the saints, and his incomparably great *power* for us who believe.

Hope, riches, and power. Notice how specific Paul's prayer is. He doesn't simply say, "Lord, bless the Ephesians this morning." We all know what it is to drop blanket prayers on people and expect that to take care of the situation. But Paul knows these people better than that. He knows that there is a danger that they could lose their vision, they could sink into indifference, they could lose sight of their hope. Yes, they have sound doctrine, but there is a danger that they could fall short of the deep, vibrant experience of knowing Christ. So Paul prays that God will enlighten their hearts so that they may know the hope of God's calling, the riches of their inheritance, and the power of God.

PAUL'S PRAYER FOR HOPE

The word *hope* is part of the great triad found in the Scriptures: "faith, hope, and love," the essentials of a well-rounded Christian experience. Hope always concerns the future. The Ephesians were in danger of losing their hope for the future. Many of us know that feeling. We all await the return of the Lord, but we don't really get very excited about it.

The hope of the believer is described for us in Romans 8:18: "I consider that our present sufferings are not worth comparing with the glory that will be revealed in us." That is the hope—a coming glory, a glory toward which we are moving day by day. Paul goes on to say, Romans 8:19–21: "The creation waits in eager expectation for the sons of God to be revealed. For the creation was subjected to frustration, not by its own choice, but by the will of the one who subjected it, in hope that the creation itself will be liberated from its bondage to decay and brought into the glorious freedom of the children of God."

That phrase, "the bondage to decay," is an accurate description of what scientists call the Second Law of Thermodynamics, the law of entropy, the scientific principle which states that everything in the universe is running down. Science and Scripture agree that the universe was once wound up, but that it is now decaying. When Paul talks about "the bondage to decay," he includes not only the natural world, with its constant decay, but the human body as well.

In Romans 8:22–25, he says: "We know that the whole creation has been groaning as in the pains of childbirth right up to the present time. Not only so, but we ourselves, who have the firstfruits of the Spirit, groan inwardly as we wait eagerly for our adoption as sons, the redemption of our bodies. For in this hope we were saved. But hope that is seen is no hope at all. Who hopes for what he already has? But if we hope for what we do not yet have, we wait for it patiently."

That was the hope these believers entertained in their minds. They knew it academically. They knew a day was coming when their bodies would be redeemed and transformed—not an uncertain dream or a faint possibility, but a guaranteed certainty. You may say (as many Ephesians Christians no doubt said), "A future hope is fine—but how does it help me now?" The answer is that our future hope is being worked out in the here and now. Our hope will not only be realized in the resurrection at the end of the age. Our hope is being realized *right now*, as we are gradually, almost imperceptibly being transformed into new creations in Christ.

Here is how the apostle Paul explains it in 2 Corinthians 4:16–18: "Therefore we do not lose heart. Thought outwardly we are wasting away, yet inwardly we are being renewed day by day. For our light and momentary troubles are achieving for us an eternal glory that far outweighs them all. So we fix our eyes not on what is seen, but on what is unseen. For what is seen is temporary, but what is unseen is eternal."

It is important too as we read these words of Paul that a little later in 2 Corinthians he lists some of what he calls, "our light and momentary troubles" that he himself had endured: beaten with rods three times; thirty-nine lashes from a whip five times; shipwrecked three times; a night and a day adrift at sea; stoned and left for dead; danger on sea and land; danger from false brethren; sleeplessness, hunger and thirst; and more. All this he gathers up in the phrase "our light and momentary troubles." All of these things, he says, work in our favor, preparing us for an eternal weight of glory beyond all comparison.

That flat tire you had yesterday which upset you so is working for you, preparing you to handle pressure, teaching you about patience, building Christlike character. All those problems you face are giving you the opportunity to exercise the power of Christ that is available to you. The lost wallet, the missed appointment, the argument with your spouse, the arthritis in your shoulder, the diagnosis you just received, the business failure you just suffered, the heart-breaking loss of a loved one—all of these are working together for your good and for your growth. God didn't cause this pain in your life, but He knows how to bring His good out of it just the same.

If you learn to look at life that way, you will never lose the hope of your calling in Christ.

PAUL'S PRAYER FOR GOD'S RICHES

Paul was concerned for the Ephesians' sense of impoverishment, so he reminded them of the riches that were theirs in Christ. He knew the dangers of self-limited thinking, and he wanted to broaden their vistas from one horizon to the other. So he prayed "that you may know . . . the riches of his glorious inheritance in the saints." Notice how he puts that. He is not asking that they understand that God is their inheritance. It is true that God is our resource and our strength—but Paul is taking a different viewpoint, God's viewpoint.

He is emphasizing the fact that we are God's inheritance, His property. He has an inheritance in us. It is His delight to use us.

If we lose sight of this truth, then we will shrink in fear from allowing God to use us. We will narrow our experience to a single well-worn rut. The Christian life, for us, will become nothing more than a gray succession of drab, dreary days.

We need to understand and welcome the adventure that awaits us when we make ourselves available to God. We need to move out, boldly take the plunge, and even take some risks for His sake! As we begin to dare great things for Christ, we will discover that life brings enrichment—the riches and rewards of adventure, excitement, and varied, delightful experiences.

Once, while I was at a conference at a beautiful estate on the Columbia River, I took a walk down a well-worn trail. As I walked, I noticed a little trail that wandered off to the side. It was obviously not as well traveled as the main path. Intrigued, I veered off and followed the trail-less-traveled to see where it might lead. It soon sloped steeply downward, and I worried that it might be difficult climbing back up. But before long the little path opened upon a lush clearing, affording a magnificent view of the river gorge, the cliffs, the woods arrayed in autumn colors, and the majestic mountains beyond. I was so glad I had taken the less-traveled path!

That's the way life is. There are riches and rewards for those who would step out of the well-worn ruts and strike out in bold directions. There are risks, it's true—but the rewards of boldly following Jesus more than outweigh the risks.

PAUL'S PRAYER FOR GOD'S POWER

Finally, Paul makes a request on behalf of his Ephesian brothers and sisters, "that you may know . . . his incomparably great power for us who believe." He knew that the Ephesians, like all Christians in every place at every time, were sometimes subject to immobilizing fear and insecurity. There was fear of a hostile society, fear of persecution, fear of ridicule, fear of failure. They were pressured without by an evil world and pressured within by feelings of inadequacy and impotence.

The answer to fear is *power*. The moment you feel empowered, fear vanishes. So Paul prayed that the Christians would see the limitless power that was theirs through Christ. The power is available to us all—but we often fail to see it, believe it, and act on it. When we feel powerless, we are quick to give up. The struggle overwhelms us and we just throw in the towel. It is because we have lost sight of the One who gives all power, and whose power was demonstrated at the resurrection, when God raised Jesus from the dead. Remember, resurrection power works best in a cemetery!

If everything is going well, if your boat is shipshape, your skies are blue, and the breeze is at your back, you have no need of a lifesaver. If everything's coming up roses, who needs a delivery from the florist? When you possess the riches of Donald Trump, Bill Gates, and David Rockefeller combined, why would you need a winning lottery ticket? It's when everything is lost that you need to be saved. It's when you face death, darkness, and despair that you need resurrection power.

Praise be to God, resurrection power is still with us today. God is alive, and He continues to work his miracles of transformation, quietly and without fanfare, bringing life out of the gloom and darkness of death.

The power that God makes available to you and me is nothing less than the supreme power in the universe, as we read in Ephesians 1:19–20:

That power is like the working of his mighty strength, which he exerted in Christ when he raised him from the dead and seated him at his right hand in the heavenly realms, far above all rule and authority, power and dominion, and every title that can be given, not only in the present age but also in the one to come. And God placed all things under his feet and appointed him to be head over everything for the church, which is his body, the fullness of him who fills everything in every way.

The power of God is far above any other force, stronger than anything that can be launched against you. So believe Paul's words! This is what the apostle is praying for—that you would truly grasp this thought and understand the true power that He offers you.

A young man once came to me in tearful emotional agony. He told me that he had been struggling with terrible feelings of lust. The feelings and temptations grew so strong that he often fell back into habits that were wrong and destructive to him and his loved ones. He feared that he would never be able to overcome those temptations to sin. So I sat down with him and talked with him about the power of a resurrected Lord, and what he has made available to us. I turned to this very passage we are studying, and I read him the words we have just examined.

"You know," I said, "God's power is made perfect in weakness. Your problem is that you are trying to feel strong. You want to feel powerful. But God says, 'No, resurrection power is the kind that works best when you feel weak.' So if you feel weak, thank God. And the next time you find yourself threatened with these attacks of lust, run to Christ in your helplessness. Say, 'Lord, I can't handle this myself. I can't control myself. If you don't help me, I'm sunk!' Just cast yourself on Him."

"Okay," he said dubiously. "I'll try."

A couple weeks later, I saw him again. This time a big, bright, triumphant smile shone from his face. "It works!" he told me. "It really works! I kept reading that passage in Ephesians, and I was struck by two words: 'far above.' It says that Christ is seated at God's right hand "in the heavenly realms, *far above* all rule and authority, power and dominion, and every title that can be given." Those two words, 'far above,' really opened my eyes. I thought, 'Hey, if God is at work in me, if He has that kind of power, then nobody else's power can get even close to me! No demonic force, no lustful urge, can be greater than the power of Jesus Christ. When I saw that fact, I was able simply to rest in the Lord—and it's been working! God has set me free!'"

NO GREAT NAME

Paul stresses the fact that the name of Jesus is greater than any name that is named. There are many names on earth that confer power and authority. A policeman acts in the name of the law. The president of the United States acts in the name of the people. A salesman acts in the name of the company. Ominously, there are some in our world who actually act in the name of Satan! But there is one name that is above every other name—the name of Jesus.

Jesus is the head of the church, and Paul tells us that the power of Christ has been made visible through His church: "And God placed all things under his feet and appointed him to be head over everything for the church, which is his body, the fullness of him who fills everything in every way" (Ephesians 1:22–23). The only place this kind of power is ever going to be manifest is in you and me, in the midst of our pressures and problems. God's power is the power to be patient in maddening situations. It's the power to love a person when he is irritating the socks off of you. It's the power to be joyful in the midst of suffering and distress. It's the power to be thankful in the midst of deprivation.

That is what Paul is talking about—the power to live as God intended us to live. God sent His Son to us so that we might have hope, and riches, and power—the power to be what He wants us to be, and the power to be what we truly want to be. It is the power to bring life out of death, hope out of hopelessness, joy out of sorrow, and beauty out of ashes. May we see it, believe it, and act on it—and may the world see God's power flowing through us as we boldly take on the challenges of our daily lives.

CHAPTER SEVEN

The Human Dilemma

Ephesians 2:1–3

We turn now to the human condition.

Of all the truth expressed in Scripture, the truth found at the beginning of Ephesians 2 is the hardest for human beings to hear, believe, and accept. Here, in these first three verses, is the revelation of a truth so difficult for us to receive that we immediately tend to discount it and water it down. The result is that we do not have a realistic outlook on the true hopelessness of our condition apart from Christ—or the true wonder of our position once we are in Christ. If you want to truly have your heart on fire with God's truth, if you want to see your own condition with absolute clarity and realism, then pay close attention to these three powerful verses of Scripture:

> As for you, you were dead in your transgressions and sins,
> in which you used to live when you followed the ways of
> this world and of the ruler of the kingdom of the air, the
> spirit who is now at work in those who are disobedient.
> All of us also lived among them at one time, gratifying
> the cravings of our sinful nature and following its desires

and thoughts. Like the rest, we were by nature objects of wrath (2:1–3).

WE ARE DEAD

In these verses we find Paul's great analysis of our problem. We are not a little misguided. We are not culturally deprived or misled in our thinking. The solution to the human condition is not better education or a social program or enhanced self-esteem. No, our problem is more fundamental and hopeless than that. Our problem is that, apart from God, *we are dead*.

It is extremely difficult for us to believe that we are dead. We seem to be getting along fine, enjoying life, getting together with friends, going to movies and concerts, eating well and exercising. How could we do all that if we are dead?

But listen to Paul's analysis and you will see what he means. Listen with a very open mind and you will see how devastatingly accurate his description of our condition truly is. The fact is that there are two basic characteristics of death which we immediately associate with a dead person:

1. Powerlessness
2. Corruption

First, let's look at the utter powerlessness of the dead. My friend Roy Bradford once told me of a time a friend of his, a mortuary worker, took him on an after-hours tour of the funeral home. The friend took Roy into a room where several bodies were laid out on slabs. He pulled back a sheet to show Roy one of the bodies and said, "Tell him about Jesus."

"I've never forgotten that," Roy told me. "A dead person is totally powerless. It's impossible to reach him. He can't do anything to respond to an appeal or to change his condition. Death is utterly final." So the first mark of death is powerlessness.

The second mark is corruption. The reason mortuaries exist is that dead bodies tend to deteriorate quickly. They decay, they fall apart, they lose their consistency. You remember that in the story of Lazarus, Martha said to Jesus, in effect, "It's too late to do anything for Lazarus. Corruption has already set in, and his body stinks. He's been dead four days!" (see John 11:39). So corruption is also a mark of death.

Powerlessness and *corruption*: the apostle uses two words that relate to those two conditions, and these two words explain why he says that, apart from Christ, we are dead. The first word he uses is *transgressions* (some translations use the word *trespasses*).

We are dead, says Paul, through our transgressions. The original Greek word in this context literally means "to miss your step." If you step in a hole and turn your ankle, or if you stumble over a step on a staircase, or if you take a long walk on a short pier, then you know what the concept is here. You have aimed your foot in one direction, thinking there would be a solid support for your step, but the result has been a stumble, a fall. You didn't intend to go head over heels and land on your face. Your intentions were okay, but the result of your actions were wrong. That's a transgression or a trespass.

That kind of action, says Paul, is characteristic and typical of humanity. We are guilty of missteps. We don't mean to do it, but things go awry nonetheless. We start out with great aims, most of us, but we miss the mark. We cannot fulfill our best ideals.

Some years ago, Os Guinness wrote a penetrating assessment of the many philosophies, ideals, and isms of our society, a book called *The Dust of Death*. He pointed out that the mass of humanity seems to swing from extreme to extreme, from naïve optimism about the future to cynical pessimism, from belief in socialist solutions for human problems to belief in free market solutions, from spirituality to materialism, and on and on. As Guinness analyzed each school of thought, he detected a fatal flaw in each one—a reason why this or that philosophy misunderstood some crucial aspect of human nature, a reason why this or that solution would not work, given the reality of human nature.

No matter how well-intentioned these approaches might be, they were all missed steps, transgressions of human nature and God's truth—and the result of each of these isms was death. Hence his title, *The Dust of Death.* Only when Os Guinness returned to the Scriptures and the resurrection of Jesus did he find a genuine solution to the human condition. The resurrection of Jesus Christ, he said, is a fresh wind blowing through the dust of humanity's hollow dreams.

That, of course, is also what Paul is saying. There is this well-intentioned but fumbling tendency in humanity—a tendency for transgressions and trespasses that ultimately mark our death. Transgressions are related to our powerlessness and limitation as human beings.

The second word Paul uses to explain why we are dead apart from Christ is *sins.* Beyond our unintentional and even well-intentioned missteps or transgressions, there are our sins, our intentional and deliberate wrongs. Sin is the violation of truth when we know it to be truth. Our sins create deterioration in our lives, and that is why sin is related to the corruption of death. There is a gradual and progressive quality to sin; it worms its way into our lives. There are sins that, at the beginning, would horrify and repulse us; but as sin seeps into our lives, our morality and standards gradually deteriorate. This is a mark of death—an increasing, progressing corruption that gradually causes our lives to reek with the stench of death.

That is Pauls' analysis. Transgression is the result of human power-lessness, a sign of human death. Sin is the result of human corruption, and corruption increases the more we practice sin—another sign of human death. Paul's analysis fits all the facts of human experience. It is a dead-on accurate diagnosis of the human condition. No other philosophy can ever explain human life adequately. This is my condition and yours. There is no escaping it. Apart from God, if we do not have a Savior, we are all dead in our trespasses and sins.

THE EXPLANATION FOR OUR DEATH

Paul moves next to explain why we are dead in our trespasses and sins. It is a three-fold answer:

1. We have "followed the ways of this world." In the original language, he says we have "followed the age of this world." The age in which we live has certain characteristics, and we are pressured by this age to adopt those characteristics ourselves. We are pressured toward conformity.

Some of us say, "I don't conform, I am a revolutionary, a noncon-formist. I reject conformity with the establishment." But if we are honest with ourselves, we have to admit that refusing to conform to one group, a majority group, only means that we have chosen to conform to a different group, a counterculture or minority group. We are all pressured and even governed by the attitudes of our peers, even if our peers claim to be "nonconformists."

The only true nonconformist who ever lived was Jesus. He was pressured to conform by the Pharisees, by the Roman government, by His family, and even by His own disciples. His answer was al-ways, "I have to be about my Father's business." So he continually sawed across the grain of his family, friends, and society. And He was criticized, hated, persecuted, opposed, and ultimately executed for His nonconformity.

To this day, the world hates genuine Christianity whenever and wherever it is practiced, because genuine Christianity does not conform to society. It contrasts. So it is attacked on all sides. One of the indications of whether your Christianity is genuine or not is whether you get attacked for your failure to conform to the corrupt norms of those around you.

2. We have obeyed the evil god of this world. Beyond the visible walls of this world, says Paul, lies something dark and evil, a sinister being, a willful force. Paul calls this force, "the ruler of the kingdom of the air, the spirit who is now at work in those who are disobedient." Notice how, with each successive phrase, Paul takes us behind the facades of our visible world and into the deeper reality of the heavenly realms. He rips the veil away and unmasks the hidden malevolent force behind so much of humanity's tragic and shameful history. Paul tells us that there is an organized realm of malevolent beings, headed by a ruler of cruel subtlety and power, whose goal is to generate and multiply disobedience against God. For that is truly Satan's stock-in-trade: disobedience.

Paul calls the devil "the prince of the power of the air." I don't think he means literally the oxygen/nitrogen mixture we breathe—although it is possible that the devil has, indeed, corrupted our physical atmosphere. At the very least, however, this is a metaphorical reference to the fact that, as the air pervades our environment yet is invisible to us, so Satan and his angels invisibly surround us, invade our minds, and manipulate the actions of the human race, leading us toward greater and greater disobedience.

Well, disobedient to what? You must have something to obey in order to be disobedient. The disobedience Paul refers to is disobedience to the truth. The God of truth is always trying to capture our attention and set reality before us. But there is an evil spirit at work in society which constantly says, "The truth is a lie, the lie is the truth. Obey my urgings and your cravings—not the truth of God.

3. We have followed the passions and desires of the body and mind. "All of us," writes Paul, "also lived among them at one time, gratifying the cravings of our sinful nature and following its desires and thoughts. Like the rest, we were by nature objects of wrath." Paul sometimes refers to this aspect of human nature "the flesh." It is our basic human nature, the way we are bodily constructed, and it is not necessarily a bad thing. God created us of flesh and bone, and it was a good creation when He made it, but something has happened to our flesh. Something has gained control of our flesh and twisted it: our sinful nature.

But there are also good things about the flesh. The basic desires of the flesh were given to us for our benefit, well-being, and survival. Among those desires are hunger and thirst, the desire for fellowship and attention, the desire to achieve and acquire, and the desire for pleasure, including sexual pleasure. There is nothing wrong with these desires in their proper place. The problem comes when they grow out of proportion, and when we seek to gratify those desires in the wrong place, in the wrong way, and with the wrong people. Eating, drinking, sleeping, working, spending, and sex are all perfectly acceptable and holy pastimes in their place. Out of place and out of proportion, they become the sins of gluttony, alcoholism, laziness, selfish obsession with status, greed, fornication, and adultery.

In discussing these passions or desires of the flesh, Paul makes an interesting subdivision between "desires" and "thoughts," between the cravings of the body and the cravings of the mind. The desires of the body have to do with satisfying and satiating the sense of the body—our sense of taste, our sense of sight, our sexual feelings. The thoughts or cravings of the mind have to do with the mind and the will. These cravings are expressed whenever we are quick to be indignant, hurt, angry, bitter, envious, resentful, or vengeful. Very often, these cravings of the mind begin with a desire for justice, to be treated fairly and decently—a normal human desire. But when our desire for justice is thwarted, our normal human desire for fairness can sour into malice, scheming, manipulating, and lusting for revenge—all sins of the mind and will.

That which produces transgressions and sins marks the death of humanity. Our condition is universal and inescapable. No one can avoid the human condition—it is a condition of hopelessness, apart from the direct intervention of God.

CHILDREN OF WRATH

The inevitable result of our condition, writes Paul, is that "we were by nature objects of wrath." We are, in our natural state, children of wrath. We are subject to the "wrath of God." We have earned punishment.

It is crucially important, however, that we understand what Paul is and is not saying here about God's wrath and God's nature. I have counseled many fearful Christians who were brought up with the idea of God as an ill-tempered cosmic judge, like a mean football referee who can't wait to blow the whistle on any player who commits the tiniest infraction so he can impose a fifteen-yard penalty. That's not what God is like and that's not how Paul wants us to think of God and His wrath.

The wrath of God, as Paul describes it for us in the book of Romans, is what we might call "the law of consequences." For every action, there is a reaction, a consequence. For every cause there is an effect. If we jump off a forty-story building, it is not God's judgmental hand slamming us to the pavement below—it is the inevitable law of gravity. In the same way, if a person contracts a disease from promiscuous sex or heart disease from a lifetime of gluttony or liver damage from years of drinking, that person should not cry out, "God, why are you punishing me so cruelly!" That person is simply reaping the consequences that have been sown by his or her own behavior.

We accept the wrath of God as it applies to gravity and tall buildings. We rebel at the wrath of God as it applies in the moral sphere of life. Many times I've heard people say, "It isn't fair! Why shouldn't I run off with my neighbor's wife? Don't I have a right to happiness? Why should I experience pain and censure and church discipline as a result of this choice?" The fact is that there is a moral law of gravity as well as a physical law of gravity. When we take the plunge into sin, we should not be surprised if, as a result, we sooner or later hit bottom.

We are children of wrath, objects of God's judgment—and with good reason. There is no amount of education, legislation, or remediation that can save us from this condition. We can rearrange the pattern but can't change the basic problem. That is why humanity struggles endlessly to correct and redeem itself but never succeeds. We are born into this condition and there is no way out.

The human condition is universal—no one escapes. It isn't a matter of race or gender, political persuasion or economic status. There is no escape whatsoever—except two little words: "But God . . . ."

That is the sudden glimmer of hope that breaks in upon us in the next verse, Ephesians 2:4. The New Revised Standard Version puts it this way: "But God, who is rich in mercy, out of the great love with which he loved us . . . ." I didn't want to close this chapter without giving you a peek into the next verse, to see that while, in our natural state, we are dead and without hope, we have good news that begins with two words: "But God . . . ."

Paul knows it is important that we first understand the depths from which we have come, the condition of death from which we need to be released. That condition is still present in our Christian lives whenever we choose not to act upon the available resources of Jesus Christ within us. But the nonChristian literally has no hope without God. This knowledge should motivate us to praise God and to share Christ with those who are not just dying, but are *dead* apart from Him.

But here, at the end of this chapter of our study, I have played for you the first two notes of a glorious symphony. Those two notes, "But God . . .", echo in our ears and bring us hope of a wonderful life beyond this condition of death into which we were born. Yes, we are children of wrath. Yes, we are dead in our transgressions and sins. *But God . . . !*

Turn the page with me and we will see what wonderful truths are embedded in those two simple words.

CHAPTER EIGHT

But God . . . !

Ephesians 2:4–6

"B ut God . . ."

These two three-letter words draw us into Ephesians 2:4, where the apostle Paul begins to set forth the story of our great salvation from the hopelessness and death of our human condition. Nothing is more important in our lives than that we grasp the enormous meaning for our lives that is contained within these brief but towering words. The New Revised Standard Version renders verses 4 to 6 in this way:

> But God, who is rich in mercy, out of the great love with which he loved us even when we were dead through our trespasses, made us alive together with Christ—by grace you have been saved—and raised us up with him and seated us with him in the heavenly places in Christ Jesus . . . .

The NIV, the version we have used throughout this study, renders the passage a bit differently. Instead of opening with the words, "But

God . . .", it rearranges the syntax slightly—but the meaning is the same:

> But because of his great love for us, God, who is rich in mercy, made us alive with Christ even when we were dead in transgressions—it is by grace you have been saved. And God raised us up with Christ and seated us with him in the heavenly realms in Christ Jesus.

Verse 4 marks a dramatic contrast in Paul's argument. We move from the gloomy picture of the human condition of verses 1–3 to a brilliant image of hope, joy, and gladness—the glory of our salvation by grace through faith in Jesus Christ. The hinge point between gloom and gladness (as expressed in the NRSV) are these two little words, "But God . . ."

MERCY, GRACE, AND LOVE

The apostle is careful to inform us of God's motivation for moving us from death to life, from darkness to light: "But God, who is rich in mercy, out of the great love with which he loved us, even when we were dead through our trespasses . . . ." We were dead—then God, driven by a heart of mercy and love as deep as time and as wide as space, began to move. God's mercy is a powerful thing.

Do you know what mercy is? Do you know how mercy differs from grace? We bandy these terms about so often in the church that I think, for some people, they become little more than theologically-sound background noise. Mercy and grace are two very specific and distinct concepts, and they are as real—no, more real!—than the page you are reading right now.

A little boy in Sunday School was asked to tell the difference between kindness and loving-kindness, because Scripture uses both those words. He put it this way: "If I ask my mother for a slice of bread and butter and she gives it to me, that is kindness. But if she puts jam on it, that is loving-kindness!" That is great theological truth! That is a beautiful illustration of the difference between kindness and loving-kindness.

There is a similar difference between mercy and grace. Both mercy and grace reach out from God to us—but for different reasons. It is our guilt that draws forth the grace of God. We deserve punishment; we receive forgiveness. That is God's grace to us. The grace of God has dealt with our guilt.

It is not our guilt but our misery that calls forth God's mercy. A parent understands this concept very well. If your child suffers from a severe cold—her throat is sore, her eyes water, her nose runs so that she can hardly breathe, she aches in every joint, and all she can do is throw her arms around your neck and cry. And what do you feel? Pity, compassion, and a sense of urgency to provide relief. Her misery calls forth your mercy. That is what Paul says has awakened the mercy of God—our misery as human beings.

We are dead in our trespasses and sin. We are corrupt and decaying. We are in bondage to Satan, an evil spirit who tempts us into self-destruction and disobedience. We blindly injure ourselves and each other, we destroy the peace in our household, we suffer heartache, despair, rejection, disillusionment, boredom, frustration, and grief. While life is often a wonderful experience, we have to admit that much of life is stained with the blood and tears of human tragedy.

God understand our condition, He empathizes with us, and the sight of our suffering awakens His love, moving Him to reach out to us. He is so moved by our plight, in fact, that He gave His only

Son as a sacrifice upon the cross for our sake. The cross, as ugly and bloodstained as it is, stands as a symbol of God's love and mercy to us. How do we know that God loved us? Because, as John 3:16 tells us, "For God so loved the world that he gave his one and only Son . . . ." That is an unmistakable mark of God's love.

What is love? A lot of people think love is a feeling, an itch in the heart you can't scratch. But the love of God is much deeper than a mere feeling. His love is a decision, a choice He made about us, expressed in action—the act of sending and sacrificing Jesus for our sakes. He did not demand that we climb up to Him; He descended to us. He is not a God of indifference or unconcern. He was touched with our misery and He came and He wept and He suffered. He became the poorest of the poor. He endured the torture and shame of the cross. He took our sins upon Himself. He did all this for us even when we were dead in our transgressions and sins.

ALIVE WITH CHRIST

The theme of "But God . . ." is not mere theoretical, theological talk. It is an immensely practical, powerful truth for our daily lives. Once we understand what God has done for us, and the riches that are ours in Jesus Christ, we have the secret of joyful daily living. As long as we ignore or fail to grasp what God has done for us, we will always be struggling and frustrated in our faith. The truth that we were dead and now alive, that we were shut up in endless gloom and now showered with glory—this is the secret of liberty, joy, and beauty of character! When we truly catch a glimpse of the length and height and breadth of God's love for us, a once-boring earthly existence becomes an exciting touch of heaven on earth.

Paul goes on to bring out three exciting facets of our new life with Christ:

1. Paul says that God "made us alive together with Christ," and he adds parenthetically, "by grace you have been saved." Our salvation is a hundred percent God, zero percent us. We cannot add a thing to what God has done for us. It is utterly by God's grace that we are made alive together with Christ.
2. We have been "raised up with him."
3. We have been "made to sit with him in the heavenly places in Christ Jesus."

These are present realities, not future theological theories. In the original Greek, the statement that God "made us alive together with Christ" is only two words. One word contains the sense of "made us alive together with" and the other word is Christ. There is a sense of immediacy and excitement in this statement that God enlivened us with Christ—and indeed, it is an exciting event!

Now, that doesn't mean that the experience is always exciting and emotional—often, it does not feel like a dramatic event at all. I have had the joy of leading scores of people to Christ, and almost always it is very quiet moment. For some, a pleasant sense of peace comes over them. Others experience a quiet sense of joy. In some cases, there is a big rush of emotion, an epiphany, even a spiritual ecstasy—but in my experience, that is very rare. Yet, even though a person's conversion experience may be a quiet one, something tremendous has taken place—a human being has crossed over from death to life.

Imagine that you had a corpse sitting in your living room for a week or two. I know this sounds gruesome, but I can really think of no more apt way to make this point! Let us say that you knew this person in life, and now he or she is utterly dead, with no ability to think, speak, hear, move, or feel emotions. Now imagine that you have the power to lay hands on this corpse and bring this individual back to life. What an astonishing miracle *that* would be—bringing a dead person back to life.

Yet that is exactly what the apostle Paul says has taken place when a person comes in faith to Jesus Christ. That which was dead becomes alive together with Christ. It is no less real and dramatic than that.

God employs numerous similes in His Word to bring this truth alive in our lives. He compares conversion to the process of birth. Becoming a Christian is likened to being born again. Before birth, there is conception, which takes place as the result of an act of love, an act of merging. It is a dramatic, miraculous event that brings life into the world. Paul wants to compel our attention, so he uses a similar metaphor here in Ephesians, comparing the conversion experience to the resurrection event, in which we who are dead receive life from Him. We are made alive with Jesus Christ.

There is a sign I always look for when a person makes a decision for Jesus Christ: a change in attitude. I find that it begins to show almost immediately. Self-centeredness evaporates; others-centeredness becomes apparent. Many times at the moment someone comes to Christ, they say, "I wish you would tell this to my brother," or, "I wish you'd pray for my parents." Immediately, their thoughts have turned away from their own wonderful experience to the spiritual need of someone they care about. That is a sure sign that this person has come alive in Christ, and passed from death unto life.

The conversion experience also produces an immediate reaction in a persons attitude toward God. I have found that most nonChristians tend to be afraid of God. They avoid church because they see people enjoying God's presence there, and it makes them feel uneasy. And that's all right—people shouldn't be expected to have to come to church to find God. Evangelism is supposed to take place in the neighborhood and marketplace, not inside the chapel walls. Church is for Christians. God reaches out to people where they are, through His own people.

NonChristians tend to be afraid of God and afraid of death. Funerals make them uneasy and nervous—"Let's get this thing over with so I can get back to my life." Death makes them think of being in the presence of God—and they don't want that!

But when nonChristians become Christians, their attitudes toward God and death change immediately. Instead of seeing God as their judge, they see Him as their Father—or better yet, their Daddy. They belong to Him, and they trust His love. They have a hunger for God, and death no longer holds any terror for them. Immediately. God is now their Father. They have a sense of belonging. And now the one Person they want above all others is God. As the Psalmist writes, "As the deer pants for streams of water, so my soul pants for you, O God. My soul thirsts for God, for the living God. When can I go and meet with God?" (Psalm 42:1).

Other examples of the change that comes over those who place their trust in Jesus: They suddenly become able to love the unlovable, endure the unendurable, and forgive the unforgivable.

Many a husband or wife has told me of reaching a point in his or her marriage of complete estrangement, of literally hating the spouse, of being unable to stand the sight of the one he or she vowed to love till death. Then, upon receiving Christ, that person discovered that a new relationship was possible. No, the struggles did not instantly vanish, but the individual was able to look at his or her spouse in a new way, and to make a Christlike decision to love, even in unlovely circumstances. I have seen many marriages saved and many nonbelieving spouses won to Christ as a result of one partner accepting Christ and discovering a newfound ability to love the unlovable.

Others are able to endure the unendurable after they come to

Christ. I remember one woman who struggled for well over a decade with constant pain that often immobilized her. She went through terrible struggles with depression, discouragement, and defeat. There were times when she considered using a bottle of pain pills as an escape from the pain of this life—but she held on, enduring the unendurable because of the power released in her by the risen Lord.

Still others have discovered, in their new relationship with Jesus Christ, the ability to forgive the unforgivable. In her Holocaust memoir *The Hiding Place*, Corrie Ten Boom tells how she and her family resisted the Nazis by hiding Jews in their home. They were ultimately discovered and sent to a concentration camp. Corrie barely survived until the end of the war; her family members died in captivity. Seared by this terrible trial by fire, Corrie's faith in God also survived, and she spent much of her time in the post-war years traveling in Germany and elsewhere in Europe, sharing her faith in Christ.

On one occasion in 1947, while speaking in a church in Munich, she noticed a balding man in a gray overcoat near the rear of the basement room. She had been speaking on the subject of God's forgiveness, but her heart froze within her when she recognized the man. She could picture him as she had seen him so many times before, in his blue Nazi uniform with the visored cap—the cruelest of the guards at the Ravensbruck camp where Corrie had suffered the most horrible indignities, and where her own sister had died. Yet here he was, at the end of her talk, coming up the aisle toward her with his hand thrust out. "Thank you for your fine message," he said. "How wonderful it is to know that all our sins are at the bottom of the sea!"

Yes, Corrie had said that. She had spoken so easily of God's forgiveness, but here was a man whom she despised and condemned with every fiber of her being. She couldn't take his hand! She couldn't extend forgiveness to this Nazi oppressor! She realized that this man didn't remember her—how could he remember one prisoner among thousands?

"You mentioned Ravensbruck," the man continued, his hand still extended. "I was a guard there. I'm ashamed to admit it, but it's true. But since then, I've come to know Jesus as my Lord and Savior. It has been hard for me to forgive myself for all the cruel things I did—but I know that God has forgiven me. And please, if you would, I would like to hear from your lips too that God has forgiven me." And Corrie recorded her response in her book:

> I stood there—I whose sins had again and again been forgiven—and could not forgive. It could not have been many seconds that he stood there—hand held out—but to me it seemed hours as I wrestled with the most difficult thing I had ever had to do. For I had to do it. I knew that. It was as simple and as horrible as that. And still I stood there with the coldness clutching my heart. And so, woodenly, mechanically, I thrust my hand into the one stretched out to me.
>
> And as I did, an incredible thing took place. The current started in my shoulder, raced down my arm, and sprang into our joined hands. And then this healing warmth seemed to flood my whole being, bringing tears to my eyes. "I forgive you, brother," I cried. "With all my heart!"
>
> For a long moment we grasped each other's hands, the former guard and the former prisoner. I had never known God's love so intensely as I did then.

That is the power of resurrection life. It is for impossible situations like that. Resurrection power baffles and bewilders the world, enabling us to love the unlovable, endure the unendurable, and for-give the unforgivable. That is what it means to be raised up together with Jesus Christ.

JOINED TO CHRIST

It is significant that Paul underscores the words "with Christ" or "with him" by repeating them three times in these verses.

1. "We are made alive together with Christ."
2. "We are raised up with him."
3. "We are made to sit with him."

The greatest fact of our entire Christian experience is that we are with Christ and He is with us—that we are, in fact, *joined* to Jesus Christ. We are one with him. Do you remember the Lord's teaching on this subject? He said, "I am the vine; you are the branches" (John 15:5). Can you tell where the branch ends and the vine starts? No. They are one plant, sharing one life together. So from here on, our identity is no longer "in Adam," but "in Christ." We are no longer ordinary human beings. We are new creations, and His identity be-comes ours.

Later in this letter, Paul will liken the church to a body of which Christ is the head. Have you examined your body lately? Tug at your fingers. Why don't they come off? Wag your head from side to side. Why doesn't it roll off your shoulders? It's because they share the life of the body. They are not buttoned, glued, stapled, or tacked on. They are an organic part of your body. That's the way it is with us and Jesus. We have been joined with Christ, and we are an integral part of His body.

An interesting package once arrived at the office of Peninsula Bible

Church. We opened it, and to our amazement and bewilderment we found it contained a supply of birth control pills. We wondered who in the world would send birth control pills to a church! We opened the card that came with the package and read:

> Dear PBC:
>
> The prescription for these pills dates to October. They are still good. Use them if you like. I no longer need them, because I am reformed. You see, I shouldn't have been using these pills because I am not married. But praise the Lord! I have made a decision to protect myself with godly chastity and virtue instead of pills—and God is upholding my decision!

The note was signed in sweet humility, "The little toe of the Body." This was the act of someone who had learned what it means to be joined to Christ. Her decision to renounce sexual immorality was a sign of a basic change in her life because she was made alive in Jesus Christ.

Finally, notice that the verbs in this passage are all in the past tense. This is something that has happened, not something that's going to happen. It is already true, and every Christian has this experience. We were made alive in Jesus Christ. We are not the same as we once were. We cannot ever be the same again.

Now, you see the radical difference that two little words make: "But God . . . ." Those two words spell the difference between gloom and glory, between darkness and light, between death and life. It is the most astounding, thrilling, life-changing statement human ears have ever heard: Once we were dead in our trespasses and sins—

But God!

CHAPTER NINE

On Display

Ephesians 2:7–10

I vividly recall a trip our family took to the De Young Museum in San Francisco's Golden Gate Park. There was a special display of paintings by Norman Rockwell, including many of the original paintings of his *Saturday Evening Post* covers. It was a rich slice of Americana, and every painting captured a unique moment, a sentimental mood, evoking either a chuckle or a twinge of nostalgia. Some of Rockwell's scenes made me laugh out loud, while others, candidly, brought a tear to my eye. That entire display of paintings was a vivid demonstration of the painter's heart, mind, eye, and workmanship.

In Ephesians 2:7–10, the apostle Paul uses this same metaphor to describe you and me. God, he says, is going to put us on display. Each one of us will be a vivid demonstration of the grace and the perfection of His heart and His character. The glory of God will be visible in us throughout the coming ages, manifested especially by His kindness toward us.

Let's look at these verses together:

> . . . in order that in the coming ages he might show the incomparable riches of his grace, expressed in his kindness to us in Christ Jesus. For it is by grace you have been saved, through faith—and this not from yourselves, it is the gift of God—not by works, so that no one can boast. For we are God's workmanship, created in Christ Jesus to do good works, which God prepared in advance for us to do.

Here, Paul explores the purpose of God in redeeming mankind. He answers such questions as, "Why did God make the decision to enter our lives? Why has He raised us up with Christ? Why has He exalted us and made us sit together with Him in heavenly places?" Paul's answer is that God made this decision about us so that, in the coming ages, He might display the immeasurable riches of His grace through His kindness to us in Christ Jesus. In other words, God's purpose was to make of us a display case to demonstrate the glory of His character and grace.

THE KINDNESS OF GOD

God has put us on display in the art gallery of His grace. Each of us is a vivid demonstration of the perfection of God's character. The glory of God is manifested, says Paul, by His kindness toward us. The kindness of God begins with the blessings he showers on all humanity— the sun and rain, the seasons, food to eat, houses to live in, productive work to do and good minds to think with, and natural wonders to enjoy. But His kindness isn't confined to natural blessings—it extends further, to God's redemptive blessings. As Paul says in Titus 3:4–6,

> But when the kindness and love of God our Savior appeared, he saved us, not because of righteous things we

had done, but because of his mercy. He saved us through the washing of rebirth and renewal by the Holy Spirit, whom he poured out on us generously through Jesus Christ our Savior.

According to the apostle, God has just begun to pour out the blessings of His kindness. Returning to Ephesians 2:7, we read that God has saved us and blessed us "in order that in the coming ages he might show the incomparable riches of his grace, expressed in his kindness to us in Christ Jesus." He has not yet poured it out upon us to the full degree by any means. His program, Paul says, is to manifest in abundance the riches of His grace in His kindness toward us through the coming ages.

Now, pause with me a moment and ponder what that means: How long is an age? Scripture identifies only two ages so far in the history of humanity. One extended from the creation of Adam to the Flood of Noah. The other is the age from the Flood to the present day. The second age will end at the return of the Lord Jesus, when another age will begin. But according to this passage in Ephesians, God has planned for many ages yet to come. How long will that be? Who can say what is in the heart and mind of God? But it is clear that God has a future in mind for us that is far beyond anything we can possibly imagine.

If you have experienced anything of what it means to be made alive in Christ, to be raised up with Him, you know how rich your life has already become. But that is just the beginning. The richness of the kindness of God will carry you on into the undreamed-of ages to come.

This is true not only of his redemptive kindness, but of his natural kindness as well. There are passages in the Scriptures which hint of the possibilities ahead in the realm of nature, in the world of physical experience—references to the new heaven and new earth, to a resurrected body, equipped to meet the demands of the human spirit in ways we have never known before.

I have always been interested in astronomy, in the breathtaking images of the universe captured at Mt. Hamilton or on Palomar Mountain in Southern California. And in recent years, these views have been eclipsed by the amazing deep-space images from the Hubble Space Telescope and other heavenly explorers. These devices are pointed right through the picture window in the front of the Father's house!

When I look into the heavens and think of the vast reaches of the universe, the innumerable whirling galaxies floating in space, it is inconceivable to me that God would create this vast universe without a plan for developing it further. And the Scriptures suggest that, in the coming ages, we who know Jesus Christ, and whose lives are bound to His life, will have an entire universe to explore. Paul does not go into detail about what our future adventures in future ages might entail, but we can be assured that in those ages to come, age upon age, there will be tremendous work for us to do—a far greater work and grander adventure than anything ever imagined by Captain Kirk or Mr. Spock on the Starship *Enterprise*!

Our present life might not always be what we'd like it to be, but we can be assured that it is only the beginning. Immeasurable possibilities lie ahead. Robert Browning wrote some lines that take on new meaning in light of Ephesians 2:7:

> Grow old along with me!
> The best is yet to be,
> The last of life, for which the first was made.

We are learning now, in this age, in order that we might be prepared to display the greatness of God's glory in the coming ages.

BY GRACE THROUGH FAITH

Next, Paul sets forth the basis for our salvation. These are verses we would do well to memorize and teach our children, because these words give us the key to a saving relationship with Jesus Christ:

> For it is by grace you have been saved, through faith—and this not from yourselves, it is the gift of God—not by works, so that no one can boast.

Notice the tense of the verb: "you have been saved." Just think of it! Our salvation has already been accomplished. This statement is the foundational link to all the other truths previously set forth in Ephesians:

> We have been made alive in Christ.
> We have been given a new identity.
> We are no longer what we once were.
> We are no longer associated with Adam, but we are in Christ.
> We are no longer children of wrath but children of God.

These realities make the difference as to how life is lived, what your days are like, and what your tomorrows will be. You don't need to chase after every new theological fad, every new book or program or movement or spiritual guru. You don't need to run after every new spiritual experience. No, you need only grasp the riches of God's grace already provided for you in Jesus Christ.

Paul stresses the fact that you had nothing to do with your salvation. It was God's action and decision alone. You did not originate it or add anything to it. It is not of human works. It is God's grace alone, which we receive directly from the hand of God.

God's grace means we can never boast. Boasting is pretending you are something you are not. Boasting is saying, "I'm my own creator, my own god, my own savior, the captain of my own destiny. I am sufficient in myself." Boasting is a lie. We are not merely insufficient, we are not merely weak, we are (as Paul says in Ephesians 2:1) *dead* in our transgressions and sins.

When we forget that our salvation is a hundred percent God and zero percent us, when we forget that we are totally dependent on His grace, then we lie to ourselves. God never allows self-deception to stand. He is an utter realist. He deals with life exactly as it is—and he wants us to do the same.

Imagine you are half a million dollars in debt. Someone comes to you and writes out a check for $500,000, saying, "This is all for you, to cancel your debt. You don't have to do anything but reach out and take it, and its yours." So you take the money and pay your debt. You are now debt-free and totally in the clear.

Question: What do you have to boast about? Can you go around bragging that you had the power and the skill and the brains to reach out and take that check? Can you talk about what a favor you did for your benefactor taking all that troublesome money off his hands? Does that make any sense?

Of course not. You received grace, nothing more, nothing less. You were impoverished; you received riches from another person. The fact that you are now debt-free is a hundred percent due to your benefactor, zero percent due to you.

Who, then, deserves the praise and glory for your salvation? Clearly, not you! You have received riches from the resources of God. His grace made it all possible.

GOD'S WORKMANSHIP,
CREATED FOR GOOD WORKS

So the apostle goes on to show us how God's grace will ultimately be displayed:

> For we are God's workmanship, created in Christ Jesus to
> do good works, which God prepared in advance for us to do.

Notice how Paul places "good works" in the proper perspective. Works are important—but they do not save. God desires our good works—but they are nothing that we can boast about. We don't obtain anything from God by working for it. We can never be deserving of salvation—the only thing we deserve is judgment. Works are important, but salvation is by grace alone.

The Greek word translated "workmanship" in verse 10 is actually the word for "poem." We are God's poetry in motion. We are His masterpiece, expressing the depths of His loving and creative heart. He is working through our lives to produce a tremendous exhibit of His wisdom, power, love, character, and joy. He is teaching us, training us, and shaping us into a marvelous masterpiece for display through the ages. The result will be that our lives will shine forth with the very thing God created us to demonstrate: good works of kindness, love, mercy, compassion, forgiveness, and service.

I once flew to Albuquerque with one of the interns of our church, Brian Burgess, for a few days of ministry in that city. We didn't know what God had planned for us, but as the plane was approaching the landing strip, Brian and I prayed together. I'll never forget his words: "Father, thank You for the good works You have already prepared for us in Albuquerque. Thank you that those good works are just waiting for us to step into them and carry them out."

This is what Paul says in verse 10: God has already prepared good works for us to do. And sure enough, God had prepared a ministry for us in Albuquerque. Brian and I met with and encouraged a missionary who had returned stateside from South America. He was so burned out and discouraged, he had decided to quit the ministry. We listened to him, studied the Scriptures with him, and prayed with him—and before we left him, he told us God had ministered to him through us, and changed his life. He decided to return to the field.

We counseled a girl who was locked in a power struggle with her parents—and God enabled her to open new channels of communication and understanding with them. We encouraged and counseled a young pastor who was dealing with division and dissension in his church. Brian led a Bible study every morning with the wealthy businessman, and it was a thrill to see this business leader sit like a child at Brian's feet, learning how to unlock the truth of God's Word. God had prepared all these good works for us beforehand—all we did was step into them.

What are the good works God has prepared for you? No one but God knows. But imagine the excitement of discovering and carrying out those good works—the works God created you to do! Give thanks to God for what He has done for you in Jesus Christ. Plunge into the adventure He has prepared for you. You are His workmanship, His masterpiece, His poem, and He has created you to display His grace and His greatness in all the ages to come!

Strangers in Darkness

Ephesians 2:11–13

In this portion of our study in Ephesians, Paul is going to confront us with yet another metaphor to describe our condition apart from Christ, our past life before we joined our life to His. Here, Paul looks back upon who we were as preChristians, as pagans (the word he uses is *Gentiles*), and he reminds us of our previous condition of darkness and ignorance. He writes in Ephesians 2:11–13:

> Therefore, remember that formerly you who are Gentiles by birth and called "uncircumcised" by those who call themselves "the circumcision" (that done in the body by the hands of men)—remember that at that time you were separate from Christ, excluded from citizenship in Israel and foreigners to the covenants of the promise, without hope and without God in the world. But now in Christ Jesus you who once were far away have been brought near through the blood of Christ.

In this passage the apostle deals with the difference between Jews and Gentiles. He identifies the Gentiles for us: those called "uncircumcised" by Jews, who are circumcised. Paul indicates that circumcision is the distinguishing mark of the Jews, and he has a good reason for doing so. He says, "You Gentiles are uncircumcised. The Jews are the circumcised people." Circumcision marked the Jews as a special people, uniquely belonging to God. So when Paul said the Jews were circumcised, he was symbolizing the advantages of the Jew over the Gentile.

CIRCUMCISION AND SEXUALITY

Circumcision—the surgical removal of the foreskin from the male sex organ—is very important in the Scriptures. It is referred to throughout the Old Testament and the New. The practice began with Abraham, who circumcised his son Isaac at God's command, signifying a special relationship to Him. The Gentiles did not circumcise. The symbol of circumcision, like all scriptural symbols, has a special meaning. Why do you think God chose to place His mark of ownership on the male sex organ? Why was this part of the body chosen as a sign that the Jewish people were chosen by God?

The answer is that our sexuality is a basic part of our humanity. The Scriptures teach this very plainly. The church has often been squeamish about teaching the plain biblical truth of our sexuality. We have often behaved in the church as if our human bodies ended at the waist, and we needn't be concerned with those so called "unmentionable" parts of us. But sex and sexuality are not unmentionable to God. He created our sexuality, and He knows it is not extraneous to our existence—it is fundamental! God's Word deals with sexual matters in a forthright, honest way that accepts the fact that our sexuality is an integral part of our humanity.

Most important of all, the Bible places our sexual nature in a spiritual context. The Scriptures teach us plainly that we are to respect our bodies and treat our sexuality as a holy gift from God. So circumcision is the recognition on God's part that what we think about sex reveals what we think of ourselves, of self-image, and our identity.

The Gentile, pagan world was called "uncircumcised" because it was characterized by two elements:

1. Sexual immorality. Like the pagans in our own society, many of the pagans in Paul's day were highly educated—what we call "civilized." But mingled with their civilization was a terrible sexual degeneracy—which I'm sure sounds very familiar to you. When you visit the pagan world, the ancient temples of Rome and Greece, you find a tremendous emphasis on sex symbols. The Greek philosophers, who are regarded as such advanced thinkers that in many ways they have never been surpassed, were quite sexually degraded. Homosexuality was widespread and widely accepted, along with other degrading sexual practices. So the pagan world of Paul's day revealed its lack of understanding and respect for its own humanity by its degraded sexual practices.

2. Religious ignorance. The Scriptures teach that you can never truly know yourself until you know God. It is knowledge of God that reveals you to yourself. Those who have come to a knowledge of God are always growing in self-understanding and the understanding of others.

All of this is implied in the classification of the pagan world as uncircumcised. It is sexually aberrant and ignorant of God. Yet Paul gives us a hint in verse 11 that the Jews, despite their many advantages, were often hypocritical. They failed to take hold of those advantages, claiming to possess what they did not actually possess. Paul explains: "Therefore, remember that formerly you who are Gentiles by birth and called 'uncircumcised' by those who call themselves 'the circumcision' (that done in the body by the hands of men)."

Paul's suggestion here is that while the Jews were called "circumcised," they didn't always live like circumcised people. You say, "So what? How does this affect me today? That was then and this is now! The first century world has nothing in common with the world today!" If that's what you believe, you are very much mistaken. Beneath the styles and technological trappings of our era, we are very much the same kind of people as those in the first century, facing the same moral issues and temptations that they face.

STRANGERS WITHOUT HOPE

Paganism is rampant in our day, and it is no different from the paganism of Paul's day. Many of us believe we live in a Christian nation, but the fact is that America today is in the grip of pagan beliefs and practices. Those of us who truly adhere to biblical ideals and morality are the minority in America today. There is no "moral majority," only a narrow slice of true, faithful Christians and the much larger pagan world.

We, as faithful Christians in America, are in much the same position as the Jews of Paul's day—even if we are Gentiles by race. We have been exposed to a great deal of truth. We have many advantages, just as the Jews had. The Jews of Paul's time had the Scriptures and traditions that should have resulted in a humble, faithful, trusting relationship with God—yet many of them did not know God at all. A lot of us, as churchgoing Americans, are in that same condition today.

Many of us in churches today have come out of a pagan environment, such as Paul describes here. We know that the pagan mindset is much the same now as then, whether that pagan is a first century cloth merchant or a twenty-first century stockbroker. So we should listen carefully as Paul describes the pagan condition, because his words are as applicable today as they were 2,000 years ago. If anything the world is a more pagan place today than ever before, as our culture rapidly sheds its veneer of Christian influence and tradition, and becomes openly idolatrous, immoral, and self-centered. Paul writes in verse 12: "Remember that at that time you were separate from Christ, excluded from citizenship in Israel and foreigners to the covenants of the promise, without hope and without God in the world."

That is paganism. The one thing that can be said of all pagans, no matter what their background, is that they are separated from Christ. If you haven't yet come to Christ, you are a pagan. You may have been brought up in a religious home. You may be trained in civilized approaches. You may be witty, intelligent, artistic, successful, well-read, educated, and urbane—in every worldly aspect an admirable and enjoyable person. But the one great fact remains: you are separated from Christ.

Without Christ you have no life from God. You may accept the fact that some Supreme Intelligence exists, but your belief does not lead to worship or friendship with the one true, living God. There are pagans in Paul's day who believed in God. They had turned from the gods of the Greek and Roman pantheons, and they accepted the Jewish creed of a one true God, the Maker of heaven and earth. But they didn't know Him. They had no personal relationship with Him. And that is so true of many today.

What a tragic thing to be separated from Christ. You may know the stories about Christ, you may love His teaching, you may admire His courage and compassion—but until you have trusted Him for your salvation, you don't *know* Him in a personal way. There is a gap of separation between you and Jesus. As long as that gap exists, it is a death-gap. You are still dead in your transgressions and sins, in bondage to the evil prince of this world, fulfilling the lusts of the flesh, a child of wrath. That is the highest thing that can be said of a pagan.

But for many it is much worse. Paul goes on to describe those who are "excluded from citizenship in Israel." Here Paul contrasts the position of the Gentiles with that of the Jews. The Jews had a nation over which God ruled—and that meant they had a national cultural sense of destiny, a sense of God's protection and oversight.

But the pagans did not have this. They were excluded from the citizenship of the Jews. The pagan world worshiped a pantheon of gods. The Greeks had their list of gods, the Romans had theirs, the Persians had theirs, and the barbarians to the north had theirs. The pagan gods were as irritable and undependable as people are. Pagans lived in a world in which they were exposed to powers they recognized as being greater than themselves, but in which there was no love, compassion, mercy, justice, or consistency. Pagans never thought of their gods as loving them, nor did they have any reason to love their gods. They felt no sense of belonging to the gods—and that is why they had no hope.

Paul goes on: Pagans, he said, were "foreigners to the covenants of the promise." These covenants were the agreements God made with Abraham, Jacob, and Moses—agreements that bound God to do certain things. God bound himself to obey certain provisions, if His people would respond to them. So every Israelite had a hope, if he would only be obedient to it. The Scriptures show that they frequently strayed from that hope, but the covenant of God was dependable, if the people would only respond to it.

There were, for instance, promises that had to do with sacrifices. Every Israelite knew that if he were burdened with guilt, there was something he could do about it. He could bring a sacrifice, and if an animal was sacrificed under proper conditions, then the conscience of that individual would be erased.

There were promises that had to do with the Messiah. Every Israelite knew that no matter how bad things got, one day God was going to send a Messiah. And even though the nation forgot God and turned away completely, God would not cut them off. He would send a Messiah who would one day restore the people.

The pagans had no such hope—and that is the contrast between the Jews and Gentiles. Pagans, in their darkness, had no hope. Their lives were ruled by the chaotic whims of unreliable, unpredictable, irritable gods. They had no solution to the problem of sin and shame. They were subject to violence, cruelty, and warfare which obsessed the pagan world. They were strangers in the world, with no hope for the future.

So Paul sums up their ultimate condition with these words: "without hope and without God in the world." Archaeologists have dug up first century cemeteries in various places in Greece and Rome and have found many tombstones that bear the Greek or Latin inscription for "No hope." How heartbreaking! Imagine living your entire life with no hope! Imagine going to your death, to that eternal night, with no hope!

The pagans looked out into the future and saw absolutely nothing significant. Their writings reveal the utter darkness, emptiness, and hopelessness of pagan life.

THE FADING OF TRUTH

Remember the words of Pontius Pilate just before he washed his hands of the Lord Jesus? Our Lord had just told Pilate that He had come into the world to declare the truth. And Pilate responded, "What is truth?" That is the hopeless cynicism of an educated Roman pagan agnostic.

We tend to think of the ancient Romans and Greeks as worshipers of many gods. Certainly, people did worship those gods. But the truth is that many Romans and Greeks were atheists and agnostics. They worshiped nothing. They didn't believe in the old gods anymore. They went through the rituals of worshiping, just as people often do in churches today, but they didn't believe in the gods. Doesn't that sound just like many of the agnostic pagans you and I know so well? Doesn't that sound like so many people around us, in our neighborhood, on our jobsite, in our schools, in our country club or gym, and even in our own churches?

The Greek and Roman thinkers, the scientists and philosophers, the statesmen and leaders of the day, looked out upon the universe and saw nothing but an enormous cosmic loneliness—a cruel and heartless universe without a molecule of pity or compassion of the strugglings of human beings. Doesn't that sound familiar? Doesn't that sound like someone you know? Perhaps someone you've been praying for and witnessing to?

We hear that the ancient world was a beautiful place, filled with great architectural achievements, works of art, drama, literature, and philosophy. Sometimes the pagan world is portrayed as an idyllic paradise—a place of exotic beauty and fascinating culture. Superficially, outwardly, this may be so—but inwardly, every pagan was in the grip of fear, hostility, hatred, superstition, and emptiness.

I once read an account of a South American tribesman who was led to Christ by a missionary. The tribesman said, "When I lived in the jungle, I was always afraid. When we woke up in the morning, I was afraid. When I went out of my house, I was afraid. When I walked along the river, I was afraid. I saw an evil spirit in every stone and tree and waterfall. And when night fell, fear came into my hut and slept with me all night long."

That is the inner life of a pagan. And that is what the world is returning to. All around us, on every side, as Christian truth begins to fade, as the nation becomes secularized and humanized, this pagan darkness settles upon the land once again.

THOSE WHO WERE FAR OFF ARE BROUGHT NEAR

But that is not the end of the story. Paul goes on to tell us in verse 13: "But now in Christ Jesus you who once were far away have been brought near through the blood of Christ." Notice that Paul does not merely say that we were brought near through the *death* of Christ, but through the *blood* of Christ. I believe Paul chose his words with care.

Death, of course, is not always bloody. You can die without losing your blood. The Scriptures sometimes speak of the death of Christ, and more often of the cross of Christ. But most often of all, the Scriptures speak of the blood of Christ. Why does God place such an emphasis on blood?

For obvious reasons, many people don't like to hear about the blood of Jesus. But God underscores it. He wants us to think about it, because blood is a sign of violence. It is extremely important that we remember that Jesus did not simply pass away. He died a painful, violent, bloody, gory, ugly, revolting death. He was tortured and beaten, then His writhing body was hammered to a rough wooden cross, the end of which was dropped into a hole in the ground with a bone-wrenching thud. The blood of Jesus streamed down His face, His arms, His sides, staining the cross and the ground beneath him.

God wants us to remember the violent death of Jesus, because violence is the ultimate result of godlessness and paganism. It is the final expression of a godless society. Cruelty arises immediately when love and truth disappear from society. God wants humanity to see that when we have done our worst, sunk to our lowest, expressed our most violent hatred and sadistic cruelty, when we have tortured and impaled Innocence personified—God is there, reaching out in love, ready to forgive. He calls to us who are far off from Him, and draws us to himself through the blood of Jesus.

This is the wonder of God's grace. In the midst of our violence and hatred, He sends His mercy and love. In the midst of our sin, He sends His purity and innocence. In the midst of our darkness, He sends His light. In the midst of our death and corruption, He sends His resurrection and life.

Here is one of the great and beautiful paradoxes of our faith: We who were dead now live because of the death of His Son. His blood makes us clean.

We are no longer strangers in darkness. We are children of the light.

CHAPTER ELEVEN

The Prince of Peace

Ephesians 2:14–18

As commander of the French forces in World War I, Marshal Ferdinand Foch was responsible for a number of Allied victories against the Germans, including the battles at Ypres (1915) and the Rhine (1918). Marshal Foch rarely gave interviews to the newspapers during the war, so reporters continually pressed those around him for any nugget of information about Marshal Foch's thinking about the war.

One man who was continually hounded by the press was Marshal Foch's driver, Pierre. The most frequently asked question: "When does Marshal Foch think the war will end?" The driver told reporters, "The Marshal never tells me anything—but if he ever says anything to me, I'll be happy to tell you."

Day by day the reporters continued to pressure Pierre for any information. Finally, the driver surprised the reporters by saying, "This morning, Marshal Foch spoke to me about the end of the war."

Pens poised above their notepads, the reporters eagerly demanded to know what the military leader said.

The driver continued, "Marshal Foch said, 'Pierre, what do you think? When is this war going to end?'"

Everywhere, for as far back as humanity remembers, the most urgent question of our race has been, "When will there be peace?" Do you remember a time in which there was truly peace in the world? When there was no major war, no brushfire war, no cold war, no war of liberation, no terrorist war, no war of guns, no war of words?

Conflict among nations is truly just a macrocosm of the conflict we see and experience daily at the microcosmic level—conflict between individuals, conflict within families, conflict within businesses, conflict within churches, even conflicts on the freeway where angry drivers engage in everything from "Same to you, fella!" tirades to actual gunfire. As human beings, we scarcely know ourselves, we don't even begin to understand all the sources of our conflicts—so how can we know how to bring about peace?

Peace is a universal longing. We all want peace—but none of us knows the way to peace.

THE GREAT PEACEMAKER

In our study of Ephesians 2, we come to a passage in which the apostle Paul deals with Christ's role as the great peacemaker among men. Here we will see him in fulfillment of the great prophecy in Isaiah 9:6: "And he will be called Wonderful Counselor, Mighty God, Everlasting Father, Prince of Peace." This exalted title belongs strictly to Jesus.

In Ephesians 2:14–18, the apostle gives us the way of peace. He uses as an illustration the fact that Jesus Christ bridged the widest chasm that ever existed between people—the gulf between Jew and Gentile. If you doubt that the Jew-Gentile division is so difficult to bridge, consider the Israeli-Arab problem in the Middle East. The greatest minds of our day have tried to work it out, and no one has gotten anywhere near a settlement. This is a classic confrontation between Jew and Gentile, and the differences are so profound, the hostilities so entrenched, that a solution appears impossible.

Paul describes in Ephesians 2:14–18 how Christ bridges the conflict and brings peace:

> For he himself is our peace, who has made the two one and has destroyed the barrier, the dividing wall of hostility, by abolishing in his flesh the law with its commandments and regulations. His purpose was to create in himself one new man out of the two, thus making peace, and in this one body to reconcile both of them to God through the cross, by which he put to death their hostility. He came and preached peace to you who were far away and peace to those who were near. For through him we both have access to the Father by one Spirit.

The word *peace* appears four times in three verses in that passage, and those occurrences of the word *peace* give us the apostle's outline of how Christ brings peace:

1. "For he himself is our peace," verse 14. That is the origin of peace.
2. "His purpose was to create in himself one new man out of the two, thus making peace," verse 15. This is the process of peace, how it is actually brought about: Jesus came and made peace.
3. "He came and preached peace to you who were far away and peace to those who were near," verse 17. He brought us to peace by preaching to us the means of peace.

I want to again underscore, as I have in previous chapters and will again in later chapters, that these truths are not mere doctrinal or theological concepts. If you are in conflict with another person in your home, on the job, in your neighborhood, in your church, or anyplace in the world, this is the way of peace, the key to peace, the secret of peace. Let's take a closer look at Paul's practical teaching on the issue of peace.

1. THE ORIGIN OF OUR PEACE

Paul starts with a definition of what true peace really is. True peace is oneness. It is not merely the cessation of hostility, the absence of conflict. Peace means being one. This is a crucial truth. Until we understand it, our understanding of the meaning of peace will be superficial at best.

Is it peace when you get two armies to lay down their weapons and stop fighting each other? Certainly, not shooting at each other is better than shooting—but a cessation of armed warfare is often little more than a lull between rounds of conflict. That's not true peace by God's definition.

Is it peace when two friends who have fallen out with each other, who have been engaged in a war of words, finally decide to simply avoid each other and remain civil but cool and distant toward each other? Not according to God's definition.

When a church outwardly maintains its rituals and programs, but inwardly festers with division, suspicion, and resentment, is that a peaceful church? No, not according to God's definition.

According to God, peace is oneness and harmony. It is sharing mutual enjoyment. It is being one. Anything else is superficial and temporary and not truly peace at all. Yet, in our personal relationships, our overwhelming tendency is to make peace only on superficial, external terms rather than in terms of real oneness. Weariness of warfare is not peace. Distance and coldness is not peace. An enforced truce is not peace. Only oneness is peace. That is the only form of peace God is interested in—the healing of conflict, the restoration of genuine unity and relationship.

Here the apostle tells us the secret of peace. The secret of oneness is a Person: "He himself is our peace." And when Christ Jesus makes peace—between individuals or between nations—that peace will be a satisfying, permanent, and genuine peace. It is a peace that will last and last. In order for you to live at peace with other persons, you must be at peace with the Person of Christ. If you have His peace, you can start solving the conflict around you. But you never can do it on any other basis. The place to start, the origin of peace, is the settling of any problems between you and Jesus Christ.

People often come to me for counseling. They are upset, troubled, discouraged, and angry—they are not at peace. They talk at great length of all the terrible things the other person has done, and all the reasons why they are justified in being so angry, and feeling so mistreated. I listen to it all, then I say, "Yes, you have a problem—but the other person isn't your only problem. You really have two problems. And the one you haven't mentioned at all is the one you must start with."

Then I have to point out that their basic problem is that they don't have any peace within. They are not at peace. They are upset, angry, and emotionally distraught. Everything they do and think is colored by that emotional state. It is impossible to solve the problem with the other person until they themselves acquire peace.

This is the promise of God to Christians: He is our peace. Once our hearts are settled and we have placed the matter in the hands of the Lord, we can begin to understand the problem more clearly and apply intelligent, caring, practical remedies to the situation that will result in true peace, true oneness. There is profound insight in the fact that Christ is our peace.

2. THE PROCESS OF PEACE

Next comes the process of peace. How does peace happen? It comes in three stages, Paul says. Three stages must take place before we experience oneness.

1. Jesus "has destroyed the barrier, the dividing wall of hostility" between Jew and Gentile. The hostility must end first. He has accomplished this "by abolishing in his flesh the law with its commandments and regulations." That is how he breaks down the wall, as we will see in a moment.

2. "His purpose was to create in himself one new man out of the two, thus making peace." His goal in destroying the barrier between Jew and Gentile was to create wholeness and unity, which produces peace.

3. Though this unification and wholeness between Jew and Gentile, He produced one body—the church—"and in this one body," says Paul, Jesus reconciled "both of them to God through the cross, by which he put to death their hostility."

Paul is talking about the ending of the great conflict between the Jews and the Gentiles of his day. He says the first thing Jesus did was to tear down the wall of hostility and separation between them. He uses a turn of phrase that refers to a feature of the temple in Jerusalem. He was a Jew, and had been brought up in that temple, and he remembered the wall, about 3 or 4 feet high, that ran through the temple court, dividing it into two sections. One section was the court of the Gentiles, an outer court, while the inner court was accessible only to Jews. There was a warning sign threatening death to any non-Jews who entered that inner court.

In fact, in the year 1871, archaeologists digging around the temple site uncovered the very stone marked with this warning. These were the actual words, translated from both the Hebrew and the Greek: "No man of another race is to proceed within the partition and enclosing wall about the sanctuary. Anyone arrested there will have himself to blame for the penalty of death which will be imposed as a consequence."

The temple partition wall is a symbol. It was destroyed when the temple was leveled by the Romans in A.D. 70, several years after this letter was written. But Paul says the hostility between Jews and Gentiles was demolished in Jesus Christ. At best, the Jews treated the Gentiles with aloofness; at worst, they despised and hated them. There was enormous hostility between these two peoples.

I once visited the Berlin Wall, which divided that great German city into a communist sector and a free sector. Walking along that wall, I could literally feel the hostility radiating from that wall like heat radiating from an open oven. Gun-toting East German guards were stationed at intervals along the wall, and they glared with suspicion across the no-man's land toward the western side. Many individuals and even entire families were killed trying to cross that ugly gray partition to the West and freedom. Wreathed crosses marked the places where they have fallen under a hail of East German bullets.

But today that partition is gone. East and West Germany have been brought together, made whole, made one. The hostility has been erased. If you want to see that wall today, you can't go to Germany—but you can find a section of it in America, at the Ronald Reagan Presidential Library in Simi Valley, California. It is decorated with a flower and a butterfly—symbols of peace and freedom—and it stands as a reminder of old divisions and a symbol of the peace that comes from unity and oneness.

The fallen Berlin Wall is a symbol of the kind of peace God wants to bring to our lives—the tearing down of partitions and barriers, the creation of genuine unity and oneness. How does Jesus Christ tear down those walls between Jews and Gentiles, between ourselves and God, and between ourselves and others? These barriers seem impenetrable—but the apostle says that Jesus Christ knows how to remove these walls. How? "By abolishing in his flesh the law with its commandments and regulations." It is the law that creates the hostility. So if you remove the law, you end the hostility.

The strength of hostility is demand. The Jews despised the Gentiles because they considered themselves better than Gentiles. "We have the Law of Moses," they said. "The Law is right and true; it reflects the character of God. You Gentiles don't have the Law." And in their self-righteous arrogance, they thought they were keeping this Law because they didn't do some of the outward, external acts the Law prohibited. And so they hated and despised the Gentiles because they thought they were superior. The Gentiles, on the other hand, hated the Jews, for their smugness and hypocrisy. So there was intense hostility between them.

Jesus' solution is to take away the Law and substitute what both Jews and Gentiles really needed: grace and forgiveness. By giving Jews and Gentiles a common ground of grace and forgiveness, he removed all reason for hostility.

So this is the way to end hostility and generate peace: Remove self-righteousness with its arrogance and demands. Put grace and forgiveness in its place. I've seen peace come to families when parents stopped insisting they never made mistakes, when parents began to apologize when they erred. When parents free themselves from the obsessive need to be seen as flawless and infallible, when they finally allow themselves to be human in front of their kids, peace becomes possible in the family. I've seen the same principle work between friends, among church leaders, and in business settings. Hostility results from self-righteous demands. Remove the demands, and hostility gives way to unity and peace.

But God doesn't stop with merely abolishing the Law and its demands. If He stopped there, He would simply be indulging and tolerating sin. God goes further than that, and His next step is an act of creation: "His purpose was to *create* in himself one new man out of the two, thus making peace." Notice the word *create*. That is something only God can do. Man cannot create. Only God is the Creator. Only God creates out of nothing. He makes a new person, a new unity which never existed before.

I know many people who have experienced this new unity in their lives. "Since I stopped trying to judge my spouse," they say, "we've come together acknowledging that we both need God and His forgiveness. We've discovered a whole new relationship I never dreamed possible." Through Christ, a new and unified relationship comes into being, something that never existed before.

Here in Ephesians, the "new man" Paul refers to is the church itself. The church is a picture of what Jesus Christ does. In the church, there is neither Jew nor Gentile. The Jew does not have to become a Gentile; the Gentile does not have to become a Jew. There is a new and fully integrated entity created. In the church today, we don't see a great deal of division between Jews and Gentiles, but we have other divisions: divisions between whites, blacks, and other races. Divisions between rich and poor, between the powerful and the powerless. Divisions between different leaders in the church (including self-appointed church bosses who demand that the church be run their way). Divisions between different philosophies of ministry. Divisions between different cultural and historical heritages within the church.

Peace comes to a church when the walls of division are broken down and the church discovers what it means to have a oneness, a unity, a fellowship of Christlike men and women who demonstrate the same grace, love, and forgiveness that was taught to them by their Lord and Savior.

Paul reminds us that the ultimate barrier—that between sinful humanity and God—has been broken down by the cross: "and in this one body to reconcile both of them to God through the cross, by which he put to death their hostility." Ultimate peace must be with God. When we recognize that we are all on the same level before God, that the ground is level at the foot of the cross, that we all stand in need of the same grace and forgiveness, then hostility is brought to an end. This is what the apostle says: "by which he put to death their hostility."

A young man once told me, "I want to tell you about my marriage. I haven't been married long, and it was only shortly after we were married that I learned my wife was not a virgin before we wed. That was very hard for me to accept. I forgave her—but inwardly, I wrestled with resentment toward her. But then I felt God speaking to me, reminding me that she and I were morally no different. She had violated God's moral law by her behavior, but I had violated God's moral law with my thoughts and attitudes. Before God, I was just as much in need of forgiveness for my failures as she was. When I saw that, then there was healing."

This is what Paul tells us. We are to see each other as no different before God. The only ground we have to stand on before God is the ground of His grace and forgiveness, and "not by works, so that no one can boast" (Ephesians 2:9). When that is our attitude, all division is brought to an end. Hearts are healed. Peace is created.

3. THE MEANS OF PEACE

In the final section of this passage, we find the means of possessing peace. How do we lay hold of peace? Well, the apostle says, verses 17 and 18, "He came and preached peace to you who were far away and peace to those who were near. For through him we both have access to the Father by one Spirit." Here we see that two steps are necessary to lay hold of this kind of peace:

1. Believing the message God has given you. "He came and preached peace," says Paul to these Ephesians. That is, "Jesus preached to you." How did he do that? He didn't come in person. He came in the person of Paul, an apostle sent by the Lord. Paul's preaching was Jesus' preaching of peace. Christ seized the initiative and sent the apostle to proclaim His peace. All that remained was for the Ephesians to accept it and believe it.

Preaching is never an argument or a dialogue. Preaching is an announcement. You can either accept it or reject it, but you can't quarrel with it. It is what God says is true. And God says that the barrier has been removed and a new relationship is available, which will be far richer than anything you've known before.

And the next step to laying hold of God's peace?

2. Communication with the Father: "For through him [Jesus] we both have access to the Father by one Spirit." This is probably the greatest statement in the book of Ephesians. I don't know a higher plateau of truth than this. Here we see the Trinity of God—Father, Son, and Holy Spirit—all working together to bring us into the closest possible relationship with God. He invites us to communicate

with him, to unload before him all the burdens and pressures of our life. And we begin to live in this new relationship with the Father.

There is nothing higher than this. When the full glory of this relationship breaks upon us, we will discover the greatest joy of the Christian life. "Now this is eternal life," Jesus said, "that they may know you, the only true God, and Jesus Christ, whom you have sent" (John 17:3). At this point, life begins to be what God intended it to be.

We've been climbing with Paul, step by step, up a great mountain. And now we have come to the very summit: direct access and communication with the Father. We can go no higher than that. Life with the Father is the most delightful of all experiences, for all that we need is provided by a Father's heart, and a Father's love.

Here, at the summit of the Christian experience, we find the peace and joy that humanity has always longed for. Hostility has ended. The partitions have been torn down. Communion and fellowship with God and one another are ours at last. We have been elevated to all God intended us to have and to be by His Son, Jesus—

The One who is the Prince of Peace.

CHAPTER TWELVE

The Foundation and the Cornerstone

Ephesians 2:19–22

Wahen humorist Will Rogers was introduced to President Calvin Coolidge at a White House reception, a friend bet Rogers that he would not be able to make "Silent Cal" laugh.

"I'll get him to laugh inside of twenty seconds," Rogers replied.

A few minutes later, Will Rogers was taken to the president and introduced. "Mr. Will Rogers, President Coolidge."

The humorist put out his hand and leaned close to the president. "Ah, excuse me," he said, "I didn't quite catch the name."

President Coolidge laughed. At that moment, Will Rogers and the president of the United States were no longer strangers—and Will Rogers had won his bet.

We come now to the concluding verses of Ephesians 2, in which Paul reminds us that, as followers of Christ and members of His church, we are no longer strangers, but members of God's household. He writes in Ephesians 2:19–22:

> Consequently, you are no longer foreigners and aliens, but
> fellow citizens with God's people and members of God's

household, built on the foundation of the apostles and prophets, with Christ Jesus himself as the chief cornerstone. In him the whole building is joined together and rises to become a holy temple in the Lord. And in him you too are being built together to become a dwelling in which God lives by his Spirit.

There are three beautiful metaphors used in this passage, one after the other, and they are designed to teach us great truths about what it means to be a Christian. There is the figure of a kingdom ("fellow citizens with God's people"), a family ("members of God's household"), and a building ("a holy temple in the Lord . . . a dwelling in which God lives by his Spirit"). These metaphors are designed to instruct us so that Paul's prayer for us in the first chapter will be answered: "I pray also that the eyes of your heart may be enlightened in order that you may know the hope to which he has called you, the riches of his glorious inheritance in the saints, and his incomparably great power for us who believe" (Ephesians 1:18–19).

NO LONGER FOREIGNERS AND ALIENS

Paul begins with a negative. "You are no longer foreigners and aliens," he says. In other words, you are no longer strangers. What is a stranger? We all have been strangers at one time or another. You probably know the feeling of moving to a new town, being the new kid in school, or the new person on the job—the sense of isolation and loneliness of being a stranger in a strange place. Perhaps you know what it feels like to be a foreigner, a stranger in an alien land, unable to speak the language, unfamiliar with the customs, maybe unable to even handle the currency or get around town.

A stranger is characterized by not knowing much about the place where he is. Once, while I was in Spokane, Washington, a man stopped me on the street and asked directions to the J. C. Penney store. "I'm sorry," I replied, "I'm a stranger here myself." In other words, I was ignorant of the advantages of that community, of all the cultural possibilities—in fact, I didn't even know where I could find a store to buy a pair of socks or a package of flashlight batteries. Strangers are ignorant.

Once we were strangers, says the apostle. We did not know what God could do for us. We were ignorant of the advantages and possibilities of knowing Him. We had no idea of the resources of peace and joy and forgiveness that could be ours for the asking. We knew nothing of His ability to quiet our fears and soothe our hostilities.

Once we were foreigners, says the apostle. A foreigner is different from a stranger. A foreigner may be quite familiar with the country in which he lives—but he is limited. He is an alien. He lives on a passport, and under certain circumstances he can be deported. He lacks the full rights and advantages of a citizen. Many in the church are like foreigners—attending regularly, familiar with the hymns, perhaps even familiar with the Bible and the language of Christianity, but without a genuine saving relationship with Jesus Christ, not a full citizen of God's kingdom.

Paul says that we who have come to Christ used to be foreigners and strangers—but no more. Now that we have come to Christ, says Paul, we are no longer foreigners, no longer strangers. We are *home*.

If we are no longer strangers and foreigners, then what are we? Three things, according to this passage:

1. "Fellow citizens with God's people." That is a great statement. It means that we have entered a new kingdom. We have changed our citizenship. We are now under new authority.

I am an American citizen. I suspect that most of us in America take for granted the rights of American citizenship, and tend to forget the responsibilities that go with those rights. As Americans, we are under authority and the government has certain powers over us. It regulates certain areas of our life, whether we like it or not. We are under certain controls, and if we do things the government has prohibited, the government can step in and take our freedom from us. We are under authority—and that is the first mark of citizenship.

The Bible recognizes two kingdoms in this world—two *spiritual* kingdoms. And every one of us belongs to one or the other. We are either under the authority of Satan or the authority of God. One or the other has ultimate dominion over our lives. When you become a Christian, you move out of the kingdom of Satan and into the kingdom of God. There is a basic change of government. Jesus often said that His kingdom was not of this world (see, for example, John 18:36–37). He meant that His government was not like that of earthly governments; His kingship is over the hearts of human beings. But it truly is a kingdom; it exercises authority over people. When we come into His kingdom, we come under a new authority, a new king, a new head. We are no longer under the bondage and power of the other. What a transformation this is!

Being citizens of a kingdom means we have certain responsibilities and privileges given to us in Christ. We owe allegiance and obedience to our King—yet we also have the power and protection of the King. That doesn't mean that our King will protect us from all problems and suffering—but He is a resource we can call upon to help us through our problems and suffering.

Jesus said, "Blessed are you when people insult you, persecute you and falsely say all kinds of evil against you because of me. Rejoice and be glad, because great is your reward in heaven, for in the same way they persecuted the prophets who were before you," (Matthew 5:11–12). He knows what to do. Furthermore, "Do not take revenge, my friends, but leave room for God's wrath, for it is written: 'It is mine to avenge; I will repay,' says the Lord," (Romans 12:19). God is saying, "When there is injustice and injury in your life, don't try to avenge yourself—I'll be your defender. I know how to straighten it out. I will resolve the problem in a way that brings about perfect, lasting peace."

Paul tells us that we have become fellow citizens with God's people—we have become close friends with the great citizens of God's kingdom, names that until now we have only read in the Bible. Jesus himself said, "I say to you that many will come from the east and the west, and will take their places at the feast with Abraham, Isaac and Jacob in the kingdom of heaven," Matthew 8:11. These are not "plaster saints," but genuine heroes of the faith—and we'll have all eternity to get to know them!

The final glory of all is that we have access to the King himself. He walks with us, tells us His plans, shares His program of history with us, and opens His mind and heart to us. These are just a few of the many marvelous privileges we have in Christ.

2. "Members of God's household." The next metaphor Paul uses to describe our position is even more exalted than the first. Yes, we are citizens of the kingdom—but more than that, we are members of God's own intimate family! The apostle John never ceased to marvel over this. "How great is the love the Father has lavished on us," he wrote in 1 John 3:1, "that we should be called children of God! And that is what we are!"

The story is told of a kingdom long ago. The king was in the throne room, holding council with his advisors, noblemen, and high ministers of state. Suddenly there was a bang and a clatter at the door of the throne room. All eyes turned as the door burst open and a young boy ran into the room.

One of the king's royal guardsmen tried to stop the boy. "Hold there, lad!" he shouted. "Don't you know you're disturbing the council of the king?"

"He's *your* king," laughed the boy, "but he's my *Daddy*!" And the boy bounced into the open arms of his father, the king.

A child of the king always outranks any nobleman, advisor, minister, ambassador, or dignitary. That is the position we have with God. That is the access we have to His throne room.

Your Father's loving concern surrounds every aspect of your life. He is not only concerned about getting justice for you. A king does that. But you are the object of his deepest, most intimate love and concern. As Zechariah tells us, "For this is what the LORD Almighty says: '... Whoever touches you touches the apple of his eye'" (Zechariah 2:8). We are the apple of God's eye, and there is no love in the universe greater than His love for us.

3. We are "built on the foundation of the apostles and prophets, with Christ Jesus himself as the chief cornerstone." Paul takes our relationship with God to an even deeper, closer level. At first, this may not be apparent, since a building seems like a rather cold and impersonal metaphor, compared with the relationship of a family. But if you look carefully you will see what the apostle had in mind. He is stressing the closeness of the members of the very habitation of God, both to one another and to the Lord.

It is possible for the members of a family to be scattered throughout the earth. You may have relatives who are across the country or on the other side of the planet. You may have relatives you haven't seen or spoken to in years. You and your relatives are family, but there is a separation there. In a building made of stones, however, there is no separation between the stones. To build a wall, stones must be joined together. If the stones are separated, the wall collapses. So the apostle describes a still more intimate relationship.

Moreover, says Paul, this building is a living, growing habitation of God. Paul's metaphor merges right into the metaphor of a body. The building becomes the body of God, the dwelling place where God himself lives. And what could be more personal, more intimate to you, than your body? This is how Paul reminds us of how close we are to God—a God of power, a God of might, a God of love. This is how intimately we are related to Him and bound to Him as He builds us into a great building, an eternal dwelling place for himself.

And what is the cornerstone? Jesus himself. When you begin to build a building, you first place the cornerstone. All measurements for the building are taken from that cornerstone. Everything relates to it. The whole building ties together because of the cornerstone. The apostle depicts Jesus as having that relationship with us. Throughout the letter to the Ephesians, everything is "in Christ," "in him," "by him," "through him," "through his blood," "by his death," and so forth. Everything comes to us in Christ. If you do not have Jesus the cornerstone, you cannot be part of this building.

Some years ago I helped a friend, Paul Carlson, build a house in northern Mexico, among the Tarahumara Indians. He hired an Indian stonemason to work on the walls, and it was fascinating to watch him work. He began with a pile of stones he had dug up and gathered from the hillside. He would examine the stones and select one he thought was the right size and shape. Then he would take a hammer and chisel, and he would knock off a piece here, smooth an edge there, then place it where he wanted. If it didn't quite fit, he would carefully chip it and smooth it until it was exactly right. Then he would cement it in place with mortar.

That is the picture Paul gives us of how God works with us. He is knocking off our rough edges, shaping us up, getting us ready for placement in His eternal dwelling place. He is building a holy temple—a beautiful, magnificent building. We are His building materials, His building blocks. The process of being chipped and smoothed for His service is often painful, but the result is going to be glorious!

I do not know any way to explain and make sense out of history—including the history of our own lives—other than from this point of view. Everything that happens in the world, from major wars and upheavals to the minor frustrations in our own everyday lives—is part of the building process of God. He is preparing His people, shaping us, smoothing us, making us just the right shape for His service so that He can fit us into place in His temple, His dwelling place, the church of Jesus Christ.

Everything else that we have built in our lives, in our civilization, will one day be blown away in the fires of final judgment. All that will be left is the permanent, eternal structure that God builds out of our lives.

CHAPTER THIRTEEN

The Great Mystery

Ephesians 3:1–6

The first paragraph of Ephesians 3 is in many ways the key to the entire letter. Here Paul begins to describe the great mystery of our faith.

We all love a good mystery. There is something about our human makeup that is endlessly fascinated by what is hidden and secret, waiting to be discovered and revealed. God understands us so thoroughly that He has embedded His mysteries in every aspect of life. There is always an element we don't understand. Even terms we use every day—"love," "joy," "life"—are fundamentally mysterious to us. We struggle constantly to understand the great realities they represent.

This is true in every area of our lives. Even physicists tell us that, hidden within every physical manifestation of the universe, there is mystery. Quantum theory, upon which much of modern physics is based, has at its heart a "principle of uncertainty," which states that it is impossible to specify both the position and momentum of a particle (such as an electron) with certainty. The measurement of the position of the particle renders the momentum of the particle a mystery; the measurement of the momentum renders the position a mystery.

Physicists can only deal in probabilities, not certainties. Truth remains a mystery.

In the Scriptures too we are confronted with mystery. "It is the glory of God to conceal a matter," says Proverbs 25:2. "To search out a matter is the glory of kings." God knows we all want to be kings, that we are made to reign. And the glory of kings is to discover that which is hidden.

A PRISONER OF CHRIST

In Ephesians 3:1–6, Paul describes the greatest mystery of life:

> For this reason I, Paul, the prisoner of Christ Jesus for the sake of you Gentiles—Surely you have heard about the administration of God's grace that was given to me for you, that is, the mystery made known to me by revelation, as I have already written briefly. In reading this, then, you will be able to understand my insight into the mystery of Christ, which was not made known to men in other generations as it has now been revealed by the Spirit of God's holy apostles and prophets. This mystery is that through the gospel the Gentiles are heirs together with Israel, members together of one body, and sharers together in the promise in Christ Jesus.

This paragraph falls into two divisions. First, Paul describes his role as a teacher of this mystery. Then, he describes the mystery itself.

Sometimes it is difficult to see the structure of Paul's argument in the English translation. This is particularly true of this passage. Paul begins with the phrase, "For this reason." This phrase actually connects with verse 13 of chapter 3. Everything between the phrase

"For this reason" and verse 13 is parenthetical—but what a powerful, exalted parenthesis it is! This is the way the apostle's mind worked. He starts out to say one thing, but then he is captured by the truth of something else he is going to say. So he pours this truth into a grand parenthetical clause, which he builds, truth upon truth, until he finally returns to his original thought and completes the statement he began to make in verse 1.

So here is how this statement should be read: "For this reason . . . I ask you, therefore, not to be discouraged because of my sufferings for you, which are your glory." Understanding how verses 1 and 13 connect gives us a context for understanding what Paul is saying in the intervening sentences.

The apostle wanted the Christians to whom he was writing to understand why he was going through persecution and imprisonment. Paul wrote this letter from a rented room where he lived under house arrest, chained day and night to a Roman soldier. Paul's Christian friends must have wondered how God could allow this great missionary to be confined in this way, his missionary voice shut up within four walls, his missionary feet in chains—reduced to conducting his ministry by letters alone.

His first statement was to proclaim himself a prisoner—not a prisoner of the Roman government, but of Christ. Paul did not think himself a prisoner of the Roman Caesar, awaiting the judgment of Nero. No, he saw himself as a prisoner of his Lord, accountable only to the judgment of God. Nero did not have the final say about Paul's life or death; God did. Paul was content to be in prison if it served Christ. He was content to live free if it served Christ. He was content to die if it served Christ. He was the prisoner of Jesus Christ. Imagine how our lives and our attitudes toward problems and suffering would change if we viewed our lives the way Paul viewed his.

Paul goes on to state that he is a prisoner on behalf of the Gentiles. This refers not only to the fact that he was arrested for preaching the gospel to the Gentiles, but also to the fact that the gospel benefited the Gentiles. The Jews were angry with Paul and charged him with sedition because Paul claimed to carry a message from God to the Gentiles. Jewish sensibilities were outraged that a Jew would treat Gentiles as equals.

Acts 21 and 22 tells the story of Paul's arrest in the temple courts after his presence there starts a riot. After his arrest, Paul speaks to the Jewish mob in his own defense. He begins by giving his testimony— the story of his encounter with the living Lord Jesus. The mob listens quietly until he says, Acts 22:21, "Then the Lord said to me, 'Go; I will send you far away to the Gentiles.'"

At that point, the crowd flies into a murderous rage. "Rid the earth of him! He's not fit to live!" What triggers the crowd's wrath? The word *Gentiles*. They would have lynched Paul on the spot had it not been for the Roman guards. So it was because of this great message of salvation, delivered unto the Gentiles, that Paul became a prisoner.

I think it is also fair to infer from Paul's words that he wanted the Ephesians to know that they were benefiting from his arrest, due to the fact that his imprisonment gave him time to write this and other letters—letters that have changed the course of history. Paul's concern for these Ephesian Gentiles was such that he would have gone to them had he been free to do so. He would have preached to them and taught them directly from the Word—but he might never have had time to write his great insights down. So it may be that one reason the Lord Jesus allowed him to remain imprisoned was in order to produce some of the great epistles of the New Testament.

THE ADMINISTRATION OF GOD'S GRACE

The second thing Paul says about himself is, "Surely you have heard about the administration of God's grace that was given to me for you." He wanted the Ephesians to understand that he was going through these trials because God had committed a responsibility to him—the responsibility of being a steward or administrator of God's grace.

A steward or administrator is one who is made responsible to manage and dispense certain goods or commodities. The commodity that had been entrusted to Paul was God's grace, and he was a responsible steward of that commodity. This is a strange statement for Paul to make, but it is in line with a statement he made to another church in 1 Corinthians 4:1: "So then, men ought to regard us as servants of Christ and as those entrusted with the secret things of God."

What is Paul talking about? The secret things of God are the mysteries that God knows about life, and which humanity desperately needs to know. Paul is not suggesting that he alone is a steward of God's secrets. *All* Christians are stewards of God's mysteries. You are and so am I. We have received the gospel, the story that explains all of life and enables us to solve the riddle of our existence. This responsibility was committed to us by God, and he expects us to dispense this secret to those around us.

Now, it is important to remember, as Paul himself makes clear in verse 3, that "the mystery [was] made known to me by revelation, as I have already written briefly." Paul was personally instructed by none other than the Lord Jesus himself. That is the source of Paul's authority as an apostle. So Paul's apostleship is not less than that of John or Peter, who also learned directly from Jesus. His apostleship and the message of the gospel were given him by direct revelation from Jesus (see also Galatians 1:12).

Some have suggested that Paul's apostleship was a secondhand apostleship, the result of a gospel he received from talking with the other apostles. But in fact Paul didn't talk with the apostles during the first few years of his Christian experience. It was three years before he ever went back to Jerusalem after his conversion, and then he only saw James, the Lord's brother, and they didn't discuss doctrine. It wasn't until fourteen years later that he had an opportunity to sit down and compare notes with all the other apostles. They didn't teach him anything, Paul said, because he already understood all facets of the gospel as they did, because Jesus had taught him directly, just as He had taught the Twelve. Paul spoke with direct authority, because he was commissioned by the Lord Jesus himself.

Notice again verse 3, "the mystery made known to me by revelation, as I have already written briefly." Bible scholars have puzzled over that last phrase, "as I have already written briefly." Some believe it is a reference to a previous letter—but we know of no other letter Paul wrote to the Ephesians. I personally believe Paul refers to a previous passage in this same Ephesian letter—chapter 1, verses 9–10:

> And he made known to us the mystery of his will according to his good pleasure, which he purposed in Christ, to be put into effect when the times will have reached their fulfillment—to bring all things in heaven and on earth together under one head, even Christ.

I believe that is the brief statement he had written to these Ephesian Christians, and to which he refers. He says in effect, "You can understand that I have a great understanding of this mystery, the secret that touches all of life and lies at the heart of human existence. It is the mystery of the goal toward which God is moving in human affairs, yet it also encompasses space, time, and matter." All of this is summed up by Paul in these few words, "the mystery of Christ." Jesus Christ is at the heart of all things.

If we listen carefully to the questions that are asked in our newspapers, on TV and radio talk shows, and over back fences all over America, it becomes clear that we live in troubled times, and everyone is seeking an answer to the mystery of life. We worry about pollution, poverty, the threat of war, racism, crime, divorce, illegitimacy, domestic violence, child abuse, AIDS, drug abuse, and more. We think our world is beset with many problems, yet they are really extensions of the one problem that has plagued humankind since the beginning.

Some propose one solution, while others propose other solutions. Some solutions are partially right, some are clearly wrong. But the reason the best and brightest minds of our time cannot solve these problems is that they have never come to grips with the core problem. That core problem is the sin problem—and the key to solving it is what Paul calls the mystery of Christ.

THE REVELATION OF THE MYSTERY

In the next sentence, Paul goes on to give us a brief summary of this great mystery that is the solution to all the problems of humanity:

> In reading this, then, you will be able to understand my insight into the mystery of Christ, which was not made known to men in other generations as it has now been revealed by the Spirit of God's holy apostles and prophets. This mystery is that through the gospel the Gentiles are heirs together with Israel, members together of one body, and sharers together in the promise in Christ Jesus.

That is the mystery.

The first thing Paul says about it is that it has been hidden in the past. The greatest men of God in the Old Testament did not understand this mystery. Moses, David, Solomon, Isaiah, Jeremiah, and the rest may have understood much of God's plan, as God revealed it to them, but they did not understand this mystery. The secret was hidden in past ages.

How was this mystery unfolded? Through Jesus Christ. The Lord Jesus himself began to unfold the mystery. In Matthew 13:34–35 we have these amazing words about Jesus:

> Jesus spoke all these things to the crowd in parables; he did not say anything to them without using a parable. So was fulfilled what was spoken through the prophet:
> "I will open my mouth in parables, I will utter things hidden since the creation of the world."

Our Lord, then, began to unfold this mystery, to tell us things that were hidden from the very foundation of the world. So it is obvious, from what the apostle says in Ephesians, that God needed to prepare humanity for the unfolding of this secret. He accomplished this preparation with the rituals and symbols of the Old Testament—the giving of the Law and the sacrifices, which helped us to understand that we human beings have something inherently wrong with us, which cannot be cured by making a few good resolutions. The only thing that can cure our sin problem is death itself. God had to prepare this race to be able to grasp and accept this terrible fact. Even then, He had not fully unveiled this mystery. A little was revealed in the past, but the great secret was kept hidden.

"It has now been revealed," Paul says, "by the Spirit to God's holy apostles and prophets." But, as we have already seen, it was the Lord Jesus who began to unveil it. Paul simply says that it was made known to all the apostles and prophets—that is, the writers of the Scriptures, such as Luke and James and others who were not apostles, but who were prophets.

In the closing verses of Romans 16 there is a very clear statement on the unveiling of this mystery:

> Now to him who is able to establish you by my gospel and the proclamation of Jesus Christ, according to the revelation of the mystery hidden for long ages past, but now revealed and made known through the prophetic writings by the command of the eternal God, so that all nations might believe and obey him—to the only wise God be glory forever through Jesus Christ! Amen (16:25–27).

JOINT HEIRS

The mystery itself consists of this great truth, as we read in Ephesians 3:6: "the Gentiles are heirs together with Israel, members together of one body, and sharers together in the promise in Christ Jesus." One of Paul's identifying traits, known well among Bible scholars who read his writings in the original Greek, is his fondness for coining new words. No other New Testament writers do that. But Paul has so much he wants to say, and the truths God has given him to convey are so exalted and astounding, that he runs out of language. The words of ordinary language are insufficient to the task, so he has to invent new words by jamming old words together in new ways. So here, in Ephesians 3:6, he invents three new words which are found nowhere else in the Greek New Testament. In English, those words are:

1. *Joint-heirs,*
2. *Joint-bodies,* and
3. *Joint-partakers.*

Upon coming to Christ, Jewish believers and Gentile believers become joint heirs together, joint members of one body, and joint partakers of the promise. What does all of that mean? In those three terms you have the answers to the greatest struggles with which humanity struggles today:

To be a *joint-heir* has to do with possessions. This term touches the whole problem of man and his universe, living in a natural world. It deals with our inability to solve our ecological riddles. In Genesis, man was created to have dominion over the earth, but with the entry of sin into the world, the ground became cursed. So the old creation is now gripped by an unbreakable law, which Paul calls "the law of decay" in Romans 8. Scientists call this the Second Law of Thermodynamics, the law of entropy. This law states that energy is becoming less available, that order is on the decline and disorder is on the rise, that everything is running down and deteriorating. We cannot get around this immutable law of nature.

But Paul says that in Christ the breakthrough has occurred. In Christ, God is beginning a new creation, one that lives by a wholly different principle and is not subject to the law of entropy. And this creation has already begun! It began with the resurrection of Jesus Christ.

The resurrection was an act of creation, the reversal of the process of entropy and death—and never in their wildest imaginings did anyone in Old Testament times foresee such an event. In the Old Testament we find a few veiled prophetic statements that we now can see refer to the resurrection of the body. For example, in Job 19:26, they read these words: "And after my skin has been destroyed, yet in my flesh I will see God." But the believers of Old Testament times didn't understand what these statements meant. They believed God would provide them with a life beyond death, but they didn't know what kind of life. The full splendor of the resurrection was hidden from them. They died hoping in God—but that hope was vague and undefined.

One crucial aspect of the resurrection life that was hidden from them is that resurrection life is available to us not only after we die, but here and now, while we still live. You never find that taught in the Old Testament. But that is what the apostles taught—that God has already broken through the old creation, and He is right now, at this very moment, bringing about His new creation. As Christians, we are to live on the basis of that new creation.

As Christians, we have the answer to the ecological crisis. We are joint-heirs with Christ, and what we inherit from God is the world. Paul tells us, "All things are yours, whether Paul or Apollos or Cephas or the world or life or death or the present or the future—all are yours, and you are of Christ, and Christ is of God" (1 Corinthians 3:21–23). And Hebrews 1 tells us that we do not yet see all things subject to Christ, but we do see Jesus, the One who has been made heir of all things, and in Him we share that inheritance, so that one day all things subject to this new law will be ours. One day there will be a reversal of the law of entropy and decay, and all creation will be endowed and imbued with new energy and a new order. All of creation will be revitalized, restored, and renewed.

JOINT MEMBERS OF ONE BODY

The next phrase in Ephesians 3:6 speaks of us as "joint-bodies" or joint members of one body. This statement answers the age-old problem of why human beings can't get along with each other. It answers the problem of family breakups, arguing and strife, church divisions, malice and hatred, racism, crime, and even war. All the struggles and battles of humanity are answered by our becoming joint members of one body.

Human divisions and strife began with the introduction of sin into the world. After Adam ate the forbidden fruit, God asked him, "Have you eaten from the tree that I commanded you not to eat from?" And Adam replied, "The woman you put here with me—she gave me some fruit from the tree, and I ate it" (Genesis 3:11–12). First Adam blamed God ("the woman *you* put here"), then Adam blamed his mate ("*she* gave me some fruit"), and thus was division created between man and God and between man and other human beings, beginning with his own mate. The rest of the Bible is the story of how the stakes in these divisions were raised from family arguments and recrimination (Adam and Eve) to murder (Cain and Abel) to racial divisions and wars.

Why can't we get along with one another? Because when we are still living in the old creation, these things are inevitable. If you fulfill the flesh, there is no way by which you can keep from living in disharmony with people around you. But in the realm of the Spirit, the breakthrough has already occurred. When we begin to walk in the Spirit, we can love, forgive, and reach out to others. The whole experience of life is transformed—not in some distant, hoped-for future, but right here, right now.

SHARERS TOGETHER IN THE PROMISE

Finally, Paul takes up the issue of power for living—the power of the Holy Spirit. He says that we are "sharers together in the promise in Christ Jesus." What promise does Paul mean? The promise of Jesus was that after He left, the Holy Spirit would come to live in us and empower us to do everything God wants us to do. Anytime we sense that there is something God wants us to do, but we don't feel like doing, we can cast ourselves upon the Lord, trusting the promise that the power of the Spirit is available to us. When we rely on Him, the power of the Spirit will come flowing through to enable us to do what otherwise we could never do.

This is Paul's explanation of the great mystery. It is a breakthrough, a new and marvelous way of life which has already begun in our experience, and which, ultimately, will solve all the problems facing humanity. Amazingly, we do not have to wait for some future fulfillment—we can experience it right now. In Colossians, Paul puts it this way: "To them God has chosen to make known among the Gentiles the glorious riches of this mystery, which is Christ in you, the hope of glory" (Colossians 1:27).

Our present civilization with its politics, its art, its science, its information technologies, and all its proud achievements can be likened to a cocoon, clinging lifelessly to the branch of history. But inside that cocoon, God is working a metamorphosis; a new creation is taking place. Someday that cocoon will open, in the springtime of the world. At that moment, a new entity will emerge, which is being created at this very moment within the cocoon.

This is a great parable that God teaches us in nature. Did you ever wonder why caterpillars crawl on the ground? Why don't they run around on four legs? Because God is teaching us things in nature, if we would only pay attention. Everything that lies in a caterpillar's path is a horrible obstacle over which it must painfully crawl. It cannot see very far, and it doesn't know which turn to take. This is an apt description of the way we live our lives as natural human beings.

But God has a wonderful program in mind for a caterpillar. The caterpillar fastens itself to a twig or branch, and its life as a caterpillar comes to an end. It encases itself in a death-shroud, a silken cocoon. Its motion ceases. It hangs limp and lifeless.

But that is not the end of the caterpillar's story. Inside that cocoon, a mystery takes place. Springtime comes and the cocoon begins to move and split—then something beautiful emerges from that death-shroud. It spreads its wings and takes flight—a beautiful and spectacularly colorful creature. It no longer crawls blindly over the ground. It soars over the fields and hills. It is a butterfly, one of God's most wondrous expressions of beauty and joy in nature.

The life of a butterfly is a great mystery. So is your life and mine. The springtime of the world awaits us. Here, within the cocoon of our daily lives, God is preparing us to be manifested, like butterflies, as creatures of God's new creation, wrapped in the beauty of His grace, the joyous splendor of His creative power.

The mystery is all around us. The new creation has already begun. You and I must choose to either become a part of His new creation— or to remain in the old. We cannot be both. If you are in Christ, you are no longer part of the old but part of that new program that awaits the dawn of a new world, a new life, and a new day. On that day, all God's people shall be one over all the earth. There will be no more sickness, no more sadness, no more death, no more war.

I can hardly wait. I am ready for that day. Are you?

CHAPTER FOURTEEN

Secret Riches

Ephesians 3:7–12

When I first became a Christian, I thought I was a pretty decent fellow. I was a young man, and I felt I had a pretty clean record. Sure, there were a few corners of my life that could stand some tidying up—but I figured that if God could straighten up those few corners a bit, I would be ready to wear my halo.

Amazingly, the older I got and the more mature I grew as a Christian, the more "untidy corners" I found. As God gradually opened my eyes to the true state of my behavior and character, I began to think myself more and more wretched—so much so that I began to feel truly repugnant in God's presence. I wondered how God could possibly allow such a sinner as myself into His church!

Carl Jung, the great psychologist, once put into words a great deal of what I began to feel about myself as I moved into the middle of my life:

> In the second half of life, the necessity is imposed of recognizing no longer the validity of our former ideals, but of their contrary, of perceiving the error in what were

previously our convictions, of sensing the untruth in what was our truth, and of weighing the degree of opposition and even of hostility in what we once took to be love.

That is an apt statement of what it means to see ourselves with honest, unsparing clarity. As we probe deeper into Ephesians 3, we will see this same brutal honesty in Paul's own appraisal of himself. In verse 7, Paul continues his discussion of the great mystery of the Christian gospel—yet he does so in a way that is intensely personal and candid. He writes in Ephesians 3:7–13,

I became a servant of this gospel by the gift of God's grace given me through the working of his power. Although I am less than the least of all God's people, this grace was given me: to preach to the Gentiles the unsearchable riches of Christ, and to make plain to everyone the administration of this mystery, which for ages past was kept hidden in God, who created all things. His intent was that now, through the church, the manifold wisdom of God should be made known to the rulers and authorities in the heavenly realms, according to his eternal purpose which he accomplished in Christ Jesus our Lord. In him and through faith in him we may approach God with freedom and confidence. I ask you, therefore, not to be discouraged because of my sufferings for you, which are your glory.

Verse 13 reveals that the reason Paul wrote this section of the letter is that the Ephesian Christians were troubled by his suffering—not so much because they felt sorry and fearful for him (though, of course, they did), but because their faith was shaken by his sufferings. They were really troubled that a great apostle—the very fountainhead of truth, as far as they were concerned—should appear to be a helpless victim of Caesar's cruelty, chained to a Roman solider day and night.

Paul writes back, and says, in effect, "You've got it all wrong. You don't understand the true nature and purpose of my troubles. You see, suffering for the cause of Christ is the sure way to victory." This mighty apostle had learned that the cross is always the pathway to a crown. Victory in Christ entails an element of sharing in the sufferings of Christ. So Paul is writing to assure them that everything is exactly as it should be. There is a point and a purpose to his sufferings.

THE WONDER OF PAUL'S GIFT

Notice his sense of amazement as he writes: "I became a servant of this gospel by the gift of God's grace given me through the working of his power. Although I am less than the least of all God's people, this grace was given me: to preach to the Gentiles the unsearchable riches of Christ." Two things that never ceased to amaze him are (1) the immense value of the gift God had given him, especially in view of (2) his own weakness and unworthiness.

This gift of the ministry of the gospel came to him by the grace and power of God. In the old creation, we were given natural gifts called talents. These natural gifts include such abilities as musical, artistic, organizational, mathematical, leadership, speaking, and writing talents. Everyone has talents. They are part of God's gifts to Adam and his race. But in the new creation, we have been given supernatural gifts, spiritual gifts.

It is one of these spiritual gifts that Paul reveals in here in Ephesians 3—the gift of an evangelist. In verse 8 he says that though he is "less than the least of all God's people, this grace was given me: to preach to the Gentiles the unsearchable riches of Christ." The word translated "to preach" really means "to evangelize." So Paul had the gift of evangelism among his many spiritual gifts, and this is what drove him to the far corners of the earth, preaching Christ to people who had never heard of Christ before. Paul had a hunger for seeing people come to salvation, which is characteristic of the gift of evangelism.

It is the Lord Jesus' prerogative to assign a ministry to every one of us, and the ministry He assigned Paul was an evangelistic ministry to the Gentiles. Both Peter and Paul had gifts of evangelism, but Peter's ministry was to the Jews and Paul's was to the Gentiles.

If you know Jesus Christ, you have spiritual gifts, and the Lord Jesus wants to lead you into the place where you will minister and utilize that gift. That is your ministry. Every believer ought to have a ministry. This is what makes the church function as God intended it to do.

You may have a ministry to children, or to old people, or to down-and-outers at the Rescue Mission, or to the up-and-outers in Brentwood or Beverly Hills, or to the Hispanic community, or to the African-American community, or to the Native American community, or to the Muslim world, or to the former Soviet bloc, or even (in view of the new millennium we are now entering) to settlers on the high frontier on Mars or the Moon. A particular gift can be exercised in all of these places, in all of these ministries. The gift opens the door to the ministry.

Paul never got over the wonder of his gift. What a glorious thing it was, he said, that God had given him the gift of preaching this tremendous message to people who had never heard the good news before.

THE WONDER OF PAUL'S WEAKNESS

Paul was continually amazed that God would entrust such a gift and such a ministry to someone as weak as himself. "Although I am less than the least of all God's people," he said, "this grace was given me: to preach to the Gentiles the unsearchable riches of Christ." I don't think this is mere false modesty on Paul's part. He is expressing the depths of his true feelings, his candid self-assessment.

I have heard people say, "Paul is so conceited! He talks about his holiness and his faithfulness and his compassion. He says, 'Imitate me, as I imitate Christ.' Man, what an ego!" That is a complete misreading of Paul's heart. If you really want to know what Paul thought of himself, here it is in Ephesians. Here again, Paul invents a new word, putting a comparative and superlative together, saying, "I am the least of all God's people." In 2 Timothy, he calls himself "the chief of sinners." This is not the self-appraisal of an egotist, but of a humble, Christlike man.

Paul is following in the footsteps of the One who said, "Take my yoke upon you and learn from me, for I am gentle and humble in heart, and you will find rest for your souls" (Matthew 11:29). What happened in Paul's life is what we so often see in the lives of the truly great saints, past and present. As they grow older, they grow in an awareness of their own sin and weakness—and this awareness produces true Christlike humility.

As Paul began to understand the full revelation of the mystery which is in Jesus Christ, the clarity of his knowledge gave him an unclouded view of himself and his own weakness. That is why he could say, in all honesty, without false modesty, "I know that nothing good lives in me, that is, in my sinful nature. For I have the desire to do what is good, but I cannot carry it out" (Romans 7:18). Though many of us would deny it, that is a candid and accurate assessment of our true human state.

Here is the glory of the mystery: Out of weakness comes strength—our weakness and God's strength.

AMAZING THE ANGELS

When this apostle could say of himself, "I am less than the least of all of God's people," he was able to go on and describe a fantastically effective ministry, which he goes on to set forth in beautiful terms:

> Although I am less than the least of all God's people, this grace was given me: to preach to the Gentiles the unsearchable riches of Christ, and to make plain to everyone the administration of this mystery, which for ages past was kept hidden in God, who created all things. His intent was that now, through the church, the manifold wisdom of God should be made known to the rulers and authorities in the heavenly realms, . . . (3:8–10).

Here, Paul discloses a threefold effect that his ministry has had:

1. Those to whom he has preached have discovered unsearchable riches in Christ. The preaching of Christ enriches the lives of those who hear the gospel—not in some time to come, but right here and right now. Wherever Paul preached, hearts were changed, hurts were healed, families were restored, the bad habits of a lifetime were broken, and lives were filled with joy, hope, love, and peace. The unsearchable riches of Christ are a present reality, not just a heavenly hope!

2. His preaching unlocks the mystery and reveals God's plan for all to see: "and to make plain to everyone the administration of this mystery, which for ages past was kept hidden in God, who created all things." In Isaiah 9, the prophet predicted that those who walk in darkness would see a great light—and he went on to prophesy the coming of the Christ-child: "For

to us a child is born, to us a son is given, and the government will be on his shoulders. And he will be called Wonderful Counselor, Mighty God, Everlasting Father, Prince of Peace" (Isaiah 9:6).

Jesus is the light that illuminates the darkness. Paul exulted in the role God had given him—a role of unlocking the mystery, of enlightening men and women with this tremendous secret. Everything good in life and society—good government, world peace, safe neighborhoods, enlightened education, progress in knowledge and technology—is directly proportional to the degree that we in society have ordered our lives by the mystery of the gospel. To reject this mystery is to embrace darkness; to embrace this mystery is to invite God's light into our lives and our society.

Notice that Paul ties everything up with the phrase, "God, who created all things." God has ordained life to be lived in accordance with His truth. The more people act out rebellion against the truth of the gospel, the faster society tilts toward anarchy, lawlessness, and spiritual darkness. When the light of God's truth recedes, the darkness of superstition, occultism, and demonism comes flooding in.

Paul knew this great secret—the secret that true enjoyment of this life, true pleasure and satisfaction in this life, comes only when the gospel has permeated our lives. So he reveled and exulted in the privilege he had been given to spread this brilliant light into the dark and weary pagan world of the first century A.D. This wonderful, illuminating mystery was hidden by God until the world was ready for it. All the ages of history before the coming of Christ were spent preparing the world for the unfolding of the mystery, for the revelation of Jesus Christ. There is nothing in all the world like this great secret—and God had to get us ready for it.

A godly Canadian scientist, Dr. Arthur Custance, put it this way:

> The processes of history have special significance because the crucifixion could not be merely an isolated event occurring in some dark age of lawlessness and barbarism, or in some corner of the earth where knowledge of it might filter back into the world only by accident. It was an event which had to be appropriated, witnessed, and recorded, which had to be performed in an orderly, legal way, according to an accepted standard of behavior and judgment to which mankind as a whole would give rational consent. It had to occur at a time when the event itself would be sufficiently public, one might say publicized, that there could never be doubt about its having happened. It had to come to pass when there was a sufficiently sophisticated and dependable means of communicating the news to a large population that was not merely numerous but fluid, so that word of it could be carried far and wide . . . . The Roman Empire guaranteed, at least for a short while, a world ideally ordered as a proper setting.

This is what Paul meant when he wrote, "But when the time had fully come, God sent his Son, born of a woman, born under law, to redeem those under law, that we might receive the full rights of sons" (Galatians 4:4–5). This was the beginning of the unfolding of this mystery, which is the secret of the governing of human lives.

3. His preaching demonstrates the unique and matchless wisdom of God. In verse 10, Paul writes, "His intent was that now, through the church, the manifold wisdom of God

should be made known to the rulers and authorities in the heavenly realms." We are surrounded by an invisible spiritual kingdom made up of both demons and angels—as Paul will explore in greater detail in Ephesians 6. These "rulers and authorities in the heavenly realms" are watching us. It is as if we are on the stage of a great theater, with the angels gathered around in rows, watching us and learning from what is happening here in the lives of believers.

This is why, in 1 Corinthians 11:10, for example, Paul says to women that their dress and demeanor should be exemplary, so as to instruct the angels. Angelic beings are watching and learning from us. What are they learning? Again, Dr. Custance writes:

> The key to the existence of such a universe as this lies, I believe, in the fact that God wished to show forth that aspect of His being which the angels have never comprehended—namely, His love—without at the same time surrendering that part of His being which they do comprehend, namely His holiness.

So the revelation of the mystery is the revelation of the love of God in ways that amaze and instruct the angels. This is why the apostle Peter says in his first letter that our salvation is so tremendous that the angels longed to look into these things. In other words, God's incredible love is demonstrated by the church in such a way as to startle and amaze the angels, as they see the *manifold* wisdom of God.

This word *manifold* is rarely used in the New Testament. What this word suggests is that the wisdom and love of God is manifest in all the hues of life—in our golden moments of glory, our green pastures of contentment, our red hours of anger and passion, our blue days of depression, our black days of grief. His many colors of wisdom are all aspects of His character. We cannot always see the full rainbow of His wisdom and love toward us, but it is always there.

As the angels watch us, they see us learning to turn from our fears, anger, and sin, as we learn to trust God. When the angels, who have seen God, see that weak and faltering humans, who have never seen God, can learn to trust and obey Him, they cannot help but praise Him. They glory in the wondrous truth captured by Charles Wesley in his great hymn: " 'Tis mystery all, the Immortal died." When the angels—especially the fallen angels of demondom—see that frail humans succeed where angels failed, loving and obeying the same God that the demons rebelled against, then the true wisdom and righteousness of God is demonstrated for all time.

THE ORDERING OF THE AGES

Paul never lets us forget that the source of this great mystery is our Lord Jesus Christ. In verse 11, Paul writes: "according to his eternal purpose which he accomplished in Christ Jesus our Lord." The New Revised Standard Version puts it this way: "This was in accordance with the eternal purpose [literally in the original Greek, the ordering of the ages] that he has carried out [accomplished] in Christ Jesus our Lord."

Jesus is the source. In Him God has ordered the ages to produce the unveiling of this great mystery. This means that all of time and all of history are woven together by the hand of God to bring these great events to pass. Paul and the other apostles proclaimed it. And it is now our privilege to declare it to the world.

Paul goes on to add, in verses 12 and 13: "In him and through faith in him we may approach God with freedom and confidence.

I ask you, therefore, not to be discouraged because of my sufferings for you, which are your glory." We, as weak, frail, fumbling human creatures, have access to come boldly and confidently before God to pour out our needs before him. We will always find Him to be a compassionate, tender, loving Father, concerned to bring to bear all His omnipotent power to work out the problems of our lives.

Is there any message greater than this that man could ever hear? What a glorious message! No wonder this apostle was so amazed at the wonder that this message should be committed to him! No wonder he told his Ephesian friends not to be discouraged over his sufferings! From Paul's perspective, the sufferings of one man didn't amount to a hill of beans compared with the unsearchable riches of Christ, the universal knowledge of the great secret that unravels all human misery and problems, the opportunity to teach the truth about God's love and wisdom to the authorities and powers of the heavenly realms.

This mystery of the ages was first revealed to the world in a stable in Bethlehem. It was further unveiled upon a wooden cross of horror and torture on a hill outside of Jerusalem. That revelation is still going on, and the reverberations are reaching out beyond the walls of our own world, penetrating to the outermost heavenly realms. It is shaking the foundations of the kingdom of Satan. It is illuminating the world and breaking the power of darkness. It is showering us with unimaginable wealth and blessing—

The wealth and blessing of our unsearchable riches in Christ.

CHAPTER FIFTEEN

Don't Lose Heart!

Ephesians 3:13–21

Composer George Fredric Handel was at the lowest point in his life. He was sick and so destitute he could not afford a doctor. His creditors hounded him daily, threatening to send him to debtor's prison. Yet he believed in the music he was writing, so every morning he dragged himself out of his sickbed, ignored the threats of the bill collectors, and persevered, laboring over his musical score long into the night.

Finally, the musical piece was finished. It was performed before a royal audience in London. The music was so moving and majestic that the King of England rose to his feet in honor of the resounding chorus. And ever since that first performance, audiences have stood for the singing of "The Hallelujah Chorus." The musical masterpiece which contains that chorus—Handel's famous oratorio *The Messiah*—not only enabled Handel to finally pay his bills, but it gave us one of the grandest, most inspiring works of music the world has ever known.

Handel didn't lose heart in the midst of his adversity, and neither should we. God is creating a masterpiece of praise in our lives. If we persevere to the end, the angels themselves shall rise to their feet in praise of the moving, majestic tribute to God that He is building out of our lives. We are His handiwork, His masterpiece, and our lives will bring Him praise and honor if we do not lose heart.

In the closing verses of Ephesians 3, Paul expresses his concern for the Ephesians. He writes in Ephesians 3:14–21,

> For this reason I kneel before the Father, from whom his whole family in heaven and on earth derives its name. I pray that out of his glorious riches he may strengthen you with power through his Spirit in your inner being, so that Christ may dwell in your hearts through faith. And I pray that you, being rooted and established in love, may have power, together with all the saints, to grasp how wide and long and high and deep is the love of Christ, and to know this love that surpasses knowledge—that you may be filled to the measure of all the fullness of God. Now to him who is able to do immeasurably more than all we ask or imagine, according to his power that is at work within us, to him be glory in the church and in Christ Jesus throughout all generations, for ever and ever! Amen.

Paul was concerned about the Christians in and about Ephesus because they were in danger of losing heart. Perhaps you know what it feels like to lose heart.

Imagine an athlete competing in a marathon—a foot-race of 26 miles requires an extraordinary level of perseverance. When a runner has been running for two or three hours straight, knowing that the finish line is still miles away, when his legs begin to turn to rubber and every breath becomes excruciatingly painful, he knows he must keep running—or fail. And when he finishes, everyone looks at him with admiration and wonder, saying, "What a great heart he's got!"

But when you lose heart, you lose your stamina, your morale, your will to persevere. You come to a place where you say, "What's the use? Why keep going? I can't make it." And you give up.

That is what Paul fears is about to happen to the Christians at Ephesus. They were about to lose heart and give up the race. So Paul says to them in verse 13, "Don't lose heart. The situation isn't the way you think it is." And he closes his great morale-boosting message with a prayer, as we see in verses 14 to 19.

THE APOSTLE'S PRAYER

The apostle Paul dealt with the issue of motivation once before, in chapter 1. There too he closed the chapter with a prayer. In verses 15 and 16 he writes, "For this reason, ever since I heard about your faith in the Lord Jesus and your love for all the saints, I have not stopped giving thanks for you, remembering you in my prayers." Then he goes on to pray that the eyes of their hearts may be enlightened, that the truth may grip their emotions and enlighten their minds, so that they will begin to see truth not merely as intellectual dogma but as living reality that will motivate their lives for God.

Paul's prayer in Ephesians 3 picks up right from that very point. The apostle makes clear that they need to have light and knowledge to begin, but more than that, they need power to continue. They not only need motivation, but they need perseverance to keep going, to continue to the end.

Isn't that what you and I need as well? We need perseverance to meet God daily for Bible study and prayer. We need perseverance to continue serving Him when obstacles and discouragement get in our way. We need perseverance to break bad habits and build good ones.

We need perseverance to continue showing Christlike love and kindness to those around us, especially those unloving, unkind, difficult personalities who rub us the wrong way. We need perseverance to deal with the problems and pain that nag at us and drain our enthusiasm, and which don't ever seem to go away.

We need perseverance more than motivation to begin. We need power to continue—and to continue and continue and continue. That is the difference between this prayer in Ephesians 3 and the prayer in Ephesians 1. Paul's previous prayer was a prayer for understanding—understanding that grips even the emotions. But here, in chapter 3, Paul prays for power—power that keeps us going and keeps us from losing heart.

So if you are losing heart right now—or if you ever have or ever might in the future—then please give careful attention to this prayer. The apostle Paul begins with this issue, with the person who has reached a point of exhaustion, depression, or despair, the person who is ready to give up or turn back. Then he prays for that person, and each step or division of this prayer is designed to encourage and motivate that person to keep on keeping on. The end result, as we find when we reach the end of Paul's prayer, is praise.

Let's look at each step of Paul's prayer in turn, beginning with verses 14 and 15: "For this reason I kneel before the Father, from whom his whole family in heaven and on earth derives its name." In other words, Paul begins with prayer. If there is one thing we all need, it is a greater understanding of the ministry of prayer—what prayer really does and how it works.

The apostle clearly understood the value and operation of prayer. Intercessory prayer permeates all of his letters. He always promoted prayer as the solution to the problems of Christians. He continually sought the prayer of his Christian brothers and sisters for his own trials and for the success of his missionary efforts. When somebody's faith is failing, when they are turning cold and dead in their spiritual experience, our first recourse must be to pray for them.

Notice the One to whom Paul prays. He says, "I kneel before the Father." It wasn't customary for the Jews to bow their knees in prayer. We think of kneeling as the common posture of prayer, but the Jews usually prayed standing upright, with arms outstretched to God. It was only when something was of deep, intense concern that they bowed the knees or prostrated themselves before God. That is the position the apostle takes here.

Of course, it really isn't important what your physical position is—God is much more concerned with the condition of your heart than the position of your knees. A poem by Sam Walter Foss, "The Prayer of Cyrus Brown," says it so well:

> "The proper way for a man to pray,"
> Said Deacon Lemuel Keyes,
> "And the only proper attitude
> Is down upon his knees."
> "No, I should say the way to pray,"
> Said Reverend Doctor Wise,
> "Is standing straight with outstretched arms
> And rapt and upturned eyes."
> "Oh, no, no, no,"
> Said Elder Slow,
> "Such posture is too proud.
> A man should pray with eyes fast-closed
> And head contritely bowed."
> "It seems to me his hands should be
> Austerely clasped in front

With both thumbs pointing toward the ground,"
Said Reverend Doctor Blunt.
"Last year I fell in Hidgekin's well
Headfirst," said Cyrus Brown,
"With both my heels a-stickin' up
And my head a-pointin' down.
And I made a prayer right then and there,
The best prayer I ever said,
The prayingest prayer I ever prayed,
A-standin' on my head."

Ol' Cyrus Brown could teach you and me a lot about praying with earnestness and sincerity! And that is precisely the point underscored by the apostle Paul as he writes, "I kneel before the Father, from whom his whole family in heaven and on earth derives its name." In other words, God is the very epitome of fatherhood, and every fatherhood in heaven and on earth that deserves the name of father derives from the fatherhood of God. He is the archetypal father—the Father from whom all true fatherhood takes its essence and its character.

Let us not mistake paternity for genuine fatherhood. We are familiar with paternity suits, in which a woman sues a man for financial support, claiming that he caused her to be pregnant, that he participated in the conception of the child. But participating in the conception of a child does not make a man a father, in the truest sense of the word. A loving adoptive father is unquestionably much more of a father than a man who simply donated his DNA in an act of passion, then left mother and child to fend for themselves.

Paul talks here about true fatherhood—the loving, caring, providing, training, guiding action of someone who truly fills the role of a father. When you are despairing, when you are about to lose heart and quit, Paul wants you to remember to turn to your loving Father. God is the very quintessence of fatherhood, and He reaches into the storehouse of His inexhaustible resources and showers upon us the riches of His glory, as Paul says in verse 16: "I pray that out of his glorious riches he may strengthen you with power through his Spirit in your inner being."

God's being is God's glory. He himself is His own treasury of glorious riches. When God wants to display His glory, He simply reveals himself in His own glorious reality. He simply shows us what He is like. God is not some cold, remote being out in the universe or up on Mount Olympus, indifferent to our needs and our prayers. He is a tender, concerned Father, who is involved in our daily lives and who answers our prayers out of the inexhaustible riches of His own personal glory.

OUR INNER BEING

Next, Paul traces, step by step, the course of recovery from spiritual depression, from losing heart: "he may strengthen you with power through his Spirit in your inner being." This is not merely a reminder that the Spirit dwells in the inner being, although that is true. Rather, the idea here is that the Spirit can infuse His own strength into your inner being.

What does Paul mean by the phrase "inner being"? He is distinguishing between our outer humanity and our inner humanity. The outer part of ourselves—our "outer being"—is the part we dress, clothe, feed, wash, dry, bandage, and smear with wrinkle cream. We are always concerned with our outer humanity—the body and its needs.

But God is concerned with our inner humanity. Many Bible commentators take this to mean the soul, with its faculties of reasoning, emotion, and will. But I don't think this is what Paul means in Ephesians 3:16. In another letter, Paul gives us a clue to what he means. In 2 Corinthians 4:16, Paul writes, "therefore we do not lose heart. Though outwardly we are wasting away, yet inwardly we are being renewed day by day." Paul says that we do not lose heart because, even though our outer humanity is aging, decaying, and deteriorating, there is a part of us—the innermost part—that is getting better, fresher, stronger, and more vital with each passing day. That is our "inner being."

You may well ask, "Well, haven't you just described the soul? Isn't the soul our innermost being?" Actually, no. The Bible differentiates between the soul and the spirit. The Greek word for soul is *psuche*, from where we get the words *psyche* and *psychology*, which refer to the human mind—not the spirit. The Greek word for spirit is *pneuma*, which is literally the breath of life.

As we grow older, our soul ages as well, and can become enfeebled by age and diseases, such as Alzheimer's disease. The soul is subject to the ravages of brain injury, alcohol and substance abuse, and physical exhaustion. The emotions of the soul can grow unstable with age, stress, and trauma. Even the human will, which is part of the soul, can become enfeebled, so we lose the drive and determination we once had in youth. So the soul is linked with the outer man, which is perishing day by day.

The inner being that Paul describes is the spirit, not the soul. The spirit does not age. It is the most fundamental and eternal aspect of our nature.

When you are really discouraged and have given up, you are said to be "dispirited." That is an accurate term. You have become "dis-spirited." Your fundamental nature is dissatisfied and utterly discontented. You are not merely bored (that is in the realm of the soul), but you are filled with a persistent sense of despair and lifelessness within. That is where recovery must begin.

Paul tells us that the Creator himself, our loving Father, gives us a fresh infusion of strength by His Spirit into our spirit—our inner being.

Remember what Jesus himself taught in that great passage on prayer in Luke 11:11–13:

> "Which of you fathers, if your son asks for a fish, will give him a snake instead? Or if he asks for an egg, will give him a scorpion? If you then, though you are evil, know how to give good gifts to your children, how much more will your Father in heaven give the Holy Spirit to those who ask him!"

Do you feel the force of his argument? When Jesus talks about how the Father will give the Holy Spirit to those who ask Him, He is not talking about how to be indwelt by the Spirit, but about how to recover from losing heart. The first step is to ask God to grant that your spirit will receive a new infusion of strength, that you can drink again of the river of the Spirit of life which is in you. This is how your spirit is restored, empowering you to live as God intended.

You may not have a strong sense of restoration in the realm of your feelings and emotions—that, after all, is part of the soul, not the spirit. But you will experience strengthening and refreshment in your innermost being, in your spirit.

ROOTED AND GROUNDED

Next, Paul prays that God grant you to be strengthened with might through His Spirit "so that Christ may dwell in your hearts through faith," verse 17. Notice the connection—Paul does not say *"and that* Christ may dwell in your hearts through faith." You are strengthened by the Spirit *so that* Christ may literally make His home in your heart. The strengthening of your spirit results in your sensing the personal presence of the Lord Jesus, as your reborn faith takes hold of his promise once again.

The key to it all is in the last two words of that statement: "through faith." Why have you been languishing and losing heart? Because your faith is failing. The reality that God has revealed to you has begun to seem unreal. Your faith is dragging. The solution: A fresh infusion of the Spirit to awaken your faith, so that you can begin to believe again.

The first thing to believe is the most fundamental fact of the Christian life—Jesus Christ has come to live in you. This fact is not dependent upon your feelings, which ebb and flow. It rests solely upon Jesus' promise given in the Upper Room in John 14. The question was put to Him by Judas Iscariot a short time before He would be betrayed by this man. Judas said to him, verse 22, "But, Lord, why do you intend to show yourself to us and not to the world?" Jesus replied, verse 23, "If anyone loves me, he will obey my teaching. My Father will love him, and we will come to him and make our home with him."

That is what Paul refers to. Faith is awakened now. You remind yourself that Jesus Christ lives in you. You are a believer. He has taken up residence in you. He will not leave you. He is at home in your heart, and you belong to Him.

Do you see how Paul is leading us, step by step, back to recovery? Though we may be in danger of losing heart and giving up, Paul shows us the way back to strength, motivation, and fresh courage. He underscores the way back with this prayer for the Ephesian Christians in 3:17–18: "And I pray that you, being rooted and established in love, may have power . . . ."

Here is yet another key to recover from a fainting heart: love! We are reassured by Jesus' promise to be with us, and we know that He loves us, He cares for us, and He will never change that relationship. Christ's love roots us in Him. It is the ground of our being. This is a statement of ultimate security. Roots are solid in the ground, dug deep into the earth, steadfast and immovable, like a tree that has sent its roots deep into the rich, life-sustaining soil.

We once had a young sapling tree on our property that seemed so spindly and frail, a stiff breeze could have knocked it over. An agronomist advised me to stake the tree and tie it firmly during the first couple years of its life. I followed his advice, and today that tree is immovable. The roots have gone so deep into the soil and have spread over such an area that it would take considerable work to kill it—and you'd have to blast the stump out of the ground to finish the job. Today it could stand a storm of near-hurricane force!

The same is true of you and me. If we put our roots down deeply into the love of Christ, we become immovable, firmly fixed, rooted and grounded. We become secure in Him. His love gives us our sense of security and well-being.

SHARING OUR LIVES

Paul takes us a step further and deeper with these words, verses 17–18: "And I pray that you, being rooted and established in love, may have power, together with all the saints, to grasp how wide and long and high and deep is the love of Christ." Here Paul shows us that a key to recovery when we are losing heart is our relationship to other believers. We are to reach out to other Christians—and as we do that, God gives us the power, along with our fellow believers, to grasp and experience the full width, length, height, and depth of the love of Christ!

All too many Christians today attempt to live in solitary confinement. They resist relating and sharing—and thus they fall into the trap of this world, which demands privacy and wallows in darkness. Christians must share their lives, not isolate themselves. They must walk in the light, not hide in the darkness. When Christians take seriously the commands of Christ to love one another and live in close community with one another, then the church becomes a force for change and healing in a world of alienation, isolation, and loneliness.

There are 59 "one another" commands in the New Testament, including 21 that say "love one another." Here is a partial list:

"Be at peace with each other" (Mark 9:50).

"Wash one another's feet" (John 13:14).

"Love one another" (John 13:34, 35; 15:12, 17; Romans 13:8; 1 Thessalonians 4:9; 1 John 3:11; 3:23; 4:7; 4:11, 12; 2 John 5).

"Be devoted to one another in brotherly love" (Romans 12:10).

"Live in harmony with one another" (Romans 12:16).

"Accept one another, then, just as Christ accepted you" (Romans 15:7).

"Instruct one another" (Romans 15:14).

"Greet one another with a holy kiss" (Romans 16:16; 1 Corinthians 16:20; 2 Corinthians 13:12; 1 Peter 5:14).

"Have equal concern for each other" (1 Corinthians 12:25).

"Serve one another in love" (Galatians 5:13).

"Carry each other's burdens" (Galatians 6:2).

"Be patient, bearing with one another in love" (Ephesians 4:2).

"Be kind and compassionate to one another" (Ephesians 4:32).

"Submit to one another out of reverence for Christ" (Ephesians 5:21).

"In humility consider others better than yourselves" (Philippians 2:3).

"Forgive whatever grievances you may have against one another" (Colossians 3:13).

"Admonish one another" (Colossians 3:16).

"Make your love increase and overflow for each other" (1 Thessalonians 3:12).

"Encourage each other (1 Thessalonians 4:18).

"Encourage one another (1 Thessalonians 5:11; Hebrews 3:13; 10:25).

"Build each other up" (1 Thessalonians 5:11).

"Spur one another on toward love and good deeds" (Hebrews 10:24).

"Confess your sins to each other" (James 5:16).

"Pray for each other" (James 5:16).

"Love one another deeply, from the heart" (1 Peter 1:22; 4:8).

"Live in harmony with one another" (1 Peter 3:8).

"Offer hospitality to one another without grumbling" (1 Peter 4:9).

"Clothe yourselves with humility toward one another (1 Peter 5:5).

The Christian is to have no private areas in his life at all. There must be, in the life of every Christian, at least one nucleus of close Christian friends with whom you can be open, honest, and transparent, and with whom you can begin to experience the height and depth and length and breadth of Christ's love.

Why does Paul describe the love of Christ in these four dimensions? Some see in them the cross, with its height and depth and length and breadth. Some see it as a description of the deep and wide extent of the love of God. But I think these dimensions refer to elements of Paul's earlier discussion in Ephesians.

The "length" is what he calls in Ephesians 1:18 "the hope to which you are called," that hope which began before the foundation of the world, and which reaches on through all of recorded time, and into the limitless reaches of futurity and eternity. That is the length of God's program of love, of which you and I are a part—the hope to which we are called.

The "width" is what Paul calls the riches of Christ's inheritance among the Gentiles. God's grace is not narrowly confined to any one group, the Jews. It is freely available to all, without discrimination or division—to Jews, Gentile, black, white, rich, poor, slave, free, male, female—it doesn't make any difference. All humanity is caught up in the riches of Jesus Christ, in the cross and in the church. That is the width of God's love.

The "height" is the place to which we are raised with Christ. He has raised us to sit together with Him in heavenly places, far above all principalities, powers, and authorities, in this age and in the age to come. It is the place of authority as a Christian, the place of power to be freed from everything that would drag you down and blunt your effectiveness for God.

The "depth," of course, is what Paul described in Ephesians 2 as death, the living death out of which God has called us. Once we were victims of death and sin; now we are victors over death and sin. Once we were children of wrath; now we are children of God, raised from the depths to heights of splendor with Christ.

All of these dimensions of Christ's love are available to us as we learn to live in close community and fellowship—what the Greek New Testament calls *koinonia*—with one another in the church. This is the kind of lifestyle we committed ourselves to as a congregation at Peninsula Bible Church. Without it, the church is barren, narrow, and isolated. With it, we experience all four dimensions of the vast and amazing love of Christ.

LOVE THAT SURPASSES KNOWLEDGE

Next, Paul tells us that a key to recovery from losing heart is to know the unknowable. He writes in verse 19: "And to know this love that surpasses knowledge—that you may be filled to the measure of all the fullness of God." Here is another of God's great paradoxes—we are to know the unknowable! How do we do that? Here is where the Christian experience reaches its full peak. You can't understand it but you can sense it, you can know it, you can feel it.

There are many things we can feel that are beyond our comprehension. A baby feels his mother's love. He knows it. But does he understand it? No—not anymore than you and I can understand the amazing love of Christ. Still, His love is ours to experience and revel in. It is ours to draw strength from, and as we experience His incomprehensible love, we recharge our spirits so that we do not lose heart.

Paul goes on to say that the knowledge of the unknowable, the experience of the inexpressible, enables us to be "filled to the measure of all the fullness of God"!

That is the pinnacle. Once God has performed this work in us, once we have been filled with the fullness of God, we have truly realized the purpose of our own creation. This is what God made you and me for. He created us as vessels, wholly filled and overflowing with God himself.

This is not a condition you attain once or twice in your Christian life. It is a condition to which you are to return again and again. This is what Paul refers to as being filled with the Spirit. It is the condition in which God is in possession and control of our lives, enriching us, blessing us, and strengthening us. Our faith is strong and vital, and we reach out in joyful ministry to others. As Paul put it earlier, we are God's workmanship, and as He fills us with himself, we discover all the great and wonderful works to which we have been foreordained.

Paul underscores the wonder and astonishment we feel as we realize the incredible work God is doing in our lives—and again, the thrill of seeing God so powerfully at work in our lives is a wonderful "heart medicine," an antidote to losing heart. Paul writes, verses 20–21, "Now to him who is able to do immeasurably more than all we ask or imagine, according to his power that is at work within us, to him be glory in the church and in Christ Jesus throughout all generations, for ever and ever! Amen."

That is the secret, isn't it? You and I can do nothing—but God, living in us, filling us, working through us, is able to do abundantly more than we can even think to ask Him to do in our prayers! What are your goals for this day, for this year, for this lifetime? God can exceed your wildest dreams—if you stop trying to manipulate, scheme, and bring it to pass in your own strength. Allow Him to live in you and through you, and the wildly unthinkable will become commonplace in your life, day after thrilling day, year after astonishing year.

We each have only one lifetime to live—so we dare not blow it. Instead of trying to run our own lives according to our own finite plans, let's turn our lives over to the One whose plan is infinite and eternal. When we are secure within His loving heart, we can never lose heart. Who could think of turning back, of giving up, when He has shown us a glimpse of the glory that lies before us?

So don't lose heart! The race is nearly won! Come on! Keep going! Don't look back—look ahead! His love carries us forward—and His glory is almost within our reach!

PART TWO

The Ministry of the Saints

Ephesians 4:1–16

CHAPTER SIXTEEN

Why the Church Exists

Ephesians 4:1–3

The noted English historian, Alexander Kinglake, was interested in the claims of Christianity—but he was also very skeptical about the truth of the resurrection and the reality of the new life in Christ. He once suggested that every church should bear an inscription over the door: IMPORTANT IF TRUE.

Though Kinglake's suggestion is cynical, perhaps even sarcastic, there is a great deal of validity in his suggestion. If what the church has to offer is true, it *is* important—vitally and eternally important! If Jesus truly has been raised from the dead, if He offers all of humanity a new quality of life on earth, as well as eternal life in the world to come, then there is nothing in the world more important than the message of the church.

We who have Christ living in our lives know beyond any doubt that the message of the church is true—and infinitely important. And that is what Paul wants to teach us in Ephesians chapter 4.

THE PURPOSE AND MINISTRY OF THE CHURCH

Paul presents us with a declaration of God's intention in forming His church. In these verses, Paul sets forth the church's purpose and ministry in the world—in every century, not just the first but the twenty-first. This passage, then, is as applicable to our lives today as it was to the lives of the Ephesian Christians to whom Paul wrote. In Ephesians 4:1–3, Paul writes:

> As a prisoner for the Lord, then, I urge you to live a life worthy of the calling you have received. Be completely humble and gentle; be patient, bearing with one another in love. Make every effort to keep the unity of the spirit through the bond of peace.

This passage is a condensed summary of the reason for the existence of the church and a statement of its function, and verse 1 is a key exhortation to those in the church as to how they are to view their calling as members of Christ's church. Paul begins this exhortation by again describing himself as the Lord's prisoner.

As we already saw when we examined Ephesians 3:1, Paul is writing from Rome where he awaits trial before the emperor on charges of inciting a riot, with the implication of treason against the emperor himself. These charges had been lodged against Paul by the Jews in Jerusalem at the time of Paul's arrest in the dramatic encounter he had with the Jewish leaders in the city of Jerusalem (as recorded in Acts 21 and 22; for a discussion of Paul's arrest, see Chapter 13: "The Great Mystery").

After languishing for two years as a prisoner in Caesarea, Paul was sent on a perilous sea voyage. Despite being shipwrecked, he arrived at last in Rome. There he lived in a private home, chained to a Roman guard day and night. Though a personal prisoner of Nero, the Roman Caesar, Paul never refers to himself as the prisoner of Rome. Instead, he looks beyond the chains, the guard, the imperial legal system, and the emperor himself. He sees only the controlling hand of Jesus Christ in his circumstances. He is, therefore, a prisoner of Christ.

The result of Paul's viewpoint is that he does not fret about being imprisoned. He doesn't feel limited by his chains. If Jesus put these chains on him, then the chains can only be a tool for furthering God's purpose and accomplishing His will. Paul's chains are not a hindrance but a help. As Paul says in another letter, "So we fix our eyes not on what is seen, but on what is unseen. For what is seen is temporary, but what is unseen is eternal" (2 Corinthians 4:18).

Paul's attitude is the same as that of Christ before Pilate. Pilate said to Jesus, "Do you refuse to speak to me? Don't you realize I have power either to free you or to crucify you?" And Jesus answered, "You would have no power over me if it were not given to you from above" (John 19:10–11).

This has a direct bearing upon Paul's theme of the purpose of the church. The reason the church often seems so confused, divided, or misdirected in our own time is that we Christians tend to look on the things that are seen instead of the things that are unseen. We see ourselves as imprisoned by events, politics, ideologies, and worldly problems. Our view of our role in the world as members of Christ's church would be transformed if we instead saw ourselves as prisoners of Christ himself. Instead of looking on ephemeral conditions and applying superficial solutions, we would live in the invisible, spiritual realm and be used as God's tools in His eternal plan.

How does Paul say the church should live in view of our invisible prisonership on behalf of the Lord Jesus Christ? "As a prisoner for the Lord, then," he says, "I urge you to live a life worthy of the calling you have received." In other words, "Christ is our Lord and Commander—so obey His orders!"

Our duty as members of the church is to take our direction from the Head of the church. We must follow the divine strategy, not the shallow counsel of men. The church is not an independent organization existing by means of its own strength, like mere human organizations.

What is our calling? What are our orders? As we have already seen in our study, the first three chapters of Ephesians are devoted to a description of what Christians have in Christ as compared with their former condition. We are no longer in death and darkness, defeated citizens of the kingdom of Satan. We have been brought to life and light, as citizens of the kingdom of God—and more, as children of God.

HOLY AND BLAMELESS

Paul always structures his letters very deliberately, beginning with foundational, doctrinal truth. The truth of God calls us to reality, to a realistic vision of life. In the first three chapters, Paul shows us our purpose in the present time and our purpose in eternity. In Ephesians 1:4, Paul says, "For he chose us in him before the creation of the world to be holy and blameless in his sight." That is our calling. The church was no afterthought; it was planned and founded from the beginning of time—and it was planned to be holy and blameless.

The moral character of God's people is essential to understanding the nature of the church. We are to be a moral example to the world, reflecting the character of Jesus Christ.

The story is told of two Americans riding a train in England. They noticed a distinguished-looking gentleman in the compartment, and one of the men thought he recognized the gentleman. In a low tone, he said to his friend, "I would wager money that he is the Archbishop of Canterbury." The other man said, "Him? The Archbishop? I don't think so! I'll take that bet." So the first man approached the gentleman and said, "Sir, would you mind telling us, are you the Archbishop of Canterbury?" The Englishman snapped, "You mind your own blankety blank business! What the blank difference does it make to you?" The first American shrugged to his friend and said, "I guess the bet's off. If he won't tell us, we'll never know if he's the Archbishop or not!"

The point is clear. Christians ought to be evident by the way they talk and live, the way they think and act. We are designed and created to live holy and blameless lives before God. That is one of the purposes of the church.

Paul also tells us, Ephesians 1:12, that our purpose as Christians is so that "we, who were the first to hope in Christ, might be for the praise of his glory." We have been destined and appointed (here is our calling) to live for the praise of his glory. The first job of the church is not the welfare of other people—serving others is important, but not the central aspect of our calling. The first duty of our calling is that we live to the praise and the glory of God. The New English Bible puts it this way: that we "should cause his glory to be praised."

What is God's glory? It is the story of what God is and does. The problem with this world is that it does not know God. The glory of God is the revelation of His reality, of what He is truly like. It is the story of who God is and what He has done. As Paul writes in 2 Corinthians 4:6, "For God, who said, 'Let light shine out of darkness,' made his light shine in our hearts to give us the light of the knowledge of the glory of God in the face of Christ."

THE BOND OF UNITY AND PEACE

We see the calling of the church to reveal God's true nature in Ephesians 1:22–23, where Paul writes, "And God placed all things under his feet and appointed him to be head over everything for the church, which is his body, the fullness of him who fills everything in every way." The secret of the church is that Christ lives in the church. The mission of the church is to declare Him, to reveal to the world the reality of the living Christ.

We see it again in Ephesians 2:19–22: "Consequently, you are no longer foreigners and aliens, but fellow citizens with God's people and members of God's household, built on the foundation of the apostles and prophets, with Christ Jesus himself as the chief cornerstone. In him the whole building is joined together and rises to become a holy temple in the Lord." This is the holy mystery of the church: the church is the dwelling place of God. He lives in His people.

We see the purpose and calling of the church reflected again in Ephesians 3:9–10. Paul says his ministry is "to make plain to everyone the administration of this mystery, which for ages past was kept hidden in God, who created all things. His intent was that now, through the church, the manifold wisdom of God should be made known to the rulers and authorities in the heavenly realms." There are other beings beside human beings who are watching—and being instructed by—the church. This is an important aspect of the ministry of the church.

The last two verses of chapter 3—the verses immediately preceding the passage we are exploring—make it doubly clear what the calling of the church is. Paul writes, "Now to him who is able to do immeasurably more than all we ask or imagine, according to his power that is at work within us, to him be glory in the church and in Christ Jesus throughout all generations, for ever and ever! Amen." The calling of the church is to declare by our word and to demonstrate by our lives the character and the work of Jesus Christ who lives within us. We are to talk to others about the reality of a life-changing encounter with a living Christ, and to demonstrate that change by an unselfish life of loving, forgiving, and serving others.

That is why the apostle goes on to say, in Ephesians 4:2–3, "Be completely humble and gentle; be patient, bearing with one another in love. Make every effort to keep the unity of the Spirit through the bond of peace." He moves from grand, exalted, doctrinal truth to the realities of our everyday existence. He links the eternal plan of God to our daily grind. In order to carry out God's eternal plan, we have to get along here on earth—in our families, in our churches, in the situations of our lives that are irritating, annoying, and downright frustrating. The unity of the Spirit is our witness to the world of the reality of our living, resurrected Lord.

THE LORD'S WITNESSES

The Lord himself told us about our calling as members of His church. Just before He ascended, He told His disciples, "But you will receive power when the Holy Spirit comes on you; and you will be my witnesses in Jerusalem, and in all Judea and Samaria, and to the ends of the earth" (Acts 1:8). There is the calling of the church: we are to be witnesses of Christ.

A witness is one who declares what they have seen. As Peter states in 1 Peter 2:9 (emphasis added), "But you are a chosen people, a royal priesthood, a holy nation, a people belonging to God, *that you may declare the praises of him* who called you out of darkness into his wonderful light." That is the job of the church. That is our calling.

Notice, this calling is always addressed to the individual Christian. It is amazing that the church is never addressed as a body in the Scriptures, but always as individual units within a body. Therefore the responsibility to fulfill this calling of the church belongs to every true Christian: We are all called—individually. We are all indwelt by the Holy Spirit—individually. We are all expected to fulfill our calling in the world—individually. The expression of the church's witness may sometimes be corporate, but the responsibility to do so is always individual.

OUR MESSAGE IS OUR PURPOSE

In Scripture, the only message that the church has for the world is the gospel of Jesus Christ. This is not to say that the church has nothing to say about politics or social justice or civil rights or abortion or any other issue on the earthly scene. Christians are called to demonstrate compassion, and the Christian who can shrug off his fellow human being and say, "I'm indifferent to the needs of others," is not truly Christian—he is horribly sub-Christian.

But we must recognize that the gospel is not a social agenda. It is a transcendent message of new life, eternal life. This is what men, women, and children need to hear. That is our message.

In the letter to the Ephesians, Paul calls us back to those great purposes of God for which the church was established. The church has no right to set its own agenda. It was placed here to carry out God's agenda. The church was not placed in the world with a mandate to correct the evils of society, but to declare and demonstrate the power of God in Jesus Christ. The great and beautiful paradox of the church is that the more it focuses on its true spiritual mandate, the more effective it is in correcting the ills and evils of society. But the more preoccupied the church becomes with a social agenda, the less effect it has in the world.

So we must focus on our message—the simple story of what Jesus Christ has done in our own lives. Ask any Christian what is the greatest event in his or her life, and invariably, without hesitation, that Christian will reply, "The moment I came to know Jesus Christ as my Lord and Savior." So if you then ask that person what is the greatest message he or she can give to others, that Christian will naturally reply, "The good news of how to have a personal relationship with Jesus Christ as Lord and Savior!"

Christians are not to witness in arrogance and rudeness, not in holier-than-thou smugness, not in sanctimonious presumption, but in a spirit of Christlike meekness. And Christians cannot bear witness to the peace, love, and forgiveness of God while living out the warring, factionalism, and grudge-bearing of ugly church fights.

Our calling, our purpose, our reason for existing as the church of Jesus Christ is to live out the character of Christ in our personal and corporate lives, and to tell forth the good news of Jesus Christ everywhere we go. We, like Paul, are the Lord's prisoners, and these are His orders. It is our joyful, glorious duty to carry them out, maintaining the unity of the Spirit in the bond of peace.

CHAPTER SEVENTEEN

Our Unity in the Spirit

Ephesians 4:4–6

To dwell above with saints we love,
O that will be glory!
But to dwell below with saints we know—
Well, that's another story!

I'm sure you've felt that way from time to time about some of the saints you know in your own church. It's impossible to be deeply involved in the life of a church without bumping elbows with a saint who's—well, let's just say a saint who puts our Christian love and patience to the test! And, if the truth were known, there's probably a brother or sister in your own church who could say the same for you!

Division among Christians brings shame and disrepute to the church, to Christ, and to His gospel. Christian unity brings glory to Jesus Christ and demonstrates the reality of God's grace, love, and forgiveness. In other words, our *oneness* is our *witness*!

As we saw in our study of Ephesians 4:1–3, we in the church—both as individuals and as a body of believers—must recognize that, like Paul, we are prisoners of Jesus Christ. We do not have the right to chart our own course. Our goal has already been set. Our purpose has been determined by our Lord. That is what Paul says in the first three verses of Ephesians 4.

He goes on in verses 5 and 6 to show us that keeping the unity of the Spirit through the bond of peace comes down to one thing: *oneness.* He writes:

> There is one body and one Spirit—just as you were called to one hope when you were called—one Lord, one faith, one baptism; one God and Father of all, who is over all and through all and in all.

Unity is *oneness.* Not sameness, but a special oneness centered on a few core essentials—one body, one Spirit, one hope, one Lord, one faith, one baptism, one God the Father. Some would seize on the word *unity* in verse 3 and say, "That's the problem with the church today! It's not unified! We need to gather all the churches and all the denominations into one big church. Then the church will have power, because there is power in numbers! Churches of the world, unite!"

From the world's point of view, such feelings certainly make sense. Those sentiments account for the great move toward ecumenism, toward a single universal church, in the world today. But those "ecumaniacs" who pursue a unification of all church bodies into a single, worldwide church body miss what the Bible teaches about the unity of the Spirit.

THE SOURCES OF OUR DIVERSITY

In verse 3 Paul declares two great facts that we must clearly understand about church unity. First, he says we must allow for differences among Christians. He says we must make every diligent effort to maintain the unity of the Spirit in the bond of peace. Clearly, there would be no need for this exhortation if differences did not exist.

The fact is, there is no group in the world so gloriously diverse and heterogeneous as the church. Its glory is that it is made up of different kinds of people. In the church of Jesus Christ, you find rich and poor, slave and free, Jew and Gentile, black, brown, and white, male and female, sitting side by side in one body, waiting upon one hope, worshiping one Lord, practicing one faith, partaking in one baptism, praying to one God and Father, unified by one Spirit.

But let's be honest: We do not ignore these boundaries easily. Friction often arises from our differences. Those frictions exist today, and they existed in Paul's time. In Philippians 4, Paul addresses two ladies in the Philippian church who cannot get along with each other. Their names are Euodia and Syntyche—though some wag has fittingly rendered their names Odious and Soon-Touchy. Paul says, in verse 2, "I plead with Euodia and I plead with Syntyche to agree with each other in the Lord."

Are these women just a couple of church troublemakers who bicker with each other because they have too much time on their hands? No, Paul makes it clear that these women are serious-minded, committed Christian workers who have labored hard for Jesus Christ. "I ask you, loyal yokefellow," Paul continues in verse 3, "help these women who have contended at my side in the cause of the gospel, along with Clement and the rest of my fellow workers, whose names are in the book of life."

Churches have been shattered by divisions over issues as small as the color of the carpet in the fellowship hall—and as large as the direction and philosophy of a church's overall ministry. Frequently, spiritual gifts (see the following chapter) are a source of friction, because God distributes different gifts in every congregation, and our natural human tendency is to disparage the gifts of others while exalting our own.

So there are differences among Christians—differences of class, race, background, viewpoint, philosophy, attitude, personality, and spiritual gifts. Those differences offer fertile ground for friction.

THE SOURCE OF OUR UNITY

But the second fact Paul brings to our attention is crucial for us to understand if we are to transcend our differences and fulfill the command of Christ that we become one in Him: Beneath our differences, there is a basic unity that is given to the church by the Spirit. That unity exists right now, throughout the church, even between Christians who are at odds with each other. The fact that they don't *feel* unified and *act* unified does not cancel out the fact that they already have the unity of the spirit among them. They simply need to act worthy of a unity that already exists.

Notice the apostle does not say we are to *produce* unity; he says we are to *maintain* a unity that has already been produced by the Holy Spirit. There is a unity that is already there by virtue of the very existence of the church, because the Holy Spirit is the bond which holds the church together. Here is the fundamental error of modern ecumenical movements. By and large, they strive to generate a man-made institutional unity, ignoring the spiritual unity that already exists in the Holy Spirit. The power of the church is not the power of numbers, but the power of *one*—one indwelling Spirit, who leads us in worshiping one Lord Jesus, in practicing one faith, in praying to one Father.

The church is not a conglomeration of individuals who happen to agree upon certain things. It is bound together as a spiritual organism in a bodily unity. It cannot therefore derive power from the sum of its numbers. It derives its power solely from the Spirit of God who binds these individuals into a unified, spiritual whole.

So we are forced to choose between two different kinds of unity. One is an external unity, a worldly unity, a unity of numbers that seeks to make its plans and enforce its will on society by the power of persuasion. The other is an internal unity, a spiritual unity, a unity of genuine oneness that is joined to God's eternal plan and manifests the supernatural power of God.

As a boy, I had two friends who were brothers, only a year apart in age. One day, while the three of us were playing, the two brothers began quarreling between themselves. I thought that one fellow was out of line, so I chimed in on behalf of the underdog. That was a big mistake! Instantly, they forgot the quarrel between them and both jumped on me! I had made a shallow judgment of their quarrel, thinking that it represented a fundamental division between them. I failed to reckon with the fundamental unity between brothers.

That is an apt metaphor describing the fundamental unity between brothers and sisters in Christ. Yes, there are quarrels and disagreements within the church, but that is transcended by an internal unity—the unity of the Spirit, which surpasses even the blood-unity between those two brothers. The unity of the Spirit is the ground of our shared life together.

We can violate that unity by our actions, we can grieve the Holy Spirit by our sinful behavior toward one another in the body of Christ, we can bring shame and dishonor to the gospel by sinning against our Spirit-given unity, but we cannot create or destroy what the Spirit himself has produced. The church can be divided organizationally, but the body of Christ can never be disjointed. As the old hymn rightly puts it,

> We are not divided,
> all one body we,
> one in hope and doctrine,
> one in charity.

In verses 5 and 6 of Ephesians 4, the apostle describes the real unity of the body of Christ, which he breaks down into seven elements:

1. One body.
2. One Spirit.
3. One hope.
4. One Lord.
5. One faith.
6. One baptism.
7. One God and Father of us all.

These three elements spell the unity of the body. It gathers around the three Persons of the Trinity—the Spirit, the Son, and the Father. It includes all the essentials of the Christian faith—the fellowship of the saints in one body, our hope of salvation, the doctrinal truths of our faith, and our baptism.

Let's examine each of these elements in turn:

1. One body

We are one body. The apostle does not say one organization or one institution; he uses a specific word-picture, describing the church as a body. This picture of the church as a body is amazingly apt. While an organization is an assemblage of departments or units, a body is a living organism. A body consists of thousands of cells with one mutually shared life. That shared life and shared unity exists despite surface divisions and distinctions, even despite differences of culture and language.

I have had the privilege of traveling around the world, meeting with Christians in widespread places around the earth. I have discovered that it is easy to recognize this fundamental unity wherever I go. I may not understand the words of an African, Latin, European, or Asian brother in Christ, and he may not understand mine—but within moments of our first handshake, we both know that we jointly partake of one body, one Spirit, one hope, one Lord, one faith, one baptism, one God the Father. We know it, we feel it, we revel in the warmth of the Spirit, who joins our two spirits together in the bond of peace.

I have felt that same bond many times when I have been with Christians from other churches. This bond transcends differences between denominations, between theological viewpoint, and even between Protestant and Catholic, where there is an official, institutional denial of unity. On various occasions, I have met with Catholic churchmen, and we have shared together about our love for Christ, and I knew as we talked that we had entered together into the experience of the unity of the Holy Spirit, produced by the operation of God's Spirit in the human spirit.

It is important to remember how a body comes about. You do not create a healthy body by stitching body parts together, as Baron von Frankenstein discovered when he stitched his monster together in Mary Shelley's classic tale. A body begins with a single cell, which divides into two cells, then four cells, then eight, then sixteen, and on and on and on until it becomes a fully formed mature body—*but every cell shares the life of the original cell.* You and I are cells in a single body—"one body," as Paul says—that extends geographically around the world and chronologically back to the very first followers of Christ.

2. One Spirit

This first exalted truth brings us to the next element: one Spirit. The Holy Spirit is the great, eternal, invisible Person who is the power behind the Christian church. The power of the church never comes from its numbers, but from the one Spirit who makes us one body. This principle is not just a New Testament principle—it is woven into both testaments of our Bible.

The prophet Zechariah, for example, was once confronted with a great mountain that God said would become a plain. When Zechariah looked around, wondering how such a thing could take place and where the power would come from to level this mountain to a plain, the word of the Lord came to him: " 'Not by might nor by power, but by my Spirit,' says the LORD Almighty" (Zechariah 4:6).

The Spirit is the true power of the church, and there is only one Spirit. He is the same everywhere, no matter where the church exists, in every place and in every age. That is why the truth remains unchangeable—the passing of time does not change it. That is why the church is not dependent on many or few, or on the wisdom of its membership. It depends on one factor only: the one Spirit.

3. One hope

Paul links the first two elements—one body and one Spirit—with the one hope. These three elements link together because the Spirit forms and prepares the body for its ultimate goal, which is the one hope of the church. That hope is expressed hundreds of times throughout the Scriptures, but nowhere more succinctly than in Paul's statement, "Christ in you, the hope of glory" (Colossians 1:27). Glory is the hope of the church. As the apostle John expresses it, "Dear friends, now we are children of God, and what we will be has not yet been made known. But we know that when he appears, we shall be like him, for we shall see him as he is" (1 John 3:2). That is our hope—a hope that one day we will no longer be frail, stumbling people as we are now, but we shall finally be like Christ.

Wherever I go, whoever I meet, I find this to be the one hope of Christians. No matter what their denominational or doctrinal stamp—be they premillenialists, amillenialists, postmillennialists—all Christian believers hold a common hope. No matter how the events of Daniel and Revelation play out, no matter what form we expect the tribulation and millennium to take place, all Christians expect a transformation, in which we will eventually be like Christ. That is our one shared hope.

4. One Lord

The next three elements gather about the second Person of the Trinity, the Son—one Lord. I think it is significant that the apostle does not say "one Savior," though it is true there is only one Savior. Everywhere in Scripture it is only when we acknowledge Jesus as Lord that He becomes our Savior. So the issue Paul centers on is that Jesus Christ is Lord.

Lord means "ultimate authority." As Paul puts it in the letter to the Philippians, "Therefore God exalted him to the highest place and gave him the name that is above every name, that at the name of Jesus every knee should bow, in heaven and on earth and under the earth, and every tongue confess that Jesus Christ is Lord, to the glory of God the Father" (Philippians 2:9–11). He is the supreme Person of the universe. There is no other Lord; there will never be another Lord.

Peter puts it bluntly: "Salvation is found in no one else, for there is no other name under heaven given to men by which we must be saved" (Acts 4:12). That is why the early Christians could not say, "Caesar is Lord," as the persecutors of the early church tried to get them to do.

Torture and the threat of death could not wring those words from the lips of a Christian, because there is no other Lord. There is only one Lord, the man Christ Jesus, who lived and loved and died among us, who rose again and lives today, the Lord of the universe. That is why John says that anyone who denies this is not a Christian, he has the "spirit of antichrist" (1 John 4:3). Paul says a man can only say, "Jesus is Lord" by the Holy Spirit (1 Corinthians 12:3).

5. One faith

The next element is one faith. This does not refer to faith in general—the ability to believe. Everyone believes in something. Atheists believe in the proposition that there is no God, even while evidence continues to mount that our universe was carefully planned and delicately balanced. James 2:19 tells us, "You believe that there is one God. Good! Even the demons believe that—and shudder"—but that is certainly not the one faith Paul talks about here.

When Paul says, "one faith," he means that one body of truth that God has revealed in His Word. There is only one body of revealed truth, only one faith. This is what the New Testament refers to as "the salvation we share . . . the faith that was once for all entrusted to the saints" (Jude 1:3).

The one faith is linked to the one Lord, because our faith is centered in the revealed truth about Jesus Christ. There may be many questions on minor details of the life and message of Christ, but there is no disagreement as to the fundamental elements of our faith—that Jesus was born, lived, died, and rose again to save us from our sins. God has not given us different faiths for different cultures—one faith for the Jews, another for the Gentiles. No, there is one faith, one total panorama of truth that God has delivered to us through the prophets and apostles, forming a seamless, self-explanatory truth.

No one can truthfully say, as we sometimes hear, "Well, I have my truth and you have yours. I have my Christ and you have yours. I have my faith and you have yours." There is only one truth, only one historic Jesus, and only one faith.

6. One baptism

The next element: one baptism. Tragically, it is here, on the issue of baptism, that many Christians divide. Some say, "Immersion is the only true mode of baptism." Others reply, "You're all wet! Sprinkling is the only way!" Some believe in infant baptism, while others say baptism is only for adults.

Despite all these arguments over the symbol that Paul calls "one baptism," all Christians everywhere believe in the importance of water baptism as a symbol of our link to Jesus, who was himself baptized in the Jordan River. We are baptized into one body by one Spirit, as Paul tells us in 1 Corinthians 12:13, and we are baptized into His death, as Romans 6:3 says. That is the one baptism of the church and it is confessed at all times and in every place by the followers of Jesus Christ.

7. One God and Father of us all

The last of these seven unities is "one God and Father of all, who is over all and through all and in all." Here is the ultimate aim of all the other elements of our Christian unity. As Paul puts it in his letter to the Romans, "For you did not receive a spirit that makes you a slave again to fear, but you received the Spirit of sonship. And by him we cry, 'Abba [Daddy], Father'" (Romans 8:15). He is approachable; He is caring; He is our loving Father.

But Paul wants us to understand that God is even more than this. God is above all, and through all, and in all. He is the end and the beginning. He is close and approachable, yet He is also vast and deep and beyond our comprehension. Once we gain an appreciation for God's love and God's infinite, awesome glory, we realize He can only be properly addressed, "Our Father in heaven, hallowed be your name" (Matthew 6:9).

That is the nature of Christian unity—not a union to be created, but a unity that already exists, gathered around certain truths that every follower of Christ holds dear. As we bring new believers to Christ, the unity of the Spirit will be produced in them by the Spirit. We maintain that unity by practicing love, acceptance, and forgiveness toward others in the body of Christ.

There will be some who are weak in the faith, who may not have all their doctrinal t's crossed and their theological i's dotted. But Paul tells us in Romans 14:1 to receive the weaker brothers and sisters. Recognize a brother who manifests the experience of the unity of the Spirit, no matter what his label may be.

Occasionally, we will encounter some within a church or a Christian movement who claim to be Christians, but who deny one or more of the seven fundamental elements we have just examined. Understand, they are moving in a different direction. They do not share the one hope and one faith that is yours through the one Lord, Jesus Christ. We cannot join in evangelistic or ministry endeavors with those who deny this fundamental unity. Why not? Because our actions are determined by our beliefs.

This is why the Israelites of old were commanded, "Do not plow with an ox and a donkey yoked together" (Deuteronomy 22:10). The two animals move at different speeds, walk with a different gait, and would chafe one another all the time. It would be cruel and counterproductive to yoke them together. This is God's symbolic way of teaching us a fundamental truth, as Paul makes plain: "Do not be yoked together with unbelievers. For what do righteousness and wickedness have in common? Or what fellowship can light have with darkness?" (2 Corinthians 6:14).

This is not to say we are to shun nonChristians. Clearly, there are areas of cooperation that we can have with those who do not share the unity of the Spirit—and in the process, perhaps they might even be won to Christ. We can join with nonChristians in the workplace, in social programs, in medical programs, in government, in education, and many other enterprises in life. We can invite nonChristians to "seeker-friendly" Bible studies and church services, where they can be introduced to biblical truth and the joy of Christian fellowship in a relaxed, informal atmosphere.

You might wonder, "Can I worship with people who don't share unity?" Yes, you can. God commands all men everywhere to worship him. Wherever someone worships God as the one true supreme God, and not as a lesser god or idol, Christians can join together in praise of Him. But in the enterprise of proclaiming the gospel, we have to be careful to maintain the purity of that message and never let it be watered down by those who are not one with us. Their understanding of the gospel is entirely different from ours, their purpose is different, and they are moving in a different direction from us.

THE BOND OF PEACE

Once we truly understand where our Christian unity comes from—that it is given by the Holy Spirit, not created by ourselves—our behavior in the church will be transformed. We begin to realize that our job is not to create unity, but to live worthily of the unity of the Spirit that is already ours. Instead of striving toward unity in our own strength, we will simply try to align our lives and our actions with the unity that already exists among us through the Holy Spirit who makes us one.

This is what Paul means when he says, "Make every effort to keep the unity of the Spirit through the bond of peace." If we begin to think of our brothers and sisters in Christ as one with us through the Spirit, then our actions will be transformed. As prisoners of Christ, we will become more aware of the fact that our quarreling and struggling against one another is at odds with the fundamental reality that we are one with each other in the bond of peace. When we are tempted to feelings of resentment or to such actions as attacking one another or spreading rumors against one another, we should stop and ask God to bless the other person.

"That person is my brother or sister in Christ," we should pray, "and we are one together in the Spirit. Lord, show me how I can reach out to my brother or sister in this time of irritation. Make me a blessing and not a hindrance in that person's life. Show me practical ways I can work to maintain the unity between us that you have made possible through your Spirit. Replace my annoyance with understanding, my impatience with forbearance, my grudges with forgiveness, my bitterness with a sweet spirit, my resentment with love, my hardened heart with a tender heart. Lord, I am Your prisoner. I am ready to take orders from You."

CHAPTER EIGHTEEN

The Gifted Church

Ephesians 4:7–12

How does your body function?

In the body of flesh and bones, there are various kinds of cells—nerve cells, blood cells, skin cells, muscle cells, bone cells, and more, each with a distinct function. In a healthy body, the cells do not get together and vote on which cell does what—they simply function according to their God-given design. In a healthy body, the cells do not revolt or go their own way. When the cells of the body revolt, the result is indigestion or cramps or even cancer. When the brain cells revolt, the result is dementia or insanity.

Only when the cells perform their proper function does the body experience true health. The same is true whether we are talking about a human body or the body of Christ, the church.

We easily forget that the church is a body. We have tried to operate the church as an institution, a corporation, a business. But the reality Paul wants us to grasp in Ephesians is that the church is a body, made up of "cells"—and the cells are individual believers, you and me and our other brothers and sisters in Christ. Each cell has a unique role to play in keeping the entire body healthy.

The role of each cell is supernaturally determined. The mysterious secret to the health, vitality, and power of the church is the fact that each cell is individually and uniquely endowed by God to perform a wonderful function in the body. This mysterious endowment of every Christian life is something the Bible calls *spiritual gifts.*

THE CHARISMATA

In Ephesians 4:7–12, Paul unfolds the most profound secret about the source of the church's power to function effectively in human society: Spiritual gifts have been imparted to each member of the body of Christ. He writes:

> But to each one of us grace has been given as Christ apportioned it. This is why it says:
> "When he ascended on high,
> He led captives in his train
> And gave gifts to men."
> (What does "he ascended" mean except that he also descended to the lower, earthly regions? He who descended is the very one who ascended higher than all the heavens, in order to fill the whole universe.) It was he who gave some to be apostles, some to be prophets, some to be evangelists, and some to be pastors and teachers, to prepare God's people for works of service, so that the body of Christ may be built up.

When Paul begins, "But to each one of us," he places emphasis on the word *each.* In the original Greek, the word *one* is in the emphatic place, at the beginning of the sentence. This is a crucial transition in Paul's argument. As he moves from a discussion of the unity of the Spirit (Ephesians 4:1–6) to a discussion of the gifts of the Spirit (verses 7–12), Paul makes an emphatic point: There are no exceptions to this universal gift. If you are a Christian, a member of the body of Christ by reason of having received Jesus Christ as your Lord and Savior, then you have a spiritual gift.

Each one of us is gifted. It doesn't matter whether we are old, young, rich, poor, talented, awkward, articulate, quiet, handsome, plain, popular, unknown—you have a spiritual gift. If you do not have a spiritual gift, you are not a Christian. If you know and exercise your gift, you contribute to the vitality and ministry of the church; if not, you rob the church of a measure of the impact and influence God intended His church to have in the world. So it is crucially important that you understand, recognize, and exercise your gift.

Paul begins by talking about "grace" that has "been given as Christ apportioned it." This grace is the gift of the Spirit to each Christian. The English word *grace* is *charis* in the original Greek language, from which we get the words *charisma* and *charismatic*. The charismatic movement in today's church takes its name from the Greek word for *grace* or *gifts*. Unfortunately, many people focus on a single gift, the gift of tongues, when there are many spiritual gifts, many forms of the Lord's *charis*-grace which He has apportioned to us. The *charis* that Paul talks about here is not just the gift of tongues (tongues, in fact, is at the very bottom of the list of *charismata* in 1 Corinthians 12).

The charismatic gifts include all the gifts of the Spirit beginning with those mentioned here—apostles, prophets, evangelists, and teachers—as well as other gifts listed elsewhere in Scripture. All of these gifts are rightfully called "charismatic gifts," because they are given by the grace of God to individuals in the body of Christ as special abilities or capacities to serve Him. The list of gifts found here in Ephesians 4 is partial; a complete study of spiritual gifts requires study of the gifts listed in 1 Corinthians 12, Romans 12, 1 Peter 4, as well as isolated references in Ephesians 3:8, 2 Timothy 1:6, and elsewhere.

Do you know what your gift is? Have you ever asked yourself, "What does the Lord want me to do in ministry to Him?" Do you know how to recognize a gift? Do you know how to develop it once you know what it is? The effectiveness of the church and your own joy and fulfillment as a Christian depends on how you answer these questions.

THE SOURCE OF POWER

Verses 8 to 10 include a fascinating and perhaps mystifying parenthetical clause: "This is why it says: 'When he ascended on high, he led captives in his train and gave gifts to men.' (What does "he ascended" mean except that he also descended to the lower, earthly regions? He who descended is the very one who ascended higher than all the heavens, in order to fill the whole universe.)"

Notice that Paul quotes Psalm 68:18: "When he ascended on high, he led captives in his train and gave gifts to men." Why does Paul place this emphasis on Christ's triumphal march, leading of a host of captives in his train? It is because Ephesians 4:8–10 is an amplification and explanation of the phrase, "grace has been given as Christ apportioned it." He is telling us what this means. A gift is one thing; the power to operate it is quite another. Here he brings the gift and the power together.

Gifts are specialized functions, the God-endowed ability to do certain specific ministries, such as teaching, preaching, helping, administering, leading, and so forth. These gifts are like so many electrical appliances. Go to any department store, and you'll find a myriad of electrical appliances, from microwave ovens to computers to VCRs to electric toothbrushes. All these appliances have one thing in common: a cord with a plug on the end that must be inserted into an electrical outlet. Regardless of what the appliance looks like or how it performs its function, the power that drives it is the same.

The same is true of spiritual gifts. Just as there are many kinds of appliances, there are many spiritual gifts, many *charismata*—but all operate on the same power, all draw energy and vitality from the same source. What is the source of power that energizes our spiritual gifts? It is not the power of a strong personality—though many would seem to think so. You do not have to have the magnetic personality of Billy Graham to be an evangelist. There are many individuals who are quiet and unassuming, yet their hearts burn with a passion for spreading the gospel. Wherever they go—on the subway, on streetcorners, in the supermarket checkout line—they quietly strike up a conversation and gently share with others about their Friend, Jesus. Like Billy Graham, they have the gift of evangelism—but they exercise their gift in a quiet way. They draw on the same power source that Dr. Graham does—but that power source is not the power of a strong personality.

Is it the power of positive thinking? We hear so often that the power of positive thinking is the key to success. But that is not the power source that energizes our spiritual gifts. Is it the power of keen intellect? The power of knowledge? The power of an educated, disciplined mind? No. Even Christians with a modest I.Q. have spiritual gifts and can exercise them mightily for the Lord.

The power that energizes our spiritual gifts is far superior to all of these other forms of personal power. Paul gives us a clue in Ephesians 3:20, when he writes, "Now to him who is able to do immeasurably more than all we ask or imagine, according to his power that is at work within us."

Paul gives us another clue in Philippians 3:10, where he writes, "I want to know Christ and the power of his resurrection . . . ." There it is: *the power of His resurrection*! That is why the apostle links the gift of God with the descent of Christ, incarnation, and ascent again to the throne of power after His resurrection. All of that was required in order for you to receive the gift. All of the mystery and marvel of the incarnation and the resurrection are involved in the fact that you have received a spiritual gift from God.

Now, perhaps, you see what a tragic waste it is to allow your gifts to lie neglected and unused in some backroom of your spirit! This is the most precious gift anyone has ever given you, requiring Christ's descent from glory down to this earth, along with all the pain and sorrow of his life, culminating in the Garden of Gethsemane and the cross, followed by the resurrection and ascension. So the operation of spiritual gifts is no small thing!

GIFTS ARE NOT TALENTS

Many people confuse spiritual gifts with natural talents. Most people have talents of one kind or another, whether they are Christians or nonChristians. Only Christians have spiritual gifts. In fact, *all* Christians have spiritual gifts, even if they do not see themselves as particularly talented. You don't need resurrection power to operate a natural talent, but you cannot operate a spiritual gift without resurrection power.

Spiritual gifts cannot be stopped by mere human will. That is why Paul, even though he was imprisoned by Rome, did not consider himself limited and bound by Rome. His spiritual gift operated by the power of the resurrection—the same power that brought life out of death, the same power that rolled away the stone from the mouth of the tomb. You cannot stop resurrection power. The only limit we have in the exercise of our spiritual gifts is the limit of our own faith to believe that God is willing and able to work through us.

The church has no lack of spiritual gifts, for every Christian is gifted for ministry. The church has no lack of power, because we have the greatest power in the universe at our disposal—resurrection power. If the church seems limited and powerless, that is only because many spiritually gifted Christians allow their gifts to go unused. They fail to draw on the resurrection power that is available to them. The church remains weak and faltering, unable to reach the world for Christ, in direct proportion of the degree that we ignore and neglect the spiritual gifts God has already given us.

Some are called to an open, public ministry; others have a quieter, less visible ministry. But we all have gifts, we all have a ministry. If your gift is going unused, the church is being weakened and robbed as a result. Your gift is greatly needed.

I think some Christians are afraid to look for their spiritual gift for fear they might find it! They are afraid that if they discover that God has gifted them for ministry, it's going to interfere with their safe and comfortable plans. But God did not create us to be safe and comfortable. He created us to do good works, to serve Him by exercising His spiritual gifts. He is the Lord, and we must learn to take our orders from Him.

Each of us shall one day stand before the Lord Jesus, and He will not ask us how much money we made or how much status and fame we acquired. He will ask us, "What did you do with the gift I gave you? I left My glory in heaven, became a man, submitted to death on the cross, and was resurrected so that you could have spiritual gifts for the service of the Father and others. The gifts I gave you were very costly. Did you use them well?" How will you answer?

The Lord has given you an amazing, irreplaceable set of spiritual gifts. No one else can exercise your unique array of gifts. No one else in the body of Christ can do what you alone can do. It's time to discover your gifts, and to begin using them as God intended.

GOD'S BUILDING AND MAINTENANCE PROGRAM

There are a variety of gifts, and most of us (I think it's safe to say) have received more than one of the gifts. Over the span of a lifetime, as we mature in our faith and explore new avenues of ministry, we may discover additional gifts we never imagined we had.

I like to think of spiritual gifts as "God's building and maintenance program." Spiritual gifts may be said to divide between two major divisions or categories: (1) the Building Gifts, those spiritual gifts that serve to lay the foundation and build the structure of the church, and (2) the Maintenance Gifts, those spiritual gifts that help to maintain the proper functioning of the body of Christ.

It is vitally important that we, as members of the body of Christ, learn how to discern these gifts in ourselves, how to recognize and affirm them in others, and how to put them to work in our daily service to God:

The Building Gifts: There are four Building Gifts, all of which are listed in Ephesians 4:11—"It was he who gave some to be *apostles*, some to be *prophets*, some to be *evangelists*, and some to be *pastors and teachers*." You may look at that list and think, *I count five gifts in that list*. The last gift in the list appears as two separate words in the English translation: *pastors* and *teachers*. In the original Greek text, however, it is actually a single concept: pastor-teacher or teaching pastor.

In verse 12, Paul unveils the purpose of the Building Gifts: "to prepare God's people for works of service, so that the body of Christ may be built up." Here, in a single breath, Paul uses two figures of speech to describe the function of these gifts—a body and a building. This is one of the several places in Scripture where Paul mixes his metaphors—rather like saying, "You buttered your bread, now lie in it." Yes it takes a mixed metaphor to convey the richness of the truth that Pau wants us to understand.

The church is a body, made up of many parts that are miraculously, mysteriously coordinated to function together. And the church is a building, set upon a foundation, constructed stone upon stone, designed to be a fitting dwelling place for God. In this mixed metaphor, the church is truly a living, organic, growing, active building!

We can never understand the church unless we understand the truth Paul is getting at here. The church is where God lives and is at work today. Those who say there is no God or that God has gone away or God is dead simply don't know where to find Him. They have lost His address. But we know where He lives. He lives in us. He is at work in us, because we are the building that was built for Him by the Holy Spirit. And the means by which the Spirit has constructed this building is a set of tools called spiritual gifts. The foundation for this building has been laid by what I call the four Building Gifts. They are:

1. Apostles. The apostolic ministry lays the foundation of this building called the body of Christ. In Ephesians 2:20 Paul writes that the body of Christ, the church, is "built on the foundation of the apostles and prophets, with Christ Jesus himself as the chief cornerstone." This is an image of the church as a building, with Christ as the cornerstone, with the apostles and prophets as the foundation, and you and I as members being stones that are built up on that foundation.

I believe this imagery refers not only to the original apostles in the Bible, but to contemporary apostles. The apostolic gift is still being given to the church today, but it functions in a somewhat secondary sense compared with that of the original apostles.

In 1 Corinthians 12:28, Paul shows us a sequence by which the gifts have been given: "And in the church God has appointed first of all apostles, second prophets, third teachers," and so forth. Paul is not ranking these gifts in order of importance, he is ordering them in historical sequence. The gift of the apostles came first, followed by the prophets, teachers, and so on. That is the order in which these gifts were introduced into the church. This is extremely important.

Any builder knows that the foundation of a building is of the utmost importance. You do not take chances with the foundation, because the entire building is going to rest on that foundation and derive its strength from the solidity of that foundation. The same thing is true in the church.

The Lord Jesus made it clear that if a man builds on the wrong foundation, his structure is in trouble (see Matthew 7:24–27). It was the task of the apostles and prophets to lay the foundation of the church. As we see in the four Gospels, our Lord called twelve men to be with Him, to learn from Him, and to be sent out in ministry. Jesus named them *apostles*, a word that means "one sent forth." The twelve apostles were sent out by the Lord Jesus with a special commission and special authority. Wherever they went they spoke with authority—they themselves were astonished by the authority they had. They came back to the Lord and told how they rejoiced when they discovered that even the demons were subject to them. That God-given authority is the special mark of an apostle.

Later, other apostles were added. Paul came after the twelve and never belonged to the original twelve. He did not take part in their particular ministry, though he was truly an apostle. This "thirteenth apostle" was sent by God to the Gentiles. So were Barnabas, Silas, Timothy, and Titus, who also shared in the apostolic ministry.

The work of an apostle is to declare the whole body of truth concerning Jesus Christ. That is the foundation of the church and the foundation of your faith—the truth that you believe about Jesus Christ. That foundation was laid by the apostles. "For no one can lay any foundation," said Paul in 1 Corinthian 3:11, "other than the one already laid, which is Jesus Christ." What the apostles say about Jesus Christ is the foundation of the church, and what they say about Jesus Christ is recorded for us in our New Testament. This is from the hands of the apostles, and the whole church rests squarely upon that foundation. If it does not rest there, it is a rickety, dangerous structure—a house of cards.

The apostolic gift is still being given today, and it is needed wherever new churches are beginning. It is not that any new truth is being added to the Scriptures, but the whole body of truth that has already been given is imparted by contemporary apostles to new churches wherever they begin. That is always the task of an apostle—to lay foundations and start new churches. We call them "pioneer missionaries" today. Through the course of church history there have been great apostles, great pioneer missionaries, laying foundations for churches again and again—apostles such as Adaniram Judson in Burma, William Carey in India, and Hudson Taylor in China.

2. Prophets. A prophet speaks for God and unfolds the mind of God. In the early church, before the New Testament was written, prophets spoke directly by inspiration of the Holy Spirit, uttering truths that are now recorded in our New Testament. They unfolded the truth of God that galvanized and motivated the body of Christ to

The Gifted Church

action. Like the apostles, prophets are engaged in laying the foundation of the church.

Prophets wrote the Old Testament, as well as large parts of the New Testament. Mark and Luke and James and Jude were not apostles, but they helped lay the foundation of the church through their writings in the Scriptures. They are New Testament prophets.

The gift of a prophet differs from an apostle in that the apostle has the word of authority and gives an authoritative declaration of the whole body of truth concerning Jesus Christ. But the prophetic gift is to interpret that authoritative word and explain it so that the truth becomes clear and compelling. The word *prophet* comes from a root word with a prefix, which combine to mean "to stand before and shine." This meaning is reflected in 2 Peter 1:19, where the apostle writes, "And we have the word of the prophets made more certain, and you will do well to pay attention to it, as to a light shining in a dark place, until the day dawns and the morning star rises in your hearts."

The church owes much to prophets. Not only were much of the Scriptures given to us by the prophets, but many of the great modern theologians of the church have possessed the prophetic gift. For example, there was Dr. C. I. Scofield, who compiled the annotations for the famous Scofield Reference Bible. He was not a clergyman, not ordained to the ministry. Rather he was a layman, an attorney by profession—but he had the gift of a prophet and his writings have been helpful to people in explaining the revelations of the apostles. He has made the words of the Bible to shine with clarity.

The same can be said for many pastors and Bible teachers today. The gift of the prophet is alive and well today.

3. Evangelists. An evangelist has a special gift for communicating the gospel of Jesus Christ in relevant, compelling terms to nonChristians. While every Christian is called to be a witness, some Christians are specially gifted with the ability to share Christ in a way that creates a strong connection and wonderful attraction.

A witness is different from an evangelist. A witness simply tells what happened to him or her. That is all. All Christians are expected to be able to give a simple testimonial of what Jesus Christ has done in their lives. This is as easy as talking about any other experience. If you can talk about what a joy it was to get married, how wonderful your husband or your wife is, or your children or grandchildren, you can witness for Christ. To talk about the Lord in your life, and to do so simply and naturally, is to witness.

An evangelist goes further. An evangelist knows how to explain the why and the how of the great redeeming story of Jesus Christ. He is able to proclaim the truths that produce a new birth. His gift enables him to make the great and compelling proclamation that God has not left man in a hopeless condition, but has made a way of salvation through the cross and the resurrection, so that men and women can be set free from the oppression of sin and experience an exciting newness of life. That is the message of the evangelist.

The gospel is a message of hope and gladness. The evangelist's task is not to denounce sin and sinners, nor to expose the horrors of hellfire and portray God as roasting sinners over searing flames. If that needs to be done at all, it is the job of a prophet, not an evangelist. The evangelist is a messenger of the overwhelming, redeeming grace of God, expressed through the life, death, and resurrection of Jesus Christ.

The gift of an evangelist does not need to be exercised in mass meetings, in big-top tents and stadiums. It often is, but that is certainly not the only kind of place evangelism happens. The gift of an evangelist can be exercised one-on-one, as when Phillip spoke to the

Ethiopian eunuch and told him of the grace of Jesus Christ (see Acts 8:26–40). An evangelist can exercise his gift anywhere.

The gift of an evangelist is linked with the next gift, pastor-teachers. Evangelists and teaching-pastors work together, just as apostles and prophets work together. In the body of believers, evangelists and teaching-pastors work with individuals within the church. The evangelist is concerned with the beginning of the Christian life, while the teaching-pastor is concerned with the development and the growth of that life. Therefore, evangelists are the "obstetricians" of the church, assisting in the birthing process of new Christians, and teaching-pastors are the "pediatricians," helping to promote and maintain the growth and health of Christians once they are born again.

Returning to our mixed metaphor of the body as a building, we can see the evangelist is the "quarryman," who digs the rock out of the earth and delivers it to the building site. The teaching-pastor is the "stone mason," who shapes the rock and fits it into place, according to the blueprint of the Architect.

4. Teaching pastors. These individuals maintain the life of the body by feeding it the Word of God, cleansing it by calling for renewal and repentance, and encouraging its growth through ministry and fellowship.

Teaching pastors are also called elders, overseers, or bishops in the Scriptures. Elders or bishops were always limited to one local church in the early Christian era. A man who was an elder in one church was not also an elder in another place. He could be an elder or a teaching-pastor only in one place.

Pastors in those days were not separated into a "clergy class" as they are today, and often were not full-time pastors. They worked at other jobs, and their service to the church was not their employment but their role within the church. In the purest, most biblical sense of the word, a *pastor* is not a clergyman per se, but is *any* person—clergy or lay—who exercises the gift of teaching and shepherding within the church.

It is an error to divide the church between "lay" and "clergy." Many people who spend their working hours in the secular world have apostolic gifts, prophetic gifts, evangelistic gifts, and teaching/pastoring gifts. Every church has members who are engaged in secular work, yet who have discovered and are using their support gifts both in the church and in the lives of the unsaved worldlings around them.

I believe a terrible error has crept into the church at this particular point. Through the centuries, the church has veered away from the simple, biblical system that made it such a powerful influence upon society in its early years. Whereas the first century church truly saw itself as a body of believers, it gradually came to be identified not with people but with buildings. We fastened our attention on the meeting place instead of the people as the symbol of God's church. In the process, we gradually transferred responsibility for the work of the ministry from the people to the clergy, the select few people who worked in the church building. Paul, in Ephesians 4, makes it clear that the ministry of the church belongs not to a few, but to the many, to all members of the body of Christ.

These four support ministries—apostle, prophet, evangelist, and teaching pastor—exist for the equipping of the saints unto the work of the ministry (our contact with the world) and unto the building up of the body of Christ (maintaining the health of the church). Who is to carry out these ministries? All the people! That is God's intention. It is not the job of the pastors. The role of teaching pastors is to train, equip support, encourage, discipline, and motivate the people to do this work. It is the people who are to do the work of the church. A view of the church that sees pastors as performers and the people as spectators is a tragic distortion of God's view of the church as found in the Bible.

I once heard the game of football described as "eleven men on a field in desperate need of rest, surrounded by fifty thousand people in the stands in desperate need of exercise." Sometimes, the church seems much like a football game. But that is not Paul's view of the church, nor is it God's. A pastor who tries to run the church like a football game is doomed to exhaustion and burn-out. Worse, he condemns his church to failure and relegates his parishioners to the role of flabby spectators. According to God's plan for the church, every member is a minister. This takes the awful unbearable pressure off pastors and keeps all members of the church well-exercised and effective in their daily Christian lives.

The Maintenance Gifts: These gifts are not listed in Ephesians 4, but are found in other New Testament writings of Paul and Peter. Here are the passages that list the spiritual gifts (the Maintenance Gifts are listed in *italics*):

1 Corinthians 12:8–10, 28–30
   Administration (Leading)
   Apostle
   Discernment
   Faith
   Healing
   Helps (Service)
   Knowledge
   Miracles
   Prophecy

Teaching
Tongues (and Interpretation)
Wisdom

Romans 12:6–8
   Exhortation
   Giving
   Leading
   Mercy
   Prophecy
   Service
   Teaching

Ephesians 4:11
   Apostle
   Prophet
   Evangelist
   Teaching Pastor

1 Peter 4:11
   Teaching
   Service

These gifts include:

1. The gift of wisdom—the ability to understand how God's truth applies to specific, practical situations. This gift and its close relative, the gift of knowledge, are found in 1 Corinthians 12:8. A person with the gift of wisdom can apply any truth—scriptural truth, spiritual truth, or even secular truth—to life's problems and opportunities and produce healthy, godly results. People with the gift of wisdom are generally looked to for wise counsel by other believers. They make excellent additions to church boards, corporate boards, legislatures and cabinets, and other decision-making bodies.

2. The gift of knowledge—the ability to understand and categorize God's truth. The gift of knowledge is often (though not always) found in the same individual as the gift of wisdom. A person with the gift of knowledge can pick out the important facts in any investigation or discussion and put them in manageable order. People with this gift tend to make wonderful Bible students, because they can compare Scripture with Scripture and correlate biblical facts into a readily understandable body of truth. They are also excellent additions to committees and task groups.

3. The gift of faith—the ability to trust God and envision grand goals that God can accomplish through His church. Some call this the gift of vision—the ability to envision grand ideas, become gripped by them, and move forward even against the odds to make that vision a reality in God's name. Every great Christian enterprise was begun by someone with the gift of faith.

4. The gift of healing—the ability to pray and touch lives in such a way that God is able to restore people to physical, mental, or emotional health. This gift goes beyond the skills of a doctor or therapist (although a healing professional could possess this gift). The spiritual gift of healing is clearly the *supernatural* ability to make sick people well. Occasionally, in the record of church history, there have been some who had the gift of healing, but it is a rare gift today, infrequently bestowed.

5. The gift of miracles—the ability to pray in such a way that God produces works that are beyond natural explanation. The gift of miracles enables an individual to accomplish natural things in a supernatural way, to short-circuit the processes of nature, as our Lord did when he turned water into wine, or multiplied loaves and fishes to feed the five thousand. This gift may still be given today, but I do not believe I have ever met a person with the gift of miracles.

Many people desire to have miraculous gifts, such as this gift of miracles, the gift of healing, or the gift of being able to speak in an unknown language, the gift of tongues. This is understandable, because it is easy to confuse the miraculous with the spiritual. We think that a miraculous manifestation indicates great spirituality or closeness to God.

It is instructive, I think, to note that John the Baptist, a mighty prophet of God, never performed a miracle in his life. Yet Jesus said of John the Baptist, "I tell you the truth: Among those born of women there has not risen anyone greater than John the Baptist" (Matthew 11:11; see also Luke 7:28). If John was so great in God's eyes, why didn't he work miracles? Because that was not John's gift. God did not choose to work through John's life in that way.

Why are the miraculous gifts given so infrequently today? The answer is in Ephesians 4:7—"to each one of us grace has been given as Christ apportioned it." The gifts are given according to His will, not ours; they are given as He apportions His grace, not according to our cravings for signs and wonders.

It is instructive, I think, to read through the book of Acts in a single sitting. One thing you will readily notice is that the beginning chapters of Acts are crowded with miracles, healings, and speaking in tongues. As you move through the book, miraculous events become rarer and rarer. The reason: When the church was in its infant stage, new believers needed to see miraculous events in order to have their faith bolstered and grounded. As the church grew and matured in its faith, its need for miraculous signs and wonders diminished. Those who need a continual display of miracles in order to believe in Jesus Christ are walking not by faith, but by sight. As we mature in Christ, our need for such displays is gradually replaced by a quiet confidence and assurance of God's presence in our lives.

6. The gift of prophecy—the ability to speak for God in a way that calls people to faith, repentance, and holiness. The gift of prophecy and the next gift, the gift of teaching, are Maintenance Gifts that overlap with the Building Gifts mentioned previously, the gifts of a prophet and a teaching pastor. Both prophecy and teaching are Building Gifts, crucial in laying the foundation of the church, and Maintenance Gifts, crucial in maintaining the health, vitality, and growth of the church.

Though easily misunderstood, the gift of prophecy is one of the greatest of all the gifts. In 1 Corinthians 14:3, Paul says, "But everyone who prophesies speaks to men for their strengthening, encouragement and comfort." When someone has this gift, his words have power to build, embolden, motivate, encourage, and impact peace to others. This is not a gift only for preachers. Many laypeople have the gift of prophecy.

Perhaps you have been in a meeting where a problem was being discussed and a decision needed to be made—but the group had reached a seeming impasse. No one seemed to have the answer. Then someone stood and spoke—and everyone realized that this individual had just spoken the answer! That is the gift of prophecy at work—the ability to speak with power and authority. The church desperately needs the exercise of this gift.

Some people confuse the gift of prophecy with the ability to foresee the future. And it is true that some of the prophets of biblical times such as Isaiah and Daniel in the Old Testament and John in the New Testament did relate portions of God's program for the future. But the gift of prophecy is not essentially the ability to foretell, but the ability to *tell forth* the truth of God at decisive moments.

7. The gift of teaching—the ability to instruct others in the Word of God, so as to encourage stronger faith, deeper commitment, and richer growth and maturity in the Lord. The teaching gift enables an individual to gather truth from the completed revelation of God in Scripture and apply it to the lives of his hearers. Luke tells us that there were both teachers and prophets in Antioch (Acts 13:1), and Paul calls himself a "teacher of the Gentiles" (1 Timothy 2:7; 2 Timothy 1:11).

The person with the gift of teaching has a love of Scripture, enjoys studying and relating biblical truth, and can communicate truth in a way that impacts lives. The fact that some Christians have a *special* gift of teaching does not relieve the rest of us from the responsibility to study the Bible and teach its truths at every opportunity. For example, all Christian parents have a joyous duty to teach the truths of God to their children. Most important of all, we are to teach not only by our words but also by our example. As Paul said in Romans 2:21–22, "you, then, who teach others, do you not teach yourself? You who preach against stealing, do you steal? You who say that people should not commit adultery, do you commit adultery?" To be godly teachers, we must practice what we teach.

8. The gift of discernment—the ability to detect spiritual counterfeits and phoniness. This is the ability to discern spirits, the ability (as

1 John 4:6 says) to distinguish between the spirit of error and the spirit of truth. This is a gift I often wish I had—and I'm glad my wife, Elaine, has it. It is the ability to see through a phony before his error is manifest to everyone by its ultimate results. When Ananias and Sapphira came bringing an offering of their land and put it before Peter, he exercised the gift of discernment when he asked why they had chosen to lie to the Holy Spirit (see Acts 5:3). Peter knew that these two individuals were lying, and many believers today have this important gift.

The gift of discernment is also the ability to read a book and sense subtle error in it. It is a crucial gift for maintaining the purity of the church and of our individual lives, especially in this age of rising deceit.

9. The gift of tongues and **the gift of interpreting tongues**— the supernatural ability to speak in other languages or to interpret for those who speak in tongues. Obviously, this goes far beyond the ability of a person to serve as an interpreter at the United Nations building—it is the ability to praise God in a language that was never learned (or to interpret that praise). This gift is never for the purposes of preaching the gospel. In the Scriptures it is always and clearly for the purpose of praising God. It is not for private use, for we read that all the gifts of the Spirit are given for the common good in the church (see 1 Corinthians 12:7). This gift is useless in the church without interpretation.

Without question, this is the easiest gift to imitate, which is why imitations abound on every hand. Whether they are manifestations of the true gift or not can only be determined by careful comparison with the Scriptures.

10. The gift of helps or service—a magnificent (and underrated) gift, exercised quietly and in the background. Many Christians with servants' hearts perform acts of helps and service in the body of Christ, never receiving or asking for attention or acclaim. Though these saints are anonymous now, they will be among the greatest of saints in heaven.

The gift of helps is one of the most widespread of the gifts. It is the gift of lending a hand whenever a need appears. It is manifested in those who serve as ushers and treasurers in the church, in those who prepare the Lord's communion table, who arrange the flowers and serve the dinners and stay after the fellowship meals to wash the pots, who help the poor and weak, who read to the blind, who nurse the sick, and who minister to others in quiet yet powerful ways. The Spirit of God is powerfully manifested in this gift because it is always exercised in Christlike humility. The church could not exist without the free-flowing expression of the gift of helps.

11. The gift of administration—the God-given ability to organize and demonstrate leadership in spiritual matters. This gift means more than just having "a good head for business." Many people, thinking they have the gift of administration, appoint themselves church bosses and proceed to call the shots and intimidate others in order to get their own way. Such people have done a lot of damage in a lot of churches. The fact is, the spiritual gift of administration must be exercised in the Spirit, with genuine humility. People with this gift have a special capacity for organizing and directing, but with a Christlike concern for the feelings and needs of others and an obedience to God's Word.

12. The gift of exhortation—the ability to motivate people to action, service, and holiness in their lives, and the ability to give encouragement and advice to people so that they feel helped and healed in their spiritual lives. Proverbs 25:11 tells us, "A word aptly spoken is like apples of gold in settings of silver." And Hebrews 3:13 shows us that exhortation has a crucial role in maintaining the purity of the church: "But encourage [exhort] one another daily, as long as it is called Today, so that none of you may be hardened by sin's deceitfulness." People with the gift of exhortation demonstrate faith in others, even when others have given up on them.

We see the power of the gift of exhortation in Acts, when Paul arrives in Jerusalem for the first time after his conversion. The church was unwilling to receive him because of his history of persecuting the church. But one man with the gift of exhortation—Barnabas, whose name means "Son of Encouragement" or "Son of Exhortation"—believed in Paul and helped to establish him as a genuine Christian and a genuine apostle.

13. The gift of giving, contributing or generosity—the ability to financially support the ministry of God. While *every* believer is to tithe and give sacrificially to the work of God, there are *some* believers who have either been materially blessed or gifted with a special ability to raise funds. They see their money not as a means of controlling the church and getting their way, but as a gift to be liberally given, no strings attached, for the support of God's work.

Amazingly, this gift does not belong only to the wealthy. You often find this gift in people of modest means, or practically no means at all! I recall one scrubwoman who worked for years in the skyscrapers of New York. She lived frugally and used her earnings to send missionaries out around the world—more than thirty missionaries over the course of her lifetime. That woman is a challenge to your generosity and mine on behalf of the Lord—and she is an example of the gift of giving.

14. The gift of mercy—a special capacity and ability to visit the sick, the poor, the imprisoned, the hurting, the dying, visibly demonstrating the love and kindness of God to those in need.

Clearly, there is a wide, panoramic range of spiritual gifts. It is important to remember that these gifts are not to be expressed only within the church walls on Sunday mornings. These gifts should be used throughout our lives, in our homes, on our jobsites, in the marketplace, wherever we go, whatever we do. Our lives are to be lived as a testament of the power of God to live through a human life, a visible, tangible expression of the Lord's body on earth.

SPIRITUAL GIFTS AND THE ONGOING INCARNATION

During my time as pastor of Peninsula Bible Church, there was a statement printed on the back of the Sunday bulletin that read:

> This church advocates both evangelism and edification. People must be saved by grace through faith, but, having been saved, they must be faithfully helped to grow in grace. The two-fold task of every church is evangelism and edification—not a lopsided stress on one but the consistent practice of both.

Here is the two-fold emphasis of the church: evangelism (which is directed outward toward the world) and edification (which is directed inward, toward building up the body of believers through teaching and fellowship). This is the two-fold emphasis we see in Ephesians 4, and every local church should maintain an absolute commitment to fulfilling these two tasks by encouraging every member to understand and exercise his or her spiritual gifts.

When the members of a church fulfill their unique, God-given roles by utilizing their unique, God-given gifts, something amazing and miraculous happens: Jesus Christ becomes physically present once more on earth. Does that sound like an astounding claim? Then let me explain:

When God chose to visit this earth to offer us a new and eternal kind of life, He did so by "incarnating" His life in a body. The word *incarnate* means "to become flesh." When Jesus was born of a virgin, God himself became flesh and dwelt among us. Jesus Christ was the incarnation of God.

But that was only the beginning of the incarnation process. The incarnation is still going on. Open the book of Acts and read the opening words, and you will find that the writer of Acts, Luke, says that he has set down "in my former book" (that is, in the gospel of Luke) "all that Jesus *began* to do and to teach." Note that word *began*. Jesus is not finished doing and teaching in the world. His work continues, even though He has ascended to the Father. The book of Acts, Luke implies, is a continuation of the Lord's doings and teachings. And what is the book of Acts? It is a record of the early years of the Christian church, the body of Christ.

The story of the book of Acts is still being written two thousand years later, as we move into the third millennium of the Christian era. And the incarnation is still continuing. Christ himself is still physically present in the world, still incarnate, still doing and teaching through His body, the church. You and I are members of that body, uniquely gifted to carry on His work because of the spiritual gifts He has given us.

What is His work? We hear it from His own lips in Luke 4:16–21:

> He went to Nazareth, where he had been brought up, and
> on the Sabbath day he went into the synagogue, as was

his custom. And he stood up to read. The scroll of the prophet Isaiah was handed to him. Unrolling it, he found the place where it is written:

"The Spirit of the Lord is on me, because he has anointed me to preach good news to the poor. He has sent me to proclaim freedom for the prisoners and recovery of sight for the blind, to release the oppressed, to proclaim the year of the Lord's favor."

Then he rolled up the scroll, gave it back to the attendant and sat down. The eyes of everyone in the synagogue were fastened on him, and he began by saying to them, "Today this scripture is fulfilled in your hearing."

We tend to read that passage and think, "This is Jesus, announcing His earthly ministry—a ministry of preaching good news, liberating the oppressed, healing the blind, and more—and making it clear that He had come in fulfillment of a prophecy first issued 725 years earlier by Isaiah."

But I would encourage you to read it again—not as a description of the Lord's ministry back then, but as your ministry now. Read it as a demonstration of what Jesus Christ intends you to do right now, today. As you read it, remember what the Lord said in John 14:12—"I tell you the truth, anyone who has faith in me will do what I have been doing. *He will do even greater things than these*, because I am going to the Father." Greater in what way? Well, anything done in the realm of the spirit is greater than that done in the body.

And why will we do greater things than Jesus did? "Because I am going to the Father." Here, Jesus specifically tells us that His leavetaking from earth, His return to the Father, will result in the sending of the Spirit. Through the ministry of the Holy Spirit, the church, the body of Christ, will perform far greater works than Jesus did in the flesh, for the works of the Spirit accomplished through the church take place in the very core of humanity, in the spirit.

Note that Jesus quotes a line from Isaiah that promises the coming of the Spirit: "The Spirit of the Lord is on me, because he has anointed me to preach good news to the poor," Luke 4:18. Notice that the coming of the Spirit upon the body of Christ instantly produces a ministry that goes out to the world—the ministry of evangelism, of preaching the good news to those who need to hear it. Our Lord always begins with the poor and needy, just as he did in the first phrase of the Beatitudes: "Blessed are the poor in spirit, for theirs is the kingdom of heaven" (Matthew 5:3). God is able to give the kingdom of heaven to those who come to him with empty hands and humble hearts. We are to exercise our gifts in spreading this Good News to those who are hungry to hear it.

Jesus goes on to read that God has sent Him (and therefore, God has sent us) to proclaim freedom to captives and the recovery of sight to the blind. Release and recovery. Liberty and light. All around us we see people who are bound by sin, by emotions of self-pity or bitterness or hopelessness. We see people who stumble blindly through life. God has anointed us in the body of Christ with spiritual gifts, and we are to use those gifts to set captives free and to restore sight to the blind.

Jesus proclaims a ministry of setting at liberty those who are oppressed, who are laboring under a crushing burden. A man once drove 600 miles round-trip to tell me of a burden that oppressed him. For over a year he had been simmering with anger and hate over an injustice that was done to him. He could barely eat or sleep. He felt no peace. He was so burdened with hatred that he had actually contemplated murder. As we sat and talked, I told him that he could be liberated from that oppressing burden by handing it over to Jesus

Christ. I proclaimed to him liberty from oppression, and he acted on it by praying with me for healing and liberation. A miraculous transformation took place in this man right before my eyes. I could see in his eyes and his face that the burden was gone, the poison of hatred had been drained from his heart, and the love of Jesus Christ had come flooding in. He had been set free.

What did I do for this man? Nothing. As a mere human being, I could do nothing for him. But the Spirit of God, operating through my God-given gifts, transcended my mere humanity. I became the body of Christ, the eyes, ears, lips, and hands of Christ, and He touched this man through me.

This man didn't have to drive 300 miles one way to find someone to set him free. God could have used any yielded, Spirit-led Christian to set this man free from his oppression. Every Christian is gifted and has access to the infinite spiritual resources of God.

Finally, in Luke 4:19, Jesus reads that the Spirit of God has anointed Him—and, of course, us as well—"to proclaim the year of the Lord's favor." This is one of the most remarkable statements of the Bible. If you look up the original passage in Isaiah from which our Lord is quoting, you find there is a comma at the point where Jesus places a period. In the original passage in Isaiah, the prophet goes on to say, "and the day of vengeance of our God" (Isaiah 61:2). The Lord Jesus did not read the rest of that sentence. He closed the book at the comma, handed it back, and announced, "Today this scripture is fulfilled in your hearing" (Luke 4:21). He implies, then, that the rest of Isaiah's statement is not yet fulfilled. The day of the vengeance of God awaits the return of Christ. That is a future day; but now is the year of the Lord's favor, the time of salvation.

People need to hear that they live in a time of God's favor, a time when the door of salvation is open to them. Most people live in the grip of fear—fear of death, fear of out-of-control events in the world, fear that God has lost control, if He ever had it. They need to know that while a day of vengeance and judgment is coming, now is the time to take refuge in the Lord. He restrains evil and calms our fears. He is in control. He loves us.

So this is the ministry that Christ proclaimed for himself during His earthly ministry—and also for us, for the body of Christ. We are to use our spiritual gifts, acting in His stead, carrying on His ministry. This may be a scary and intimidating idea to you. "I don't have time to evangelize the world," you might say. "I have to earn a living! Using my spiritual gifts sounds impossibly hard!"

Actually, it's easier than you think. Spiritual gifts are a God-given part of you, so using this part of you is perfectly natural. You simply have to be yielded to God in every aspect of your life. You use your spiritual gifts in your home, at the office, and everywhere you live your life. You simply make sure that Jesus Christ is the Lord of your entire life, not just the Lord of your Sundays, your margins, and your spare time. Remember, the most important figures in the Bible are not pastors and priests but ordinary "working stiffs"—shepherds, fishermen, soldiers, tentmakers, carpenters, physicians, and tax collectors. You can carry out the ministry of Christ and exercise your spiritual gifts over lunch with a friend, around the water cooler with a co-worker, or in the car pool on the drive home.

We must put our gifts to work. The Lord Jesus has given us a precious gift, and we dare not waste it, as the unfaithful steward did in our Lord's parable. The Lord will one day demand an accounting for our stewardship, our use of the gifts He has given us. He will ask us, "What did you do with the gift I gave you—the gift I bought for you with my earthly life, death, and resurrection? Did you value it? Did you put it to good use? Did you multiply it in the lives of others? Or did you ignore, neglect, and reject it?"

The matter of spiritual gifts is a serious matter. We exist for the purpose of serving God with our gifts and praising Him with our lives. Our faith means nothing if we neglect this crucial, core issue of what it means to be a Christian, a member of the body of Christ.

But as serious as it is, the matter of spiritual gifts is also a matter of *joy.* As Christians today discover what it means to literally become the living, bodily extensions of Jesus Christ on earth, then life becomes gripping and exciting—an adventure beyond human imagining. You and I, as members of the body of Christ, prove to the world that God is not dead—He is alive and active in the realm of human lives and human events.

So now, I trust, you begin to catch a glimpse—just an introductory glimmer—of how eternally, universally important it is that you understand and exercise your gift. The spiritual gift within you is unique and irreplaceable. It may be lying dormant in you. So it is critically important that you discover and develop your gift, and that you learn how to fulfill that gift in the power of the Holy Spirit—not in the power of the flesh.

IN THE SPIRIT—OR THE FLESH?

You might be surprised by the suggestion that it is possible to use a spiritual gift in the power of the flesh. The fact is that each of us begins life on the basis of the flesh, we live our lives fully in the flesh until the moment we receive Christ as Lord and Savior, and we easily revert to living in the flesh even throughout our Christian lives. That is the inner war that Paul describes in Romans 8—the fact that every Christian is a walking battleground in a war between the spirit and the flesh.

The world operates on the basis of the flesh. We who are in Christ are to operate in the power of the new life in Jesus Christ, the power of the Holy Spirit. When we exercise our gifts in the power of the Spirit we become the Lord's hands, feet, and lips on earth, spreading His healing touch and saving message wherever we go. When we exercise our gifts in the power of the flesh, what issues from us is not ministry, but corruption.

Perhaps you have heard preachers speak in the flesh—exercising the gift of preaching but doing so out of a self-centered desire for self-exaltation and self-advancement. Such preaching often attracts hundreds or thousands, and sounds very pleasant, but it does not spring from the power of the Spirit. Such preaching ultimately produces death and corruption. Nothing is more tragic and wasteful than to exercise a spiritual gift in the power of the flesh.

We need the help of the Scriptures to see what the flesh is, and who the Holy Spirit is, and how He operates in our lives and through our gifts. We must continually immerse our minds and hearts in God's Word, allowing Him to open our eyes to new and deeper insights into the gifts He has given us and how He wants us to use them.

We need to put our gifts to daily use, exploring the unique capabilities with which God has endowed us. And as we use those gifts, we will encounter joys and successes—and we will also encounter obstacles and setbacks. Don't be discouraged—the obstacles and setbacks can be even more important to your maturity and understanding of your gifts than the joys and successes. God knows that, gifted as we are, we still have rough edges. We need to be planed and sandpapered and smoothed. God has several grades of sandpaper, running from extremely fine to extremely rough! Our job is to cooperate with him in having our corners rounded, and our coarse and scratchy surfaces polished to shiny perfection.

DISCOVERING YOUR GIFTS

The next question that naturally occurs to us is: "How do I discover my own gifts?" There are two ways that we discover our gifts. First, we discover by doing. This is the same way people discover they have a natural talent, such as musical or athletic ability. You'll never know that you have what it takes to be a great concert pianist until you first sit down at a piano and take a few lessons. You'll never know if you have what it takes to be a great quarterback until you at least pick up a football and throw it a few times. Everyone has to start somewhere.

The person who volunteers to help lead a Sunday school class or youth group could one day find himself pastoring a church. A visit to a hospital or soup kitchen could lead to the discovery of a gift of mercy. Volunteering to serve on the church finance or personnel committee could lead to the discovery of the gift of administration.

In the process of placing yourself in various ministry situations, you will see other Christians exercising their gifts. From time to time, you will find yourself being drawn to what you see. You may think, "I have an affinity for that kind of ministry as well. Perhaps God is leading me in that direction." I believe that what you enjoy doing is usually what God gives you the privilege of doing, because there is joy in exercising our spiritual gifts and in performing the ministry God designed us to do. People take great pleasure in exercising their gifts, because it is fulfilling and satisfying to carry out our God-given function.

The second way we discover our gifts is by having those gifts observed in us and affirmed in us by other Christians. When other Christians—particularly those fellow Christians you see as wise and mature—see God's gift in you and encourage you to use it, it is a message to consider carefully and prayerfully. Equally important, our fellow Christians can often be helpful in pointing out that we don't have the gift we think we have. I remember Dr. H. A. Ironside used to speak about those pathetic fellows who thought they had the gift of preaching, but were frustrated that no one had the gift of listening! So other Christians have an important role in holding up a spiritual mirror to us, so that we can see our unique range of gifts more clearly.

Of course, the key to discovering our gifts—whether we discover them through doing or through the affirmation of fellow Christians—is that we ask God in prayer to open our eyes and reveal our gifts to us. These are *spiritual* gifts, not natural talents, so we urgently need the guidance of the Holy Spirit, who leads us into the fullest knowledge and richest expression of our unique, God-given *charismata*.

In the next chapter, we will see how the Holy Spirit uses these gifts to accomplish a two-fold purpose: equipping us for ministry and making us spiritually mature.

CHAPTER NINETEEN

Shaping Up the Saints

Ephesians 4:11–16

Saints can be very difficult at times.

Contrary to popular belief, saints are not statuettes made of plaster. Saints are human beings—sinners saved by grace. They are not made of "sugar and spice and everything nice." Fact is, most saints are made of very resistant and even abrasive materials. They can be harder than diamonds, more stubborn than a mule, and slower than Christmas.

God makes saints out of whatever material he has at hand—even out of stuff like you and me! And sainthood is a never-ending process of being chipped and whittled and sanded and smoothed. God is continually knocking off the rough spots and puttying up the nicks and holes, polishing and finishing—and he is gradually restoring His image in us, the image that was defaced by sin. He is conforming us—slowly and painstakingly—into the image of His Son Jesus Christ.

FIRST RESULT: PREPARE US FOR MINISTRY

In the previous chapter, we took a quick survey of the subject of spiritual gifts. In this chapter, we will discover how God wants to use our gifts to "shape up the saints," to produce two profound results in our lives: (1) prepare us for ministry, and (2) make us mature in Christ. In Ephesians 4:11–16, Paul writes:

> It was he who gave some to be apostles, some to be prophets, some to be evangelists, and some to be pastors and teachers, to prepare God's people for works of service, so that the body of Christ may be built up until we all reach unity in the faith and in the knowledge of the Son of God and become mature, attaining to the whole measure of the fullness of Christ.
>
> Then we will no longer be infants, tossed back and forth by the waves, and blown here and there by every wind of teaching and by the cunning and craftiness of men in their deceitful scheming. Instead, speaking the truth in love, we will in all things grow up into him who is the Head, that is, Christ. From him the whole body, joined and held together by every supporting ligament, grows and builds itself up in love, as each part does its work.

In verse 12, Paul says that the purpose of the gifts is "to prepare God's people for works of service." That word *prepare* is rendered *equip* in some translations. In the original language that verb is *katartismon,* from which we get our English word *artisan*—an artist or craftsman, someone who works with his hands and accomplishes good and lasting works. We first find this Greek word in the New Testament in connection with the calling of the disciples. When Jesus walked along the Sea of Galilee, as related in Matthew 4:21, Jesus "saw two other brothers, James son of Zebedee and his brother John. They were in a boat with their father Zebedee, *preparing* their nets."

The word *preparing* in this place is *katartizo*. So these men were preparing their nets, getting them ready for service.

So God has given these gifts to prepare the saints for service, to equip them for action, to shape up the saints for the work God has planned for them. How does God shape up His saints and prepare them for ministry? The apostle Paul gives us an insight when he describes his own ministry in Colossians 1:28: "We proclaim him [Jesus], admonishing [or warning] and teaching everyone with all wisdom, so that we may present everyone perfect [or mature] in Christ."

Paul presents a wonderful sanity of balance in this explanation. We are not simply to teach, to impart doctrinal or theological information. Teaching begins with admonishing or warning. At first, we might think the order should be reversed: teach first, and if the people don't receive the teaching, then issue a warning. But the word translated "admonishing" or "warning" in this verse comes from a Greek root word which means "to put in mind"—that is, to call people's attention to something. Paul is saying you must first capture people's awareness—then you can teach them.

UNDIVIDED ATTENTION

Too often our teaching is weak and powerless because we try to impart it without first capturing the interest of our hearers. It is like the story of the old mule herder who went out to train a mule. The first thing he did was lift a big two-by-four and whack the mule a good one right between the ears. As the mule was reeling and shaking off the effects of the blow, a man ran up to the mule herder and said, "You there! What do you think you're doing?" The mule herder replied, "I'm training a mule." The other man was flabbergasted. "But why did you hit the animal with a board?" The mule herder answered, "When you aim to train a mule, you first have to get his undivided attention." And that—in a purely figurative sense—is what we have to do when we teach the Word. We have to get the undivided attention of our listeners. Their interest must be awakened so that they will hear our teaching.

The Lord Jesus always captured the people's attention when he taught. There is the story of when He taught the people that He is the bread of life. Evidently the twelve apostles were among the crowd, and Jesus saw them yawning and restless, apparently thinking, "We've heard this before." Jesus realized He needed to get their attention. So after His message, He sent them out into the sea. Soon a storm arose with howling winds and crashing waves that threatened to engulf the boat. As the disciples were fearing for their lives in the midst of the storm, they peered through the darkness and saw the Lord coming to them across the water. Suddenly, He had their undivided attention. When He got into the boat, the first thing He said to them was, "You of little faith, why did you doubt?" (Matthew 14:31). Now they were ready to listen—and they never forgot that lesson.

When the apostle Paul went to Athens to preach to the sophisticated Greeks, he went to Mars Hill and began to preach and teach—but he didn't begin by saying, "Ladies and gentlemen, I have come to speak to you about the superiority of Christianity to paganism." He would have lost his audience before reaching the end of his sentence! No, he took a fascinating approach.

Even before he preached, he began by walking around the city, keeping his eyes open, and taking careful note of the culture and mindset of his audience. Then he went to Mars Hill, and when he began to speak, it was as if he had hit his audience over the head with a two-by-four—he had their undivided attention!

"Men of Athens!" he began, "I see that in every way you are very religious. For as I walked around and looked carefully at your objects of worship, I even found an altar with this inscription: TO AN UNKNOWN GOD. Now what you worship as something unknown I am going to proclaim to you" (Acts 17:22–23). He awakened their interest—not by finger-wagging or condemning, but by "putting in mind," arresting their attention, telling them that he had come to proclaim to them the identity of the "unknown god" to whom they had built an altar. That's the key to true teaching: awaking interest, arousing attention.

TRUTH IN BALANCE

Someone has defined preaching or teaching as "the art of afflicting the comfortable and comforting the afflicted." That is how Jesus and Paul both conducted their teaching and preaching ministries. Jesus could literally "preach up a storm," and Paul knew how to take something familiar to his listeners—an altar to an "unknown god"—and use it as a starting point for evangelism. The message must be fitted to the audience. A message delivered to the comfortable should begin with affliction, admonition, a word of warning to shake people out of their comfortable complacency—that is how you "put in mind" your teaching for a comfortable, complacent audience. A message to the afflicted should begin with comfort and hope, which the afflicted long to hear—that is how you "put in mind" your teaching to a needy, hurting, afflicted audience.

One of the weaknesses of the American church is that we love to come only to hear someone say what we already know. Why? Because we love to think, "This is for the fellow behind me, or that lady over there. Thank God, this is not something I need to hear. Thank God, I don't need to make any changes in my life." Too many Christians go to church to say, "Amen!" Too few go to church to have their lives and hearts redirected toward God.

The truth ought to get under our collars and into our hearts and bother us greatly at times. When there is sin or error in our lives, the truth ought to itch and chafe and drive us crazy! Ultimately, the truth brings comfort, delight, and joy—but before it can bring us comfort, it must afflict us and disturb us and awaken us to our sense of need.

Once the teacher or preacher has our attention, it is time to teach the Word. It demands being faithful to the whole counsel of God, not riding theological hobby-horses. True teaching and preaching means expounding the whole truth of God, not picking out a few favorite themes or verses. That is why expository preaching and teaching—exploring an entire book or section of a book, leaving out nothing, commenting on everything—is the best way to preach and teach.

Scripture should not be taught piecemeal, but should be presented as an integrated whole. That is the way Scripture is written, and that is how it should be taught. As the prophet Isaiah observes, the Word of God is "rule on rule; a little here, a little there," (Isaiah 28:13). You don't find in the Scriptures a chapter on justification and another on sanctification and another on baptism. God's truth is woven seamlessly together. Whenever you take a sizable section of the Word of God and comment on every point in it, you are more likely to present His truth in balance than if you "cherry-pick" your way around the Bible.

It is *truth in balance* that truly prepares the saints for ministry. Only the Word of God can penetrate the hardness of our rationalizing hearts, cutting, melting, and ultimately healing our hearts so that we are fit for God's service.

SECOND RESULT: MATURITY

The second result that God produces through the gifts He has given us is to make us mature in Christ. In Ephesians 4:11–16, Paul writes that these gifts were given "so that the body of Christ may be built up." The first result that we just examined—preparing the saints for ministry—is directed outward, to the world. But the second result—building up the body of Christ—is directed inward, toward the church itself. The ultimate goal of building up the body of Christ is that "we all reach unity in the faith and in the knowledge of the Son of God and become mature, attaining to the whole measure of the fullness of Christ."

That is a great statement—in fact, it is a startling statement. The apostle is telling us that the goal of all God's far-flung work in history is focused on us, members of the body of Christ, the church. What is that goal? You might think it would be the evangelization of the world. Certainly, as Christians, we believe in carrying out the Great Commission to preach the gospel to everyone around the world. That is a crucial function of the church, but that is not the *supreme* function of the church!

Nor does Paul suggest that the supreme purpose of the church is to usher in the millennium, or bring about world peace and justice. These events will be accomplished, but they are not God's ultimate goal for the church. Nor is it that we become white robed, monkish ascetics or erudite theologians.

The one goal God seeks to accomplish, above all else, is our *maturity*—and Paul goes on to explain that our maturity means that we attain "the whole measure of the fullness of Christ." He desires that we may become grown up, responsible, well-adjusted, absolutely Christlike human beings, as God intended us to be.

It takes the church to do that. You cannot be all that God created you to be unless you are part of the church, functioning as God intended you to function, with the church functioning as God intended it to function. Deep down, this is what we all desire: To be whole, complete, mature, and fulfilled.

We all have a mental image of ourselves as, at least to some degree, whole and mature. We all think of ourselves as more mature than we really are, for we have an enormous capacity for self-deception. Occasionally, there are times when we are forced to be brutally honest with ourselves. We make a major mistake, we get caught in a terrible sin, we cause pain to someone we truly care about—and then our self-image is shattered like a broken mirror. We despise ourselves and say, "I'm nothing but a stupid, stubborn, immature fool!" We want so desperately to be mature and Christlike, but we so easily fall short.

Why do we so often delude ourselves into thinking we are mature when we are not? Because we measure ourselves against the wrong standard. We compare ourselves to the measuring stick of the world, which is false.

We are like the little boy who ran in and told his mother, "Mom! Guess what! I'm eight feet tall!" The mother knew her son was only half that. "How do you know you're eight feet tall?" she asked. "Because I measured myself with this!" said the boy—and he showed her the six-inch ruler he had used.

That's what we do. We compare ourselves with other people around us, then assure ourselves that compared to this person or that person, we are doing okay. But we're not okay. As Paul says in 2 Corinthians 10:12, we are unwise and self-deceived to compare ourselves with others. The people around us are just six-inch rulers; only Jesus Christ measures a full twelve inches—and when we measure ourselves against Him, we see how far short we truly come.

IMMERSING OURSELVES IN CHRIST

Here in Ephesians 4, Paul tells us what the true measure of maturity is: "the whole measure of the fullness of Christ." That's the only realistic measuring stick in the universe. In fact, just to make sure we don't miss his point, Paul tells us again, in verse 15, that God intends that we "grow up into him who is the Head, that is, Christ." The Lord

Jesus Christ is the One by whom God measures us, and the One by whom we are to measure ourselves.

At this point, we see how crucial it is that we immerse ourselves in the story of Jesus. As we study the Gospels we discover the rich, strong humanity of Jesus our Lord. He epitomized and idealized what it means to be a man, and what it means to be human. To measure ourselves against Him and to learn what it means to be like Him, we must come to see Him as a constant companion. The more time we spend with Him, the more clearly we see Him in all His sturdy manhood, His tenderness and toughness, His humor and humility, His delightfulness and discipline, His serenity and His authority. The more you gaze at the Man, Christ Jesus, the better you can measure your life against His—and the more you'll grow to be like Him.

If we never truly learn to know Him, we can never become more than a pale and shabby parody of Him—a copy of a stereotype. But as we get to know Him in His true reality, as we obey Him and cast ourselves in faith upon Him, we begin to appropriate His life. We take Him into ourselves and onto ourselves—not merely hearing Him, but doing His will and His work. That is how we attain "to the whole measure of the fullness of Christ."

You cannot truly know Jesus Christ until you follow Him. The disciples were *acquainted* with Jesus Christ before they became His disciples, but they never really *knew* Him until they left everything and followed Him. That's when their journey toward maturity began. So it is with us. We get to know Jesus by following Him, by obeying Him, by walking in His footsteps. Simply reading about Jesus is not enough.

It's like trying to learn how to swim by reading a book about swimming. You'll never learn to swim that way. You have to get into the water. You have to immerse yourself. You have to flounder around and bob up and down and maybe swallow a little water—but in time, you learn to float and kick with your feet and stroke with your arms and get it all synchronized. And in time, you become a swimmer! That's what spiritual growth is like—immersing yourself in the Christian walk and Christian service as you learn to become more and more like Christ.

You might be thinking, *How can I be like Christ? He's the Son of God, I'm a mere mortal human being. He's perfect, I'm a failure, prone to sin. If the perfection of Jesus is the standard, I might as well just give up. I'll never be like Him.* But there is no need for discouragement. Notice how we reach maturity—not in a single lightning-flash of sainthood, but through a gradual process of growth. Paul writes in verse 15, "Instead, speaking the truth in love, we will in all things grow up into him who is the Head, that is, Christ." God doesn't expect us to instantly transform and become Christlike—rather, He has provided a process by which we grow up into Christlikeness.

I know many new Christians who are disturbed and disappointed that their conversion did not instantly transform them into angelic creatures. They get down on themselves when they find old habits, old attitudes, and old sins jumping up to bite them. They don't know what to make of this. Sometimes they even wonder if they are Christians at all. Of course, they are. They just need to be reassured that, having placed their faith in Christ, they have embarked on a lifelong process of growth toward Christlikeness and maturity.

Paul goes on to describe a day-by-day, moment-by-moment growth process of the church, which parallels the growth in an individual Christian life. In verse 16, he writes, "From him the whole body, joined and held together by every supporting ligament, grows and builds itself up in love, as each part does its work." Here we clearly see that growth is God's method. As individuals, growing toward Christlikeness, we support one another, encouraging each other's individual growth and our collective growth as the church of Jesus Christ. Individually and collectively, we become more whole and mature, not only as spiritual beings but as complete human beings.

I love to see eagerness for growth. I once asked a boy how old he was. Quick as a flash, he said, "I'm twelve, going on thirteen, soon to be fourteen." What a wonderful, eager attitude! We need to have that same attitude toward our spiritual maturity—"I just can't wait to be more like Christ!" That kind of eagerness is wonderful if it makes us eager to dig into the Word, eager to serve God, eager to pattern our lives after the Lord.

But sometimes we get over-eager—and that sets us up for discouragement. We want to be mature, but some error or setback throws us and makes us feel like total failures, like spiritual babies. In our impatience for maturity, we pray, "Lord, what's wrong with me? Why don't you hurry up this growth process? I'm so tired of being immature." Have you ever felt that way? I have, many times.

But God has his own timetable, and most of us will take an entire lifetime to grow up fully. Certainly, some reach relative maturity within a few years of conversion, but even those are still in for a lifetime of spiritual discoveries that lead to greater growth. God expects the process to take some time. After all, it takes God years to grow an oak tree—but He can grow a squash in three months! God is not interested in growing Christian squashes. He wants to make sturdy oaks out of your life and mine.

GROWTH BY STAGES

Did you ever watch a child grow up? If you are a parent, you know from firsthand experience that growth follows a pattern of discernible stages. The same is true of the Christian life. There is a definite progression evident in the Christian life, and definite characteristics of each stage along this line. We grow stage by stage, and we can measure our growth by looking in two different directions. We can look back to the childishness of immaturity, noting our progress away from immature attitudes and outlooks, and we can also look at our present situation and see if the factors that indicate growth are now present.

Growth does not come by trying. You cannot say, "Now I am going to try to grow." Children would love to do this, but they cannot. So how do you grow? By making sure that factors for growth are present in your life. Paul explains it in Ephesians 4:14: "Then we will no longer be infants, tossed back and forth by the waves, and blown here and there by every wind of teaching and by the cunning and craftiness of men in their deceitful scheming."

In that verse Paul characterizes a childish, infantile attitude. In this description, we recognize two characteristics of childishness and immaturity. First, there is fickleness. Children have a short attention span. You cannot interest them in one thing for very long; soon, something else captures their attention. Children are flighty, inconsistent, and unstable.

I'm reminded of a time I took my daughter to Baskin-Robbins for an ice cream cone. She was only four at the time, and I held her up so she could see all thirty-one flavors and make her choice. After ten minutes of my daughter's indecision, my arms began to get tired. Finally, she made her choice: plain vanilla!

Young Christians show this same kind of instability—and so do Christians who are chronologically old, but spiritually immature. There is a flightiness and instability to their lives that Paul describes as being "tossed back and forth by the waves, and blown here and there by every wind of teaching and by the cunning and craftiness of men in their deceitful scheming." They dash in a dither toward every new religious fad, they seem more excited about the latest religious book than about the one Great Book, they rush from seminar to conference, hanging on to the words of the latest Christian guru, they change their spiritual doctrinal mindset as often as they change their socks. With them, prophecy becomes a hobby and spirituality becomes the latest craze. That is a mark of spiritual immaturity.

Spiritual babyhood is also manifested in a lack of faithfulness and dependability. Immature Christians may take on a task in the church, but before long their interest wanes and they become discouraged and disinterested. Soon, they don't show up at all, or they call and ask, "Could you get someone else to do this?" That is always a mark of immaturity, and it contrasts with the fruit of the Spirit called faithfulness.

Christian immaturity is also marked by sporadic attendance at worship and Bible study. Most new Christians began their Christian lives with an eagerness to join in worship and fellowship with other Christians. They love to hear the Word of God, and can't get enough of His truth. But after a while, their immaturity asserts itself as a growing apathy, a loss of attention, a loss of interest in the things that once gave them joy and excitement. And they begin to fall away from regular attendance and close fellowship with other Christians.

The second mark of childishness is a lack of discernment and awareness of danger. We clearly recognize this mark of childishness in our children. They may play in dangerous situations and be quite unaware that there is anything threatening them. They don't hesitate to walk into the street, or pet strange dogs, or stick fingers into electrical outlets, or drink from yucky-smelling bottles marked with a skull and crossbones!

In the same way, immature Christians seem unaware of the spiritual dangers around them—and sometime fall prey to spiritual traps.

Peter exhibited exactly this kind of immaturity when he swore undying allegiance to the Lord just hours before the crucifixion—then denied Jesus three times when the pressure was on. He had no idea of the perils that awaited him, and all his earnest but immature zeal was worth exactly nothing when the chips were down.

In immature Christians, you often see an uncritical acceptance of whatever comes. They don't test what they hear against Scripture. They are not skeptical and discerning. Instead, they listen to anybody who sounds good and who can quote Scripture. Many such people end up dead in places like Jonestown or Waco.

Mature Christians have learned to walk with the Lord in fear and trembling, conscious of their own weakness and fallibility. They realize that the enemy is subtle and can easily trap them. So they test every claim and every assertion, delving into the Scriptures, seeking wise counsel, covering every decision with prayer. They put their trust in God and His Word, not in any glib-sounding human preacher or teacher.

HOW MATURE ARE YOU?

Now comes the question: How mature are you? You may have been a Christian for years or decades—but are you mature? Have you grown beyond childish tantrums, attitudes of inconsistency, undependability, and spiritual gullibility? If you have, then you are maturing in Christ.

And there are other ways to measure our growth. We see one set forth in verse 15. We measure our growth by observing whether or not we are "speaking the truth in love." In the original Greek, the phrase "speaking the truth" is all one word, which we might render as "truthing." Are you "truthing" in love? Are you living the truth in love? Are you living honestly? Is you life an open, unposturing attempt to be real, to be Christlike? Do you live a life of sincere Christian love? Do you find that you increasingly exhibit Christlike acceptance, patience, forgiveness, and love in the annoying and frustrating times of your life?

If so, then you are "truthing" in love—and you are becoming more mature in Christ. That is a crucial measurement of spiritual maturity.

Paul mentions one final aspect of maturity in verse 16, where he writes, "From him [Christ] the whole body, joined and held together by every supporting ligament, grows and builds itself up in love, as each part does its work." The apostle uses a word here that appears in only one other verse in Scripture—and that verse is also in this letter, Ephesians 2:21. It is the word that is translated as "joined and held together," and Paul actually coins this word by jamming three Greek words together. He takes the Greek words that mean "a joint," "with," and "to choose" (speaking of God's choice to place us in the body of Christ). Paul is telling us that one of the factors that makes for growth is the acceptance of the ministry of other Christians in our lives. We are to join our lives together in the body of Christ. Immature Christians try to go it alone; mature Christians seek deep and active Christian fellowship. Maturity recognizes the need for a mutual ministry, one with another.

You may find this hard to take. There may be Christians in your church who rub you the wrong way. But understand this: God put you with those Christians because He knows you need them in your life. Some of them may be hard to love, but God knows that you need to learn how to love your brothers and sisters in the Lord. This is exactly the kind of exercise you need to become more mature and Christlike. Everyone in the body of Christ is an individual, with a unique personality and unique gifts. They have the right to be different, and in their own way, they are growing toward Christlike maturity, too. So do not reject God's instruments. Allow Him to use them in your life, and allow Him to use you in theirs.

All too often, Christians get tired of putting up with this or that problem in a church, so at the first sign of trouble, they pull up stakes and move on to the church down the road. Certainly, there are times when God leads you to a new church—but a pattern of church-hopping is simply not consistent with the New Testament pattern. God put you where you are for a reason, so maturity demands that you stay there and learn to live with God's people in that church. Without question, God will use that to produce growth and maturity in your life so that you might become well-rounded and complete in Jesus Christ. That is what He wants in our lives.

Notice, finally, that Paul again uses that linking phrase "in love" in verse 16: "the whole body . . . grows and builds itself up *in love*, as each part does its work." Christlike love is the key to Christlike maturity. As we live in love—love that is not just a feeling or a sentiment, but a relentless decision to do good to others even in annoying, frustrating, and downright horrible situations—we will experience something amazing. Day by day, hour by hour, moment by moment, we will discover that the Spirit of God is producing a miracle in our lives. We will gradually find that we are shedding our childish ways. We are becoming fully-formed and mature, well-adjusted and stable, faithful and dependable. In short, we are seeing God's supreme goal being accomplished in our lives.

We are growing more and more like Jesus.

PART THREE

The Christian in the World

Ephesians 4:17–5:20

CHAPTER TWENTY

Putting Off the Old, Putting On the New

Ephesians 4:17–24

What a confusing world we live in!

Turn on your TV and you are assaulted by stories of wars and rumors of wars in the Middle East, scandals in high places, accusations and counter-accusations between right and left, crises of leadership, questions of whom to believe or disbelieve, rumblings in the U.N., strife in our inner cities, and on and on and on. From the talking heads on our TV screens comes a cacophony of voices, a riot of opinions and alleged facts.

Who knows what to believe? No wonder many are confused today. No wonder so many people are willing to follow any voice that seems to offer reality and hope in this senseless world. In these uncertain times, people crave certainty—and despair of ever finding it.

But here, in Ephesians 4, the apostle Paul has a clear and definite word to say. His is not just another voice, like those of the television talking heads. His voice is authoritative, his word comes from God, and his message is precise, concise, and laser-focused on the problems you and I face in our lives today.

THE FUTILITY OF THE WORLD'S THINKING

After spending the first part of Ephesians 4 dealing with the nature of the church, spiritual gifts, and Christian maturity, Paul turns in verse 17 to the issue of living as a Christian in an unbelieving world. Unfortunately, you and I don't have the luxury of choosing to live on Mars, or in the Andromeda Galaxy, or in Shangri-La. We must live in the real world—and despite the passage of two thousand years, the world we live in is amazingly similar to the world of Paul's time. So Paul's word to us is as forceful and applicable today as it was then. In verse 17, Paul writes:

> So I tell you this, and insist on it in the Lord, that you must no longer live as the Gentiles do, in the futility of their thinking.

Notice the force of that exhortation: "So I tell you this, and insist on it in the Lord." That means that Paul is not merely offering human advice, but divine revelation. This is part of the revelation of the mind of God given to the apostle Paul in what he calls "visions and revelations from the Lord" (2 Corinthians 12:1), when the Lord Jesus himself appeared to Paul and instructed him in the message to the church. This is the finger of God placed squarely at the root of a human problem.

Paul goes on to say, "you must no longer live as the Gentiles do, in the futility of their thinking." The word *Gentiles* could also be translated "nations"—it is translated in this way in other places in Scripture. Paul is not talking about the cultural distinction between Jews and Gentiles, but the spiritual distinction between those who are in Christ (you and I as Christians) and those who are outside of Christ—the worldlings. "You Christians," Paul tells us with intensity and clarity, "must no longer live as nonChristians live."

How do nonChristians live? In the futility of their thinking, says Paul. The J. B. Phillips modern paraphrase gives us additional insight into Paul's meaning in this verse: "Do not live any longer the futile lives of gentiles. For they live in a world of shadows." And the New English Bible puts it this way: "Give up living like pagans, with their good-for-nothing notions." These are accurate and apt renderings for Paul's meaning in this verse: The thinking of the world is pointless.

So we must live differently from nonChristians—and Paul begins with the issue of the mind. He does not start with our actions, but with our thought-life. He does not begin with the outward, but with the inward. He declares the thinking of the world to be empty and futile, and he contrasts the world's philosophy of living, the world's values, with the philosophy and values of God.

Here we see the fundamental fracture between Christianity and the world. Here we see why the Christian cannot love the world and God the Father at the same time. This is why friendship with the world is enmity with God, according to James 4:4. This is why Jesus himself says, "What is highly esteemed among men is abomination in the sight of God," (Luke 16:15 KJV).

Paul rubs our noses in the fundamental issue, and we must face it squarely: Either God is right or the world is right, one or the other. It cannot be both. The Christian must choose on which basis he is going to live his life. If he is to follow Christ, he must be wiling to have his thinking transformed. That is the first issue a new Christian faces: a completely altered outlook on life. Christianity is not merely an add-on philosophy or a little different way of looking at things. It is a revolutionary alteration of one's worldview and way of living. Christianity is diametrically opposed to the mindset of this world.

DARKENED UNDERSTANDING

Next, Paul analyzes the problem at the core of the world's faulty mindset. Why is human thinking futile and pointless? Paul explains in verse 18:

> They are darkened in their understanding and separated from the life of God because of the ignorance that is in them due to the hardening of their hearts.

The mindset of worldlings is futile because their understanding is darkened. Just as a cloud may pass across the sun and darken its light, so the thinking of man in his fallen state is obscured and darkened. Scripture continually uses these terms—light and darkness—as metaphors for truth and ignorance. Truth is light; ignorance is darkness. Here, Paul declares that human thinking is shadowed with ignorance. It is pointless because it stems from ignorance.

Why are we human beings ignorant? Because there is a part of our being that does not function—our spiritual life. The human spirit is blank, darkened, and obscured. In our natural state, apart from God, there is a part of our being—the part that God intended at creation to be the key to life—where nothing takes place. The spirit of humanity, lost in sin, is dead. As a result, all human knowledge is broken, unrelated, incomplete. That is the picture Paul draws.

We tend to take pride in our great civilization with its accomplishments, knowledge, and technological wonders. But we have to ask ourselves: What has this vaunted civilization really done for us? Do we feel safe on our streets at night? Have we solved the problems of crime, political corruption, racism, immorality, and war? Are we any happier as a society than the ancient Egyptians, the ancient Mayans, the ancient Greeks? If so, why are so many of us going to psychiatrists, taking drugs, getting drunk, getting divorced, battering spouses and children, and committing suicide? Why are all of these problems rising instead of declining?

I once read a newspaper article with the headline " 'Religion Fading" says Psychiatry Professor." That caught my attention! Reading the article, I read that a noted professor at the UCLA Neuropsychiatric Institute had said that religion is on the decline in today's society. He called that a "hopeful sign of our times." He went on to declare:

> The decline in religious feeling among civilized people is an indication that man is steadily becoming more rational and less subject to superstition and therefore less likely to kill and maim those who disagree with him.

I read that statement a second time, just to make sure I hadn't misunderstood him. Then I scratched my head and wondered what world this professor lived in—because the world I live in is filled with hatred, violence, racism, brushfire wars, and Desert Storms. As the influence of religion waned in the world, these horrors seemed to be on the rise! Without question, the twentieth century—with its two World Wars, its Stalinist purges, and genocidal slaughter from Armenia to Nazi Germany to Cambodia to Iraq to Bosnia—has been the bloodiest, most tortured century in human history!

Then I realized that this man's statement was simply a confirmation of the apostle Paul's analysis of human thinking as futile. The mind of fallen man is darkened, blinded, and does not see things as they really are. It ignores the obvious truth of the human condition and persists in a faulty hope that humanity is getting better all the time.

We see the darkened understanding of humanity in talk of moral relativism, of "tolerance" for sexual perversion and promiscuity, in the declining level of moral and ethical behavior among our leaders, and a general attitude of "if it feels good, do it." People are increasingly becoming slaves to animal passions, addicts to pleasure, faithless to commitments and covenants. This is the darkening of the fallen mind.

In their ignorant blindness, human beings think they are okay in their own strength, in their own goodness, and God is of either marginal importance to their lives or no importance at all. As a result, says Paul, they are "separated from the life of God because of the ignorance that is in them." Paul is not blaming or condemning humanity—he is simply analyzing the human condition. He is not criticizing—he is simply stating a fact.

By ignoring or rejecting God, we cut ourselves off from the one thing we need to be fully human. Both nature and Scripture concur that humanity is incomplete without God. We were designed and created to be the dwelling place of God. It is God in us that makes us fully human as God intended us to be. This fact is demonstrated by the life of the Lord Jesus Christ. It was the indwelling of the Spirit and His moment-by-moment dependence upon the Father that enabled Jesus to be fully human as God intended Him to be. The life of God being lived through us, we are blinded, weak, and ignorant.

But there is yet another level of depth to Paul's great analysis. If humanity was cut off from God because of ignorance alone, humanity could well be excused. We cannot be held accountable for a truth we have never been informed of—but ignorance is not the end of the human story. Humanity is born ignorant and cut off from the life of God—but humanity *remains* in that condition only because of the hardness of the human heart. Human beings are "separated from the life of God because of the ignorance that is in them," Paul goes on to say, "*due to the hardening of their hearts.*"

A young Christian once said to me, "Why do we have such a hard time selling the world's greatest product?" It's because humanity resists the truth, rejects the light, turns from God's love, clings to error—and in the process, the human heart gradually grows harder and harder until it is completely unable to respond. All of these factors mark the darkened understanding and futile, empty thinking of the world.

Paul's message to us as members of the body of Christ is clear: "You Christians must no longer think this way. You are in the world, but you must not think as the world thinks, nor live as the world lives. You must turn away from these dead attitudes and reflect the light of God's truth."

CHRISTIANS IN A WORLD OF WORLDLINGS

We see the next step of Paul's analysis in verse 19. He writes:

> Having lost all sensitivity, they have given themselves over to sensuality so as to indulge in every kind of impurity, with a continual lust for more.

Paul makes the same point in Romans: "Furthermore, since they did not think it worthwhile to retain the knowledge of God, he gave them over to a depraved mind, to do what ought not to be done" (Romans 1:28). Paul goes on in that passage to list the awful crimes humanity commits on a daily basis, and they sound as if they are culled from the pages of your morning newspaper. Why do people do such things? Because human beings are futile in their thinking. Even the best and brightest of human minds—the leaders, the artists, the Nobel Prize winners—are darkened.

The good news of the gospel is that God reaches even these kinds of people. He pierces, penetrates, and softens human hearts. Rather than blaming those around us with darkened minds, we must remember that we, too, had the same mind, the same outlook on life. As Paul says in Colossians 1:21–22, "Once you were alienated from God and were enemies in your minds because of your evil behavior. But now he has reconciled you . . . ." Our minds were once darkened, too, and it is only because God's love reached out to us that we have the light of truth. So we have no right to be judgmental. Darkness and ignorance are the basic human conditions to which the gospel makes its appeal.

The only hope of helping others who are blinded by their darkened minds is to demonstrate a different pattern of thought, a wholly different set of values. The implication is clear that if we live as the world lives and think as the world thinks, there is not a thing we can do to help those who are lost in futility.

There is a story of a boy who thought he would teach some sparrows to sing like a canary. So he put the sparrows in a cage with the canary, hoping the canary would teach them to sing. In a few days he found the canary chirping like the sparrows! We must not be like that canary. While we live in a sparrow-filled world, we must retain our canary-like thoughts, our canary-like ways, our canary-like life. We are Christians in a world of worldlings—and we must not allow ourselves to be absorbed back into the darkened existence of worldliness.

ADEQUACY IN CHRIST

In verses 20 and 21, we come to the reason Paul speaks so strongly. He writes:

> You, however, did not come to know Christ that way. Surely you heard of him and were taught in him in accordance with the truth that is in Jesus.

In other words, you must not live like the Gentiles, because in Christ you have a different principle of living, a different way of thinking. In Christ, you have the truth by which you can test and judge all other ideas, concepts, philosophies, claims, and assertions. You have found in Jesus Christ the simple truth about life, about yourself, about the world, about the makeup of science and nature, about human behavior. You have found the One "in whom are hidden all the treasures of wisdom and knowledge," as Paul tells us in Colossians 2:3.

The Lord Jesus made the same case to the people in Jerusalem when He said, "I am the light of the world. Whoever follows me will never walk in darkness, but will have the light of life" (John 8:12). A Christian does not need to walk in uncertainty and shadows. A Christian need have no lack of essential knowledge. Jesus is the light, and He reveals to us the light of truth.

It is very much in vogue today to claim that nothing can be known for sure. The evil god of this world has sold the lie that there is no black or white, that there are no moral absolutes—only confusing shades of gray. That is the futility and emptiness of the world's thinking. If there are no final answers, no ultimate knowledge, no ultimate truth, then people don't have to reorder their lives according to God's truth. They have rationalized their way out of God's demand for righteousness and truth—or so they think.

This illusory mindset has even infected the church. I once heard a pastor say that all knowledge is tentative at best. We can never know the truth for sure. Biblical Christianity repudiates that idea utterly. Christ has come precisely so that we might know the truth. That doesn't mean everything there is to know, but it does mean we know everything we *need* to know to find meaning and purpose in life. As Jesus said to His disciples, "If you hold to my teaching, you are really my disciples. Then you will know the truth, and the truth will set you free" (John 8:31–32). Truth is absolute, it is sometimes difficult and not what we want to hear, but it is always realistic—and that is why the truth tears away the veil of illusion and sets us free.

This is not to say that everything a worldling thinks is wrong. God's truth can be found in the realms of physics and mathematics—but it is not the ultimate truth that gives meaning to life. A worldling may have vast and accurate knowledge about how to repair a Chevy engine or design a suspension bridge or construct a space shuttle—but that kind of knowledge, as true as it may be, does not result in salvation. To say that a worldling's mind is darkened does not disparage in any way the knowledge he or she has in other compartments of life—but it does means that he or she lacks the most crucial and all-important truth of all: the truth of Jesus Christ.

The truth of Jesus is superior to the truth of great thinkers such as Archimedes, Einstein, Voltaire, Teng Shih, Newton, Socrates, Nietzsche, Eddington, Huxley, Feuerbach, Bertrand Russell, Descartes, Hegel, Plato, Confucius, Zeno, Thales, Darwin, Fermi, and Oppenheimer. The truth of Jesus is superior to the truth of great theologians and preachers such as Augustine, Thomas Aquinas, Luther, Tillich, Barth, Bultmann, Billy Sunday, Dwight L. Moody, Oswald Chambers, Dr. H. A. Ironside, and Billy Graham. The truth of Jesus is certainly far superior to anything Ray Stedman has to say. I prefer the truth of Jesus to my own blind guesses, based on my own inadequate understanding and faulty data. Jesus alone is the authority over all truth.

There is adequacy in Christ for any situation. God has placed you where you are because He wants you to live the Christian life right here, right now, in these very circumstances. Those around you will never have a chance to see the tremendous, revolutionary difference that Jesus makes unless they can see Him shining through the circumstances of your life right now.

This is where we are to begin to live, and this is why Paul says we must no longer live as the Gentiles do, in the emptiness of their minds. Our lives are not empty, because we have tapped into a storehouse of resources far beyond the dreams of any worldling. When those around us see the fruitfulness and glory of Jesus Christ manifested in our circumstances, they will ask, "What has this person got that I haven't got? What kind of a faith is this? What do these people have that enables them to live like this?"

THE UNDERLYING ERROR OF THE WORLD

If you know how to balance a checkbook (I never mastered the art myself, but I understand the general principle), then you know how one little error can upset all your calculations and change the entire picture. You do not need a lot of errors to find yourself in a lot of trouble. Just one transposed figure, one error in subtraction—and all the rest of your absolutely faultless calculations can be thrown into error. A single slipped digit in a column of figures can cause a dozen checks to bounce like ping-pong balls!

That is the way it is with the error that underlies the thinking of the world. There is much truth and cogent logic in the world's reasoning—but human thinking is mingled with error. Unless we know how to distinguish the true from the false in the calculations of our lives, we will inevitably find ourselves in a moral and spiritual catastrophe.

In Ephesians 4 Paul tells us that a fundamental error has crept into human thinking. The basic premises and assumptions of human thinking are distorted. So we cannot begin with those premises and assumptions, and simply add Christianity onto our worldly worldview. We must completely alter our way of thinking. We must shed the old ways of thinking, and start over with new premises and assumptions, which come from God himself.

PUT OFF OLD LUSTS AND URGES

How do we do this? Paul comes to grips with this question in Ephesians 4:22–24. He writes:

> You were taught, with regard to your former way of life, to put off your old self, which is being corrupted by its deceitful desires; to be made new in the attitude of your minds; and to put on the new self, created to be like God in true righteousness and holiness.

You can't put it any plainer than that: Put off the old and put on the new. Paul begins with a recognition that the old life constantly tugs at us. The old self, the former way of life, can find its way back into our lives through deceitful desires. It is not merely evil deeds that we must watch for, but the old outlooks, attitudes, and corrupt desires.

The apostle Paul makes his point abundantly clear with these two phrases, "put off" and "put on." If you have a soiled garment, you put it off and put on something new. He uses the simplest of terms to illustrate a profound truth. We must reject those basic assumptions that lead to error and destruction, just as you would put off a pair of dirty work jeans. From these wrong attitudes comes corruption.

Paul goes on to explain how to recognize the attitudes we must put off: by the way they operate. They are "deceitful lusts." Unfortunately this word lust is greatly misunderstood in our day. We associate the term with sexual desire. But Paul uses this word in a much broader sense, meaning any urge or basic drive. These deceitful urges are constantly coming to us as we react to various situations in which we find ourselves.

These urges may include sex urges, of course, but they can also refer to our desire to acquire, which is expressed in an orgy of spending. We are self-deceived when we think we can make ourselves happy by owning more things. There is the urge to use others for our own advantage—the urge to manipulate people to do what we want, or the urge to hurt people through backbiting and gossip. There is the lust for power and fame, the urge to attain mastery and status in the political world, the business world, or the church. There is the urge to lie or cheat to get by, to gain an advantage, to avoid responsibility. There is the urge to criticize and blame others, the urge to indulge in self-pity, the urge to explode in anger or impatience with others, the urge to react defensively and abrasively when things don't go our way. There is the urge to attack and undermine those who are different from us or who do not do things the way we do or think the way we think. There is the urge to appear holier and better than others around us.

These are the urges and lusts Paul warns against in this passage.

THE SECRET

The Christian is to put off the old self because he has discovered a secret. He still feels these old urges as strongly as he did before he became a Christian. He feels them as strongly as the worldling does—but the secret he has learned is this: Those lusts and urges are part of the old life, the old self, which was judged on the cross of Christ.

That is what the Lord's Supper portrays. It is a vivid reminder to us that Jesus did an amazing thing on the cross. As 2 Corinthians 5:21 tells us, the One who never knew sin actually *became sin* for us. Jesus *became* our old life, our old egocentric self. Jesus became all of that on the cross. If the Word of God didn't tell us that, we would never be able to understand the depths of the mystery of the cross.

Why did God place such terrible judgment on this innocent, holy man? Why did this terrible convulsion of moral, spiritual, and physical nature take place? Why these impenetrable mysteries? It comes down to one truth: Jesus became sin for us. When He became sin, He was put to death. The sentence of death was executed upon Him. This is God's eloquent way of saying to us that all those urges that arise from the old self are futile and valueless. They are deceitful. They promise much, but they deliver nothing.

The Christian is not told to put the old self to death. He is told that the old self has *already* been put to death in Christ upon the cross! What we are doing here is claiming, in personal experience, what God has already done in the reality of the cross and the resurrection. So the process of putting off and putting on is based upon what Christ has already accomplished for us. The old self is dead already. It remains only for us to claim that truth and make it real in our own daily experience. Our prayer should not be, "Lord, slay the old self within me," but, "Lord, help me to live by the truth that the old self is already nailed to the cross!"

So the first step in experiencing what God intends for us is to put off the old self—throw it off, lay it aside, give it no more place in our lives. But that is only the first step.

There is another half to the picture, and that is to recognize the wonderful possibilities of the new life, the new self. Paul says—and I will translate it differently here to get at what I believe to be a truer understanding of Paul's meaning—"having been renewed in the spirit of your minds, put on the new nature, created after the likeness of God in true righteousness and holiness." Here we see the fundamental difference between a Christian and a nonChristian.

While it is true, of course, that nonChristians sometimes realize that things are wrong in their lives, that their attitudes and actions are sometimes wrong or destructive, they don't have the means to completely put off the old self and put on the new. They can only change from one expression of the old self to another. They can alter the outer form, but the inner problem remains the same.

But Christians—and only Christians—have the capacity to transcend the old and put on the new. That is the testimony of Scripture. When we believe in Jesus Christ and receive Him as Lord, we are renewed in the depths of our spirit. Christ is our life now, and a radical transformation has taken place. The new self is in the likeness of God, the image of Jesus. You are not identified with Him.

If you are a Christian, the life of Christ lives in you. The new urges that come with the new self are urges to love, to understand, to forgive, to accept difficult people, to endure difficult situations, to gently correct those who need correction, to be faithful at all times. The new self is real and genuine. It is love unfeigned. It is not something put on for a moment, not a painted-on smile masking a hostile heart. It is righteous. It is true. It is holy.

Now, I know that the word "holy" makes some people squirm. We usually think of some pious Joe who looks like he has been soaked in embalming fluid. But that's not holiness—that's sanctimoniousness. Holiness really means *wholeness*, being fully and completely what God designed us to be. Holiness results from having the life of the Lord Jesus living within us. How do we achieve that kind of wholeness and holiness? We achieve it through the twofold process of putting off and putting on.

Our problem is that we are afraid to put off the old man for fear we will be left with an empty husk of a life. We fail to understand that we must put off before we can put on. The Holy Spirit is waiting for us to put off the old self so that He can rush in and fill us with the holiness that God intends for us—the wholeness of Christ.

Putting off the old man is like squeezing the water out of a half-drowned man's lungs. You do this not to empty his lungs, but to enable his lungs to fill with air, the breath of life. The Scriptures tell us that the old egocentric life, the old self, has been asphyxiating us, killing us. The only air we were designed to breathe is God.

It all comes down to an appeal to the will. Put off, put on—that is the choice we must make. Reject the old, accept the new. Throw out the clutter of old urges and lusts, and make way for the Spirit to come in and set up housekeeping.

NO EXCUSES

At this point, many people object and say, "Well, I've tried this, but it doesn't work for me. I can see that it works for other people, but not for me."

That is the flesh speaking, the old self putting the blame for failure onto God. It is really a subtle way of saying that God shows partiality, giving some people help while denying help to others. That is a lie of the flesh within you. When we make that excuse, we are denying to ourselves the fact that we never really wanted to put off the old self to begin with—we enjoy it too much. We cling to the pleasures of the egocentric flesh. And as long as you cling to the old self, you cannot put on the new life that God wants you to have.

"Well, I do my best," is another excuse. Again, that's the old self speaking—and the best of the old self is hardly better than the worst. You cannot tie a pink bow on a pig's tail and pass it off as a poodle. If you want to win a prize at the dog show, you need to trade in that pig for a pooch! There's no point in prettying up and disguising the old self. You have to put off the old and put on the new.

There's no room in the Christian life for half-way measures or self-justifying excuses. The choice is either/or, all or nothing—not a little bit of both or, "Well, I tried." God has given us an absolutely sure and foolproof pattern for achieving dramatic change in our lives—and His plan is not subject to half-way results. It works.

Put off, and you can put on. Put on, and you must put off. There is no other way. The choice is extreme, it is black and white, it is utterly simple.

And it is your choice to make.

CHAPTER TWENTY-ONE

Practical Christianity

Ephesians 4:25–29

A preacher had been trying for months to coax his unbelieving neighbor to come visit a church service. Finally, just to get the preacher off his back, the neighbor agreed to come. That Sunday morning, the unbelieving neighbor sat in the very front pew, just in front of the pulpit. The preacher got up and began to preach his sermon with brisk evangelistic fervor, hoping in particular to reach the heart of his unsaved neighbor.

As he preached, the preacher gestured so vigorously that his arm knocked the water glass off the pulpit, sending a shower of water across the first pew. Several people, including the pastor's unsaved neighbor, got drenched. Flustered and embarrassed, the preacher apologized, then went on with his sermon as best he could.

At the end of the service, the unsaved neighbor came up to the pastor and chuckled, "Well, Reverend, you may have baptized me—but you still haven't converted me!"

In his wry and cynical way, this unsaved man pointed up an important distinction: Outward signs, such as baptism, are of secondary importance, compared with the truly primary issue of Christianity: inward change.

The Christian faith was never intended to make us religious. It was intended to change the way we think and the way we live our lives. Religion is outward, but faith is inward. Religion involves our Sunday rituals, but faith pervades our daily obedience. There is nothing God desires more than our reverent, worshipful obedience. There is nothing God dislikes more than mere religion.

Religion alone is an empty shell. Both the Old and New Testaments tell us that religion alone is detestable to God. But genuine, obedient faith—lived out in the real-life situations of our families, our workplaces, our schools, and our neighborhoods—is what Christianity is all about.

A PRACTICAL GOD AND A PRACTICAL FAITH

In the previous section, Paul revealed to us the principle of "putting off and putting on"—the need to put off the old self so that the Holy Spirit can come in and fill us with the new self. In Ephesians 4:25–29, Paul applies the principle of "putting off and putting on" to specific areas of living. He writes:

> Therefore each of you must put off falsehood and speak truthfully to his neighbor, for we are all members of one body. "In your anger do not sin": Do not let the sun go down while you are still angry, and do not give the devil a foothold. He who has been stealing must steal no longer, but must work, doing something useful with his own hands, that he may have something to share with those in need. Do not let any unwholesome talk come out of your mouths, but only what is helpful for building others up according to their needs, that it may benefit those who listen.

Our faith must always focus on our deeds. Our God is a practical God, and our faith is a practical faith.

It is important to understand at the outset that this kind of living is not possible unless you are a Christian. Paul's words are not addressed to people in general, but to those who have been born again and regenerated. The Word of God recognizes that no one who is not yet a Christian can fulfill these demands. People think they are capable of meeting these demands in their own strength, but that is the deceitfulness of the natural heart. If you try, you'll find you can only do so in a limited and incomplete way. The inner life remains unchanged.

The nonChristian cannot put off the old life, because it is the only life he has—he has no new life to put on. The new life is Christ. If we do not have Christ, we do not have a new life. If you have never had the experience of giving your life to Jesus Christ, then that is the place to begin.

PUT OFF THE URGE TO LIE

The apostle begins with what is probably the most universal temptation in human experience: the temptation to lie. Or, as we sometimes say, the temptation to "shade the truth." Or "exaggerate." Or "fib." Or "miss-speak." We have all kinds of euphemisms for this most common of human activities, don't we? But even a euphemism is ultimately a lie, an attempt to mask an ugly truth we do not wish to face. Paul writes in verse 25, "Therefore each of you must put off falsehood and speak truthfully to his neighbor, for we are all members of one body."

Now why does Paul start with the issue of lying? Because this is the most far-reaching and widespread characteristic of the old life. He has already told us that the old life is characterized by deceitful urges. These urges within us deceive us, and that in turn makes it easy for us to turn right around and deceive others. Lying is the most basic characteristic of the old self, because it traces directly back to the devil. Jesus said, ". . . the devil . . . was a murderer from the beginning, not holding to the truth, for there is no truth in him. When he lies, he speaks his native language, for he is a liar and the father of lies" (John 8:44).

Did you go to school to learn how to lie? Of course not. You came by it quite naturally. We learned even as little children that while a lie is an abomination to the Lord, it is a very present help in time of trouble! At least that was our philosophy.

But now as Christians we are to put off the old self with its basic urge to lie. We are to put off lies and put on truth. I am not suggesting that every worldling invariably lies and all Christians invariably tell the truth. It is quite possible for worldlings to tell the truth. But the motivation for telling the truth is different between Christians and nonChristians. The old self generally tells the truth to avoid getting caught or tripped up—in other words, to avoid trouble and consequences.

But Christians are on a different basis. We are to stop lying not to avoid trouble, but because lies are part of the old life which has been totally judged and crucified upon the cross. We have made a decision to speak the truth because the life of lying and cover-ups must be completely put off in order for our lives to be flooded by the Spirit of Truth.

So Paul says, "each of you must put off falsehood and speak truthfully to his neighbor." That is how we put on Christ. You see how practical that is? If you reject lying, and make a conscious, deliberate commitment to speak the truth—even if it hurts you—then you are living the new life and walking in the Spirit. This is not a mystical concept, but practical truth for living.

Paul goes on to explain the reason for putting away lies and putting on the truth: because "we are all members of one body." In the body of Christ, as members of Christ's life, we do not live only to ourselves. When we lie to one another, we hurt each other, and we wound the body of Christ. This is true even if we lie to someone outside the body of Christ, since we are all injured when any one of us lies. The lie of one Christian brings dishonor upon all Christians and upon Christ.

More than once I have heard people say, "You know, when I'm doing business with someone and he tells me he's a Christian, that's when I grab my wallet. I've been burned so many times by Christians, I've decided I can never trust a Christian." Why do some people have that impression of Christians? Because there are Christians who have lied. Those lies injure the cause of Christ. Because you and I are members of one another in the body of Christ, we must put off all falsehood and deal only in the truth.

But what about "little white lies"? Aren't some lies harmless? The fact is, so-called "little white lies" can be the cruelest of all! Sometimes we lie to spare a person's feelings (which actually means that we are too cowardly to speak the truth). If someone asks, "How do I look?" and you shrink back from saying, "There's a big piece of spinach stuck in your teeth," are you really doing that person a favor? Is that kindness—or cowardice?

And there are situations where the stakes are much higher. We don't wish to offend a friend, so we fail to speak the truth that needs to be spoken: "It's wrong for you and your girlfriend to live together unmarried." Or, "You are in no position to care for that child as an unmarried teenage mother; you need to consider allowing your child to be adopted into a loving, Christian, two-parent home." Or, "That joke you told was immoral and unpleasing to the Lord." Or, "I'm taking you aside privately to tell you that I was offended by the way you spoke to the pastor during the meeting." Or, "No, I don't think it was smart to cheat on your taxes. You need to ask God's forgiveness and make amends to the government for what you did." Or, "No, I don't think there are many paths to God. Jesus said, 'I am the way, the truth, and the life; no one comes to the Father but by Me,' so I am praying that you will turn your life over to Him."

We are to speak the truth with each other in the church, and with those who are outside the faith. The only way we can grow as Christians is if others in the body of Christ tell us the truth about ourselves. And the only way nonChristians will come to Christ is if Christians tell them the truth they need to hear. Truth is the sign of the new life, the new self.

We must put off falsehood. We must put on truth.

BE ANGRY—BUT DO NOT SIN!

Next, Paul moves to another issue that touches us all—the problem of anger. In verses 26 and 27, Paul writes: " 'In your anger do not sin': Do not let the sun go down while you are still angry, and do not give the devil a foothold." The New Revised Standard Version puts that opening phrase in very strong terms: "Be angry but do not sin." That is not a misprint! It really does say, "Be angry."

How can that be? Simply, this means that God understands our capacity for anger. Anger can be expressed in sinful ways, but anger is not sin as such. In fact, our human capacity for anger is part of the image of God in us! God gets angry—and rightfully so. If you do not get angry from time to time, there is something wrong with you. There are unjust, unrighteous things that happen in the world that should make our blood boil! So Paul says, "Be angry but do not sin."

Yes, there is a sinful kind of anger. How do we know when anger is righteous and when anger is sinful? Well, selfish anger is sinful anger.

If we lash out in anger because our pride has been wounded, because we feel slighted or insulted, that is sinful. This doesn't mean we are to be doormats for others to wipe their feet on. Sometimes, when rude, abrasive, or abusive people try to push us around, it is in their own best interests that we stand up to them and tell them that what they are doing is sinful and destructive—that is speaking the truth! But before we unleash our anger, we need to make sure that our anger is not merely rooted in our own pride and selfishness.

Justifiable anger is that which is concerned with the wounds and hurts of others. We should be angry with injustice, hatred, crime, racism, immorality, blasphemy, and other sins against the innocent or against God. You see this kind of righteous indignation in the life of the Lord Jesus. He was angry with the Pharisees who opposed His healings on the Sabbath (see Mark 3:5). He was angry when the disciples kept the children away from Him (see Mark 10:14). He was angry with the money changers who had dishonored the Temple, His Father's house (see Matthew 21:12; Mark 11:15; John 2:15).

Yet we also see that when Jesus was reviled, when He was personally attacked, He did not respond with self-defensive anger. "When they hurled their insults at him, he did not retaliate," says 1 Peter 2:23. "When he suffered, he made no threats. Instead, he entrusted himself to him who judges justly." And Paul teaches us in Romans 12:19, "Do not take revenge, my friends, but leave room for God's wrath, for it is written: 'It is mine to avenge; I will repay,' says the Lord." So we are to put off selfish, self-defensive anger that arises from a deceitful urge.

Yet, Paul makes it clear that even righteous anger must be managed in a righteous way or it becomes sin. "Do not let the sun go down while you are still angry," he writes, "and do not give the devil a foothold." Paul is saying, "Do not hold a grudge, do not let your anger carry over to another day." And let's not be slavishly literal about this advice. Let's not take it to mean that we can explode in anger at 6 a.m., and think, "Well, I've got twelve hours till sundown, so I've got a whole day to nurse this grudge before I have to resolve it." Paul is saying that after the first flush of anger subsides, let reason and righteousness prevail and resolve the matter quickly.

Anger can be a useful motivator at times. It is occasionally needed to prod us into action, to get us moving as we should. When we hear of some gross injustice, it is right that we become angry and that we act to remove that in injustice. So don't condemn yourself for your righteous indignation—but at the same time, don't let righteous anger fester and turn to sinful, destructive bitterness, which only poisons your life and your relationships. The holiest, most righteous anger is that which arises not out of hatred toward your enemy, but out of love toward someone who is being unjustly treated.

Paul adds a final word of warning regarding anger: If you do not deal with anger promptly and righteously, you give the devil an opportunity. An opportunity for what? To create bitterness in your own life and the lives of others. The writer to the Hebrews puts it this way: "See to it that no one misses the grace of God and that no bitter root grows up to cause trouble and defile many" (Hebrews 12:15). Unresolved, unrighteous anger can give Satan a foothold in our lives which can metastasize and spread like cancer throughout a family and throughout a church. We need to make sure that Satan has no opportunity to move into our lives and set up housekeeping.

STEAL NO MORE

While he was prime minister of Great Britain, Winston Churchill once hosted a posh state dinner, attended by dignitaries from around the world. At one point, he was taken aside by the head butler, who quietly informed him that Lady So-and-so had been observed stealing a silver salt-shaker and placing it in her purse. "How do you suggest this matter be handled?" asked the butler.

"Leave it to me," replied Churchill. The prime minister then made his way across the room, pausing along the way to pick up the matching pepper shaker from the dinner table. He stepped up to Lady So-and-so, took her by the arm, and guided her out of earshot of the other guests. Then he pulled the pepper shaker from his pocket and showed it to the woman. "My dear lady," he said in a guilty-sounding voice, "I think we've been seen! Perhaps we'd better *both* put them back!"

The next practical issue Paul addresses in Ephesians 4 is the issue of stealing. "He who has been stealing," he says in verse 28, "must steal no longer, but must work, doing something useful with his own hands, that he may have something to share with those in need." The King James Version puts it, "Let him that stole, steal no more. Let him labor with his hands."

I recall one fellow who tried to take advantage of the fact that, in the original Greek language of the New Testament, there were no paragraphs, sentences, or punctuation marks in the text—just words that ran together unbroken on the page. So this fellow got the idea of altering King James text to his own advantage by rearranging the punctuation. In his version, that verse read, "let him that stole steal. No more let him labor with his hands." Perhaps this is an indicator of how far the sinful heart will go to justify itself!

But the true sense of this verse is an unequivocal demand that Christians stop stealing. At first glance, we are tempted to respond, "Well, that's a strange command to issue to the church! There are no professional thieves in my church!" But Paul is not only addressing the professional thief. He is talking to amateurs as well.

Who is an amateur thief? Well, it's the shoplifter. It's the tax dodger. It's the person who fudges the bookkeeping—just a bit. It's the person who borrows without returning, or who says nothing when the clerk at the grocery store gives back too much change. It is the small businessman who embellishes his advertising with "over-enthusiastic" (that is, false) claims. It is the individual who hides the defects in the home or car he is selling, then rationalizes his deception with the phrase *caveat emptor*—let the buyer beware.

Paul says, "He who has been stealing must steal no longer." Why? Because all theft, whether it is a billion-dollar break-in at Fort Knox or making unauthorized copies on the copy machine at work—is an expression of the old, fallen, egocentric life that has been crucified on the cross. It is the old self that craves unearned gain, and looks for any shortcut to riches. That is a deceitful urge, an urge that lies to you.

When Jesus hung on the cross, He was hung between two thieves. At that moment, when He was made sin on our behalf (see 2 Corinthians 5:21), He became a thief. He also became a liar, a drunkard, a murderer—He was made sin, so that all our sins could be crucified in Him. When He became what we are, God put Him to death, because that is what this old self deserves. There is nothing good in it and nothing good can come from it. That is what stealing always manifests—a total self-absorption and an utter lack of concern for someone else, for their feelings, needs, and wants.

What does the rest of the verse say? "He who has been stealing must steal no longer," writes Paul, "but must work, doing something useful with his own hands, that he may have something to share with those in need." That is putting on Christ. We are not merely to put off stealing, we are to put on Christ. Putting off is a necessary but negative step; that is, it is stated in the negative: "steal no longer." But simply not stealing is not enough. We must take a further step, a positive step. We must put on Christ, and the way we put on Christ is by demonstrating generosity, by actively demonstrating a positive concern and compassion for the less fortunate.

When we put on Christ, our motive for giving is transformed. Out of a Christlike heart, we want to give joyously, generously, hilariously. That is why Paul writes to the Corinthians, "God loves a cheerful giver" (2 Corinthians 9:7). There is no joy like the joy of giving, for it manifests a heart of love and concern for the interest of others. And that is positive, practical Christianity—not merely putting off the old but also putting on the new, putting on Christ.

EVIL CONVERSATION

There is an old joke about a witness in a court trial. As the trial begins, he is called to the witness stand to be sworn in. "Put your hand on the Bible and raise your right hand," says the bailiff. "Do you swear—"

"No," the witness interjects, "but I know all the words!"

In this corrupt and evil age, we have to acknowledge that we, like that witness, know all the words, rude and objectionable words, insulting words, hurtful words, careless words, unwholesome words. But those words should never come out of the mouth of a Christian who has put off the old self and has put on Christ. So the issue Paul now brings before us is the issue of evil conversation. In verse 29, Paul writes, "Do not let any unwholesome talk come out of your mouths, but only what is helpful for building others up according to their needs, that it may benefit those who listen."

In the original Greek, Paul literally says, "Let no rotten words come out of your mouths." That covers the whole range of evil speech, from vile obscenities to idle rumors and careless gossip. Rotten words are words that are corrupt, and that spread corruption.

Our society is drenched with pornography, filth, and lewd speech. It assaults us in print, on our TV screens, and on our home computer screens, via the Internet. The tendency of the world today is to throw off all restrictions, all boundaries of decency, as if notions of modesty are a form of slavery. In reality, corrupt and evil speech are manifestations of a much more profound and horrible slavery—the slavery of being bound by sin, egocentrism, and the old unredeemed self.

So Christians are to shun all forms of unwholesome talk, which arises from the old life. You cannot put on Christ while at the same time indulging in loose talk and corrupt conversation. Paul will return to this subject in Ephesians 5:4–5:

> Nor should there be obscenity, foolish talk or coarse joking, which are out of place, but rather thanksgiving. For of this you can be sure: No immoral, impure or greedy person—such a man is an idolater—has any inheritance in the kingdom of Christ and of God.

There is no room in the Christian life for evil speech. It is a part of the old self. It must be put off in order for the life of Christ to be put on.

A friend of mine, the owner of a print shop, was once at the counter when a customer came in to have some cards printed up. My friend saw that the content of the card was obscene. "I don't print this kind of thing," said my friend.

"Oh, come on!" the would-be customer cajoled. "Don't be like that! Everybody likes this stuff—it's just that some people are embarrassed to admit it! Come on—deep down, you know you like to look at stuff like this!"

"Sure, I admit it," said my friend. "In my old self, my sinful nature,

I'm tempted by things like this. But when I committed my life to Jesus Christ, I made a decision to put all of these kinds of things out of my life. I'm human like everyone else, and there's a part of me that can easily lust for this kind of thing—but I don't intend to feed it."

My friend understood what it means to put off the old and put on the new. He would not let any unwholesome communication come out of his mouth—or out of his printing press.

Here again we see that it's not enough to avoid evil speech. That is merely putting off the old. We must take a positive step. We must put on the new. We must give ourselves to good speech, positive speech, constructive speech. As Paul says in verse 29, we must actively, aggressively, volitionally commit ourselves to speech that "is helpful for building others up according to their needs, that it may benefit those who listen."

It is not enough to put off evil. We go a step further and put on the good. It is not enough to put away falsehood. We must aggressively speak the truth. It is not enough to simply avoid sinful anger. We must use righteous anger to motivate us to seek justice. It is not enough to simply stop stealing. We must live productive lives and give generously out of our productivity to improve the lives of others. It is not enough to simply stop "cussing" or spreading vile rumors. We have to use our power of speech to build others up and benefit those around us.

THE KEY TO PRACTICAL CHRISTIANITY

Genuine Christianity is always demonstrated by a concern for the well-being of others, and for the influence we have on others. The apostle James deals pointedly with this issue in his epistle:

> We all stumble in many ways. If anyone is never at fault in what he says, he is a perfect man, able to keep his whole body in check.

When we put bits into the mouths of horses to make them obey us, we can turn the whole animal. Or take ships as an example. Although they are so large and are driven by strong winds, they are steered by a very small rudder wherever the pilot wants to go. Likewise the tongue is a small part of the body, but it makes great boasts. Consider what a great forest is set on fire by a small spark. The tongue also is a fire, a world of evil among the parts of the body. It corrupts the whole person, sets the whole course of his life on fire, and is itself set on fire by hell.

All kinds of animals, birds, reptiles and creatures of the sea are being tamed and have been tamed by man, but no man can tame the tongue. It is a restless evil, full of deadly poison.

With the tongue we praise our Lord and Father, and with it we curse men, who have been made in God's likeness. Out of the same mouth come praise and cursing. My brothers, this should not be (3:2–10).

James goes on at considerable length on the subject of unwholesome speech—and his conclusion is the same as Paul's in Ephesians: Those who belong to Christ, who have put on the new self, must not allow the old self to rule their speech. Out of the same mouth should not come praise to God and curses against other people. Either the old self rules or the new. Either the flesh is in control or the Spirit. If the Spirit controls our speech, then the evidence of the Spirit is not merely the absence of cursing but the presence of God's words of peace, blessing, and edification.

As members of the body of Christ, we are not just people who put off the old, we are people who put on the new. Being a Christian means more than merely doing no harm. We are called to be a positive force for good in the lives of one another, and in the world.

I once heard a fable that dramatically expresses this truth. It is the story of a man who was given the opportunity to visit both hell and heaven. He was transported by God to hell, a terrible place filled with incredible suffering. There, the man saw thousands of people who were starving, thirsting, wretched, and miserable. Most of all, he was struck by the fact that everyone in hell had stiff arms that would not bend at the elbows. As a result, they could not minister to their own needs. The people of hell could not feed themselves. They could not dress themselves. They could not clean themselves. They could not do anything for themselves. It was the most distressing sight this man had ever seen, and it broke his heart that he was unable to do anything to help the lost men and women who were doomed to such an existence. He couldn't wait to get away from hell.

When the man had seen enough, God transported him out of hell and into heaven. Once in heaven, the man was shocked to see that, like the people in hell, the people in heaven had stiff arms that would not bend at the elbows. They could not minister to their own needs, nor could they feed or clean themselves. The people of heaven were just as helpless as the people of hell—yet they seemed well-fed, well-dressed, clean, and completely happy. Heaven seemed to be exactly as it ought to be—a place of utter joy and bliss.

"How can this be?" the man wondered. "These people have stiff, unbending arms just like the people of hell—yet they are happy and healthy!"

Then the man noticed the Tree of Life, loaded with luscious fruit. There were people gathered around the Tree. With their stiff, unbending arms, they were picking the fruit, even though they were powerless to bring the fruit to their own lips and feed themselves. Seeing those people with the fruit in their hands, the man finally understood the difference between the people of heaven and the people of hell.

The people of heaven were *feeding each other*!

That is the great difference between the old self and the new self. The old self is egocentric, selfish, wretched, and miserable. It is rightfully condemned and nailed to the cross because it does not reach out to others. It is powerless to transcend its own limitations.

The new self, which is Christ living in us, transcends the self and reaches out to others. It is focused on serving others and obeying God. That is the key to the new life, the heavenly life. That is the key to living out the joyful demands of practical Christianity.

CHAPTER TWENTY-TWO

Forgive, Love—and Live!

Ephesians 4:30–5:2

There is an oft-quoted prayer of an anonymous child who prayed, "Lord, make the bad people good and the good people nice." I think we all empathize with that prayer. So often it seems that being religious has a souring effect. We all know people who are undeniably "good" in the sense that they are moral, honest, upright, and truthful—yet they are often cold, rigid, and unpleasant to be around. Such people are not nice at all!

If you are that kind of Christian, then you have not yet entered into New Testament Christianity. A holy but not-nice Christian is an incomplete Christian—he or she has not experienced all the spiritual growth and spiritual joy that God intended for us. When we put off the old self and put on Christ, we did not put on sour personality—that is not what our Lord Jesus Christ is like at all! A genuine Christian demonstrates not only the morality and truth of Christ, but the character of Christ—his warmth, graciousness, and love.

As I read through the four Gospels, I am struck by the fact that Jesus was extremely popular and in demand. People wanted to be around Him. His personality was a magnet that drew people to Him like flies drawn to honey. Clearly, Jesus could not have attracted thousands with a gloomy and intimidating demeanor. Yes, He felt the hurts and needs of others so deeply that the prophet Isaiah pictured Him as a Man of sorrows, acquainted with grief (see Isaiah 53:3). But it was the warmth of His radiant personality that penetrated and lifted the gloom of others. That was one of the principle reasons He was so loved and sought-after.

That same character is reflected in the one who learns to put off the old self and put on Christ. Being a Christian must make a definite, definable difference in your life. Authentic conversion is evident in a changed life. Most of us think of this change in negative terms: A Christian does not lie, does not fly into a rage, doesn't steal, and doesn't indulge in unwholesome talk. But is that all there is to being a practicing Christian?

I remember as a young Christian hearing a jingle that satirized Christians of the "thou shalt not" variety:

> Rooty-toot toot! Rooty-toot toot!
> We are the boys from the Institute.
> We don't smoke and we don't chew
> And we don't go out with girls that do.

That is the impression that the world gets of Christian negativism, a kind of smug, self-righteous pietism that completely misses the point of authentic biblical Christianity. The faith that Jesus came to give us is not a negative faith. It is not concerned primarily with taboos against smoking, drinking, dancing, gambling, or movies. Genuine Christianity is a joyful faith.

THE PRESENCE OF THE SPIRIT

In Ephesians 4:30–32, the apostle Paul reveals to us the key to a changed, positive Christian life: the presence of the Holy Spirit:

> And do not grieve the Holy Spirit of God, with whom you were sealed for the day of redemption. Get rid of all bitterness, rage and anger, brawling and slander, along with every form of malice. Be kind and compassionate to one another, forgiving each other, just as in Christ God forgave you.

In that opening sentence, the apostle Paul puts his finger on the heart of the whole matter: "do not grieve the Holy Spirit of God." The key to all human behavior lies in our relationship with God, not our relationship with our fellow human beings. Once our relationship with God is what it ought to be, all our other relationships can come into alignment. The key to the Christian life is the presence of God, in the Person of the Holy Spirit.

We have difficulties in getting along with people. There are those who irritate us, and whose personalities clash with ours. There are those who constantly sabotage our plans, either by their thoughtless actions or by their deliberate destructiveness. The place to begin solving our troubled human relationships is not with other people but with our relationship to God. Our relationship with our brother or sister will inevitably reflect our relationship to God. It always does.

Paul says we must not grieve the Holy Spirit. What does that mean? The word *grieve* is related to love. It is impossible for you to grieve someone who does not love you. If someone who does not love you is offended by what you do, he is not grieved, but angry and enraged.

Grief is always an indication of love. So this word reveals that God loves us. The Holy Spirit is in us, as Christians, in order to help us, to bless us, to strengthen us, and to teach us how to live. Because He loves us, the actions that grieve the Spirit are those actions that bring harm to us.

SEALED BY THE SPIRIT

Why should we not grieve the Holy Spirit of God? Because, says the apostle Paul, Christians are sealed by Him unto the day of redemption. What does that mean? A seal is a protective device, designed to prevent loss.

As a boy, I lived along the main line of the Great Northern Railroad in North Dakota. My friends and I often played along the tracks. I discovered as a boy that the railroad used seals to protect their boxcars. The railroad seals were long aluminum strips with a ball on the end and a slit in the ball. When the free end of the strip was brought through the door and fastened in the slot of the ball, there was no way to pull it out again. The box car was sealed and protected for the length of its journey—all the way to its destination.

That's the sense of the phrase Paul uses here. The Holy Spirit is given to us as a protective seal for the length of its journey, a guarantee that we will arrive at our destination, which is "the day of redemption"—the day of the resurrection and the completion of God's activity of salvation for human beings. We see this clearly in Ephesians 1:13–14, where the apostle writes:

> And you also were included in Christ when you heard the word of truth, the gospel of your salvation. Having believed, you were marked in him with a seal, the promised Holy Spirit, who is a deposit guaranteeing our inheritance

until the redemption of those who are God's possession—
to the praise of his glory.

We learn from this that the Holy Spirit has been given to everyone who believes in Jesus Christ. The seal of the Spirit is the mark of
a Christian. So, from a biblical point of view, it is incorrect to apply
the label "Christian" to someone who is not indwelt and sealed by
the Holy Spirit. As Paul says in Romans 8:9, "You, however, are
controlled not by the sinful nature but by the Spirit, if the Spirit of
God lives in you. And if anyone does not have the Spirit of Christ,
he does not belong to Christ." You may be a church member, you
may have been religious all your life—but unless you have believed
in the Lord Jesus and received the gift of the Holy Spirit, you are
not a Christian.

The seal of the Holy Spirit is not something you feel. Rather, the
Spirit takes up quiet residence within you at the moment you commit your faith and trust to Jesus Christ. When the Spirit takes up
residence within you, He does so permanently. He has promised
that, even if you grieve and offend Him, He will not leave you—even
though you might think He has, because your guilt-stricken conscience will tell you that a wall of silence has gone up between you
and the Spirit within you. The Spirit will never leave you, but if you
grieve the Spirit, you will have to live with a grieved Spirit within you.

Do you know what that is like? Have you ever sensed what it
means to live with a grieved Spirit within you? Let me describe it to
you—and I'm sure you'll recognize the pattern. First, there is a sense
of inner conflict, a tension, a restlessness. The Holy Spirit is pulling
you in one direction, while the lusts of the flesh pull you in another
direction. Paul, in Galatians, describes this tension as a civil war that
rages within us. The Spirit lusts against the flesh, and the flesh against

the Spirit, so that we cannot do the things we know in our spirit we want to do (see Galatians 5:17).

If nothing is done about that sense of turmoil and tension, if those feelings go unheeded, then we become fragmented and divided against ourselves. Soon we become unhappy and depressed, joyless and listless. This is why Christians sometimes seem to drag themselves and force themselves to do their "Christian duty." This is why Christians often seem to lack energy for their ministry tasks. Christianity was never intended to be a chore carried out under a burden of duty. When our lives are in harmony with the Spirit of God, we feel energized for the tasks God has given us to do.

The Spirit of God is described in Scripture as the energizing force within us as Christians. In Colossians 1:29, Paul speaks of his ministry as "struggling with all his energy, which so powerfully works in me." So the Spirit is our driving force, and there is something wrong if we find ourselves continually having to drag ourselves and force ourselves to do what we ought to do. The Spirit of God is a driving energy.

Certainly there will be times when we are physically or emotionally tired, and feelings of weariness at such times are understandable and normal. But when we are lethargic and lukewarm for weeks at a time, it indicates that something is wrong. We need to search ourselves and ask God in prayer if we have done something to grieve the Spirit of God.

Another sign that we may have grieved the Holy Spirit is fear—a numbing, nagging sense of anxiety and dread. It's tragic but true: Some Christians live for years at a time in such a state, haunted by fear. The Bible makes it clear that we were never intended to live with fear. Again and again, Jesus said to His disciples, "Fear not." Why? "For I am with you."

Feelings of anxiety and dread indicate a rift in the relationship between ourselves and God. "There is no fear in love," says 1 John 4:18. "But perfect love drives out fear, because fear has to do with punishment. The one who fears is not made perfect in love." If there is fear gripping our hearts, it is a sign that something has interfered with the flow of the perfect love of the Holy Spirit within us.

Another indication that the Holy Spirit is grieved within us is when we become cold and hard toward one another. The Spirit is like a fire, and fire is warm and attractive. The Christian who is cold and forbidding has a blockage that interferes with the flow of the love of the Spirit in his life. He has grieved the Holy Spirit.

THE TWO STEPS OF FORGIVENESS

In verse 31 Paul begins to list for us the kinds of attitudes and actions that grieve the Holy Spirit: "Get rid of all bitterness, rage and anger, brawling and slander, along with every form of malice." Certainly, the sins Paul described earlier in this chapter cause the Holy Spirit to grieve, but sins such as lying and stealing are obvious and easily discerned. More subtle and deceptive are those sins we harbor within, where others can't see. Bitter attitudes, simmering anger, slander, and malice can easily be masked by an insincere smile. What are these sins?

Bitterness is a hard, cynical outlook toward life and toward other people. Rage is a hotheaded, explosive passion we refuse to restrain. Anger is a boiling inner desire to punish others and take revenge in your own hands. Brawling is a loud, confrontational attitude toward others, an eagerness to get in someone's face and intimidate them. Slander is speech that injures others—a crafty, subtle rumormongering that destroys reputations. Malice is malignity—a dark, brooding hunger for seeing others hurt. We may rationalize these feelings as justifiable because of what someone has done to us, but these sins are destructive to ourselves and others. They bring grief and sorrow to the Holy Spirit within us.

Paul goes on to give us the solution in verse 32: "Be kind and compassionate to one another, forgiving each other, just as in Christ God forgave you." That is the essence of Christianity. That is the nature of the Holy Spirit within us. The more we give ourselves over to the control of the Spirit, the more kind, compassionate, and forgiving we become—and the more *Christian* (that is, Christlike) we become.

"But Ray," you might protest, "you don't know what I'm up against! You don't know what this person or that person has done to me! If you were in my shoes you wouldn't be able to forgive either! I *can't* forgive that person—so don't ask me to!" I have heard many Christians say that to me over the years. And there may well be a sense in which this is true.

When you feel you cannot forgive someone, it is because you are trying to take step two before you have taken step one described in Ephesians 4:31–32, where the two steps are given in their proper order. Step one, as stated in verse 31, is to deal with the bitterness, rage, anger, brawling, slander, and malice in your own life. So first you must deal with your own sin, your own attitude. Then you can go on to step two, forgiveness. You cannot forgive while your attitude is all wrong. That is where the Christian must begin.

But that's not where we want to start, is it? We want to start with the other person, with the irritation, pain, and humiliation he or she has caused us. But God says, "No, first remove the big wooden beam of sin in your own eye—then you will see clearly how to remove the dust-mote of sin from your brother's eye" (see Matthew 7:3–4 and Luke 6:41–42). Begin with yourself and your own sins. That is the first step. Then you will be able to take the second step, forgiveness.

And how are we to forgive? "Just as in Christ God forgave you." Our forgiveness is to be patterned after that of the One who forgave us. His forgiveness—which He expressed toward the woman caught in adultery (John 8), the paralytic (Matthew 9, Mark 2, Luke 5), and those who crucified Him (Luke 23:34)—was instantaneous, abundant, and complete. He didn't forgive as we usually do, making sure that the other person has suffered and squirmed enough first. We take great pleasure in extracting our pound of flesh before we reluctantly and grudgingly say, "Well—all right, I forgive you." The forgiveness of Jesus was an immediate release of a sinner from condemnation. That is the pattern He has set for you and me.

Have you forgotten how God forgave you in Christ? The Lord's Supper is designed to remind us of all He has forgiven us, in order that we would forgive each other the same way. Think of it. He forgave you before you repented, didn't He? He forgave you before there was any sign of turning on your part. The moment you turned to Him in repentance, you discovered that His forgiveness was already there.

We see His forgiveness illustrated in the Parable of the Prodigal Son and the Loving Father. That father's heart yearned after the offending son, despite the boy's selfish, willful, stubborn rebellion. The father stood on a hill every day, hoping for his boy's return, longing to take the boy in his arms and open to him a heart overflowing with forgiveness. The moment he finally saw his son off in the distance, returning home, the father ran to the boy and flung his arms around the boy's neck and showed him forgiveness.

Not only did God forgive us even before we repented, but He forgave us despite all the hurt we have caused Him. We say, "I know I should forgive, but you don't know how much that person hurt me!" But God *does* know—and He has forgiven you of all that and more.

He has forgiven you of a lifetime of sin and rebellion that was so black and evil that it caused His Son to be nailed to a cross. But God does not desire revenge against you. He forgives you and loves you and wants to embrace you as His child.

God has forgiven everything you ever did against Him, and He will never remind you of it again, and never remember it himself. We will remember, but God won't. Paul called himself the "chief of sinners," because he was once a persecutor of the church. Paul never forgot that—but God did. God forgave him completely, through and through.

That is what our forgiveness is to be like. That is how our Christianity is made manifest to the world: "Be kind and compassionate to one another, forgiving each other, just as in Christ God forgave you."

BE GODLIKE

The task of Christianity is not primarily to get us ready for heaven—that is the easy part. We achieve salvation by grace through faith in Jesus Christ. The tough part is not heaven but earth. The major task of the Christian faith is to equip us for life here on this planet. So the theme of the Scriptures is how we are to handle life, with all its stress and pressure, temptation and allure, heartache and suffering, confusion and fear.

We are not here, either as a collective church or as individual Christians, primarily to make the world a better place to live in. Instead, we are to be better people in a terrible world—and as a by-product of becoming the kind of people God wants us to be, we will make the world a better place. And we have been given the secret that makes us the kind of people God wants us to be. Paul states the great secret of Christian living in the next two verses, Ephesians 5:1–2:

> Be imitators of God, therefore as dearly loved children
> and live a life of love, just as Christ loved us and gave him-
> self up for us as a fragrant offering and sacrifice to God.

What does Paul mean, "Be imitators of God"? In the original text, the word for *imitators* is the Greek word that means "to mimic," to be a mimicker of God. Mimics are those who follow the pattern or the example of God. That is what we are to be. In a word, we are to be "Godlike." We are to be Godlike people in an ungodly world.

Paul adds to this word *imitators* the word-picture "as dearly loved children." This suggests the idea of the little child who looks at Daddy's example, Mommy's example, and wants to follow those big footsteps. If you're a parent, you remember the day your child came up to you perhaps with Daddy's big shoes on his feet or Mommy's big hat or scarf on her head, and said, "Look! I'm going to be just like you!" Remember how your heart went out to that child? That is how God looks upon us, His dearly beloved children, when we put on His characteristics—His love and forgiveness, for example—and we come up to Him and say, "Look, Heavenly Daddy! I'm going to be just like you!"

How are we to be Godlike? Obviously, this does not mean we are to be like God in terms of His omnipotence, omniscience, or omnipresence—we are limited by our humanity in those regards. The New Agers and occultists would have you believe we can be like God in those ways, imbued with supernatural powers and knowledge—but that is all a lie of the devil. We cannot be like God in those ways, but we can be like God in terms of His character. That is how we are to mimic and imitate God. We are to be holy, righteous, forgiving, kind, and loving as He is.

When we imitate God in this way, He gives us Godlike power to do great things. As Paul will later tell us in Ephesians 6:10, "Finally, be strong in the Lord and in his mighty power." There is no strength like God's strength. His is the greatest strength there is. Ultimately, to be Godlike is to be strong and filled with power to do the unbelievable and the unimaginable. It's not the same power that the world admires and desires. The power of God is quieter and less visible than political power or the power of the dollar or the power of a strong personality—but God's power is far mightier than these.

How, then are we to imitate God? Verse 2 explains that the key to living Godlike lives is to "live a life of love, just as Christ loved us and gave himself up for us as a fragrant offering and sacrifice to God." That is the key: Self-sacrificing love.

Do you know what it means to love? It means that you begin to see others as people instead of things—people with needs and feelings, people who are made in the image of God. Instead of seeing people as either objects of usefulness to you, or obstacles that hinder you, you put yourself in their place, realize that they have difficulties, heartaches, problems, joys, annoyances, yearnings, and aspirations just as you do.

When you begin to truly love, you become aware that the individual who seems so poised, confident, and maybe even arrogant is really just a scared child inside, putting up a big front. That enables you to understand and even reach out to this person who may be an annoyance or an obstacle in our life. You find that it is possible to look past the abrasiveness and see that person's need of love and understanding.

When you begin to truly love, you become aware that the cruel, cold, callous person who intimidates you was once badly hurt by life. His rough exterior is a defensive shell to prevent him from being hurt again. He's not tough—he's wounded. He needs love and understanding as much as anyone you've ever known.

When you begin to truly love, you begin to see qualities and worth in people you once wrote off as weak or boring or not worth your time. You take an interest in people you never noticed before. You appreciate people not just for what they can do for you or how attractive you find them, but simply because they are God's children, uniquely made in His image. You discover that you want to help them, to uphold them, to take an interest in their lives—and in the process, you discover that your life has become enriched by their presence. That is what Godlike love is all about.

Paul closes this with a wonderful illustration: "Christ loved us and gave himself up for us as a fragrant offering and sacrifice to God." The Lord Jesus Christ revealed to us what a Godlike life is all about, in that He is truly God and truly human. As the Son of God, He emptied himself and endured the cross in order to save us. That is love to the utmost, love that sacrifices all for the sake of another. Obedient to God, thinking of you and me, forgetful of himself, Jesus stretched himself out upon the rugged beams of that instrument of torture and took your place and mine beneath the righteous judgment of God. That is love to the Nth degree.

That is the pattern we are to imitate. There is no room in the Godlike life for the ugly attitudes and sins that belong to the old life—bitterness, rage, anger, brawling, slander, and malice. These are poisonous to your soul. Rid yourself of those poisons *now*. Paul's message to us is clear:

Forgive, love—and live!

CHAPTER TWENTY-THREE

Live as Children of Light

Ephesians 5:3–14

A college coach in a Christian school once told me of a young man in his school who said, "I'll follow the school rules in almost everything, but nobody is going to tell me what to do with my sex life." This attitude used to be an exception. Today it is the rule.

When I was a young man, it was called promiscuity. In the 1960s it was called "the New Morality." By the 1990s, society had proclaimed that moral absolutes had been replaced by "moral relativism"—you have your morality, I have mine, and no one should ever judge or criticize another person's moral (or immoral) choices. In keeping with the "nonjudgmental" mood of the times, the word *promiscuous* was replaced by the nonjudgmental phrase "sexually active." The slogan of the times has become, "If it feels good, do it!"

Today, living together unmarried is considered normal. Public schools teach sexual techniques in sex ed classes, take teenage girls out of class to get abortions without their parents' knowledge, and distribute condoms to teens in the belief that, "They're going to do it anyway." Gone are the days when the public schools teach values, self-respect, and self-control. Promiscuous sex is a regular topic in our music and on TV sitcoms in the family hour. Sex scandals regularly rock our political institutions and even our churches and Christian ministries. Our media and our society is drenched in illicit sex. Rarely do we see sexual issues addressed in our culture from the viewpoint that sex is God's gift to be practiced in marriage.

As we consider the sexual overload that bombards our senses, we are tempted to think we have reached unprecedented depths of cultural decay. The truth is that the present state of our society today is strikingly similar to conditions found in the first century A.D., when Paul's letters were being written. In Romans 1, Paul describes the sordid and lewd society he lived in:

> The wrath of God is being revealed from heaven against all the godlessness and wickedness of men who suppress the truth by their wickedness . . . .
>
> Therefore God gave them over in the sinful desires of their hearts to sexual impurity for the degrading of their bodies with one another. They exchanged the truth of God for a lie, and worshiped and served created things rather than the Creator—who is forever praised. Amen.
>
> Because of this, God gave them over to shameful lusts. Even their women exchanged natural relations for unnatural ones. In the same way the men also abandoned natural relations with women and were inflamed with lust for one another. Men committed indecent acts with other men, and received in themselves the due penalty for their perversion.
>
> Furthermore, since they did not think it worthwhile to retain the knowledge of God, he gave them over to a depraved mind, to do what ought not to be done. They have

become filled with every kind of wickedness, evil, greed and depravity. They are full of envy, murder, strife, deceit and malice. They are gossips, slanderers, God-haters, insolent, arrogant and boastful; they invent ways of doing evil; they disobey their parents; they are senseless, faithless, heartless, ruthless. Although they know God's righteous decree that those who do such things deserve death, they not only continue to do these very things but also approve of those who practice them (18, 24–32).

Sounds familiar, doesn't it? After two thousand years, these conditions are as rampant as they ever were. Paul has not written a musty document of only historical interest. Inspired by God, he has written a document of truth that blazes its way into our own century, our own society, our own hearts and lives. Now we come to Paul's treatment of the issue of sexual morality in Ephesians 5. Paul writes:

But among you there must not be even a hint of sexual immorality, or of any kind of impurity, or of greed, because these are improper for God's holy people. Nor should there be obscenity, foolish talk or coarse joking, which are out of place, but rather thanksgiving. For of this you can be sure: No immoral, impure or greedy person—such a man is an idolater—has any inheritance in the kingdom of Christ and of God. Let no one deceive you with empty words, for because of such things God's wrath comes on those who are disobedient. Therefore do not be partners with them.

For you were once darkness, but now you are light in the Lord. Live as children of light (for the fruit of the light consists in all goodness righteousness and truth) and find out what pleases the Lord. Have nothing to do with the fruitless deeds of darkness, but rather expose them. For it is shameful even to mention what the disobedient do in secret. But everything exposed by the light becomes visible, for it is light that makes everything visible. This is why it is said: "Wake up, O sleeper, rise from the dead, and Christ will shine on you" (3–14).

Paul makes it abundantly clear: Sexual immorality and Christianity do not mix. God's intention for man is either marriage, with complete faithfulness to the partner, or total abstinence from sex. The Bible allows no third option.

FIVE REASONS FOR SHUNNING IMMORALITY

Paul goes on to give us five illuminating and logically consistent reasons why sexual immorality must be shunned by those who belong to Christ. Let's examine each of Paul's reasons, one by one. The first reason is given in verse 3: "But among you there must not be even a hint of sexual immorality, or of any kind of impurity, or of greed, because these are improper for God's holy people."

Reason Number 1: Sexual immorality defiles and debases our humanity. Note the terms Paul uses: *immorality, impurity,* and *greed. Immorality* is the most commonly used term in the Bible for any kind of sexual misconduct. *Impurity* is literally uncleanness, and refers to anything that is filthy or obscene. The word *greed* (some translations use *covetousness*) refers to greed for another person's body. Another word would be lust. Paul says that all of these things are forbidden to be even named among saints. It is not only the acts themselves that are prohibited, but talk of sexual expression outside of marriage is to be shunned.

Understand, Paul is not saying we should never talk about sex. He is saying we should not talk about distortions and perversions of God's gift of sex. The prudish sanction against frank talk about sex does not come from the Bible. If you read the Bible from beginning to end, you see that there is a lot of frank talk about sex. God likes sex. It is His invention, His creation, His gift to us to be used wisely. The Bible makes it clear that sex within marriage is beautiful, wholesome, and approved by God.

But the Bible is equally clear that sex outside of marriage is debasing and sinful. It defiles our basic humanity. God's prohibitions regarding sex are not designed to keep us from something good, but to enable us to enjoy the best and most wholesome sexual expression possible. So Paul calls us to honor marital sex and our own sexuality by not only shunning immorality, but by shunning even discussion of the sordid details of sexual immorality.

This statement was made in a day when sexual immorality was as widely tolerated and approved as it is today. In the city of Ephesus, there was a temple to a pagan goddess, and the worship of this goddess was conducted by the means of prostitute-priests and prostitute-priestesses. The whole city accepted and applauded sordid sex acts as a form of worship, a sign of religious dedication. So the admonition of Paul regarding sexual immorality runs directly counter to the culture the Ephesian Christians lived in.

We are told today that all sex is beautiful and natural, that if we feel an itch, we should scratch it, and if we feel an urge, we should indulge it. We are told that having sex whenever, wherever, and with whomever we please is simply the way we were made, and we should do so without shame or apology. This idea that sex, all sex, is natural and beautiful is a lie.

You could think of sex as a wonderful sandwich, piled high with ham and turkey, Swiss and provolone cheese, alfalfa sprouts, lettuce, tomato, peppers, the works. Set it on a nice clean plate on a table with a checkered tablecloth, and it's a wonderful feast. But what if you found that same sandwich out in the trash dumpster? Would you pull it out of the mounds of garbage, shoo away the flies, and begin eating? Why wouldn't you? Because, when you take something as wonderful as that sandwich and put it in a dirty place, it becomes defiled. If you feed yourself from a trash dumpster, no matter how good the food may taste, you can expect to get sick.

Sex is wonderful, alluring, and satisfying for human needs—in its proper place. It is a feast for all the senses. But having sex outside of God's plan for marriage is like eating a sandwich from the dumpster. It's bound to make you sick. It may make you physically sick. It will undoubtedly sicken your relationships with the people you care about. And it will make you spiritually, morally, and emotionally sick. It will, above all, sicken your relationship with God.

It is a lie of Satan that, since the sex drive is a natural urge, it should be indulged whenever or wherever it arises. We have many natural urges, but we regulate them all. We all experience hunger and thirst—but we don't go up to our neighbor and snatch the sandwich and soda can out of his hands and begin eating and drinking. "Hey, I was hungry and thirsty!" is no excuse for such behavior. Neither is "I had a natural urge" an excuse for taking sexual advantage of our neighbor's husband or wife.

The sex drive is a natural urge, but it requires regulation and restraint. And the intended regulation of sex is marriage. Any other sexual expression is a violation of Christian morality and of our basic humanity as well.

Sex is obviously the most complicated of our natural urges. It requires a partner, which no other urge does. And it is not only a physical union, but an emotional union as well. In fact, the emotional union is the more significant of the two. I have counseled many couples who have experienced the physical union of marital sex, but who are emotionally separated from each other. Their lives are empty and barren as a result. Sex is a complicated process, intended to be a total union of two beings, and only in marriage is such a total union possible. As C. S. Lewis observes,

> The monstrosity of sexual intercourse outside of marriage is that those who indulge in it are trying to isolate one kind of union (the physical) from all the other kinds of union which were intended to go along with it and make up the total union. The Christian attitude does not mean that there is anything wrong about sexual pleasure, any more than about the pleasure of eating. It means that you must not isolate that pleasure and try to get it by itself any more than you ought to try to get the pleasures of taste without swallowing and digesting, by chewing things and spitting them out again.

It is important to note that verse 3 is a continuation of the thought begun in verse 2. It begins with a conjunction *but*, which connects it to the previous sentence. So to properly understand Paul's thinking, his complete thought should be read as a whole:

> And live a life of love, just as Christ loved us and gave himself up for us as a fragrant offering and sacrifice to God.
> But among you there must not be even a hint of sexual

immorality, or of any kind of impurity, or of greed, because these are improper for God's holy people.

The word *but* at the beginning of verse 3 puts everything in verse
3 in contrast to verse 2. What the apostle is saying is that any sexual
immorality is a violation of Christian love. You cannot truly love another person and practice sex with that person outside of marriage. It
is impossible.

We often hear the excuse that sex outside of marriage is justified
as long as love is present. But Paul says that is impossible. If you really love someone, you don't have sex with that person outside of the
commitment of marriage. It is easy for a young man to tell a young
woman he loves her—and it's easy for her to believe him. But there is
a saying that "true love waits," and that is true. If a young man uses
the words "I love you" as a means to get sex, he is not showing love
for her—and he is certainly not showing *Christian* love! Rather, he
is demonstrating his own selfishness. True love is concerned about
another's welfare, not one's own urges.

Dr. Henry Brandt says, "Becoming involved sexually short-circuits
the judgment, and one of the most important decisions of your life—
whom you will marry—is made under pressure of disappointment,
one-sided affection, or over-involvement." This contradicts the common misconception that it is necessary to experiment with sex before
marriage to make sure the marriage will work. This misconception
is based on the false assumption that the physical union of sex is the
central pillar of a marriage, which it is not. Moreover, it is impossible
to test marriage that way because the essential conditions that make
up marriage are not there.

"Testing" marriage with premarital sex is like "testing" a parachute
by jumping off a ladder. A ladder doesn't give you enough room to

deploy a parachute, and a premarital affair does not give you the time to truly test the durability of a marriage. You can only prove the durability of a marriage over the long haul, by making a commitment before God, then working on fulfilling that commitment, one day at a time.

Reason Number 2: Even talk about sexual immorality is pointless and wasteful. In Ephesians 5:4 Paul goes on to give us another reason for the incompatibility of sexual immorality and Christianity: "Nor should there be obscenity, foolish talk or coarse joking, which are out of place, but rather thanksgiving." When the apostle says "out of place," he means inappropriate, wasteful, and pointless. In other words, the apostle is asking us: What is to be gained by such talk? What good does it do anyone to be exposed to jokes, films, magazines, or computer material of a sexually perverse nature?

Answer: Nothing is to be gained. It is pointless and wasteful. It's a dead-end street. You never learn the true nature of sex by studying its perversions or distortions. You only learn the true nature of sex from God's revelation. There we see what sex was intended to be from the One who created it.

Like a river, the sex drive is designed to be channeled and kept within bounds. When it breaks over its boundaries and overflows its banks, the sex drive becomes a flood that inundates the whole landscape. Soon, we are all hip-deep in a slurry of vile talk, smutty jokes, pornography, and scandals.

Eventually, those who immerse themselves in illicit sexual material find that normal sexual relations lose their attraction. They find that it gradually takes increasingly more obscene, perverse, and evil stimulation to achieve the previous level of sexual excitement. Like a drug addict, the sex addict descends into ever more vile and degrading practices the longer he practices his habit.

Reason Number 3: Continuance in sexual immorality reveals an unregenerate heart. In verse 5 Paul gives us the third of his five great statements about the Christian and improper sex:

> For of this you can be sure: No immoral, impure or greedy person—such a man is an idolater—has any inheritance in the kingdom of Christ and of God.

Notice that Paul revisits the same three categories he referred to in verse 3—immorality, impurity, and greed (or covetousness). As we have seen, *greed* here refers not to being covetous for money but for passion and the body of another person. Anyone who practices immorality, impurity or sexual greed, Paul says bluntly, has no inheritance in the kingdom of Christ and of God!

In other words, sexual immorality is incompatible with Christian faith because continuance in it reveals an unregenerate heart. Notice that Paul reinforces this idea, making sure there is no room for misunderstanding or rationalization, as he adds, verse 6: "Let no one deceive you with empty words, for because of such things God's wrath comes on those who are disobedient." So you cannot be a Christian and knowingly, deliberately practice sex outside of marriage, for the one cancels out the other.

Yes, a Christian can commit sexual sins. The record is all too clear in this regard. Even in the Scriptures we have the account of David who, after years as a faithful believer, as a man after God's own heart, fell into the sin of adultery and took another man's wife. But the point the apostle makes is that no professed Christian can do this repeatedly, defiantly, or shamelessly, and really be a Christian. The true Christian, if he does fall into this kind of folly, will abhor himself and loathe his sin. He will repent and forsake it. The man who defends, justifies, and excuses this kind of activity, or even glories in it as a mark of personal liberty, gives evidence that his professed Christianity is a sham.

That does not mean that such a person is beyond the reach of God's grace. In 1 Corinthians 6 Paul lists a number of sins, including homosexuality and other sexual sins, then adds, "And that is what some of you were. But you were washed, you were sanctified, you were justified in the name of the Lord Jesus Christ and by the Spirit of our God" (1 Corinthians 6:11). God's grace reaches out even to those who practice these sins, if they repent and turn to Christ. But no one who professes Christ can continue in these sins, for his deeds deny his claim to being a Christian.

Reason Number 4: A Christian no longer has any excuse for indulging in sexual immorality. In verses 6–10 Paul gives us the fourth of his five statements about the Christian and sexual immorality:

> Let no one deceive you with empty words, for because of such things God's wrath comes on those who are disobedient. Therefore do not be partners with them.
>
> For you were once darkness, but now you are light in the Lord. Live as children of light (for the fruit of the light consists in all goodness, righteousness and truth) and find out what pleases the Lord.

Paul's argument is that all sexual misconduct is incompatible with Christianity because a Christian no longer has any excuse for indulging in it. He is not a child of ignorance anymore. He is not caught up in the web of deceit that is woven throughout our society. He is not self-deceived or brainwashed by the subtle propaganda of our age.

He knows the truth about the God-given gift of human sexuality. So it is unthinkable that he should deliberately go back from light into darkness.

Notice how clearly the apostle draws this picture. If a man or woman is born again by faith in Jesus Christ, he has been translated out of the kingdom of darkness, out of the power of Satan. He has been brought into the kingdom of light, into the power of God. This is the whole Christian gospel. So it is unthinkable that a Christian, who has been delivered from darkness and brought into the light, should turn his back on the light and return to the darkness.

The Christian should know that sexual misconduct will be the subject of subtle and deceitful propaganda. That is why the apostle warns, "Let no one deceive you with empty words." We are being assaulted by a tremendous barrage of propaganda, all subtly designed to make us think that God's moral standards are outdated and limiting. Most of our media—from books and magazines to films and television to music and advertising to the Internet—are bent toward keeping our minds focused on immorality and illicit sex.

But the Christian knows what the world denies: Sexual six evokes the wrath of God against the society that permits or encourages immorality. That is why Paul says, "for because of such things God's wrath comes on those who are disobedient."

As we discussed in Chapter 4: "The Work and Blessings of the Spirit," the term *God's wrath* is greatly misunderstood today. The wrath of God does not refer to God's judgment coming down upon sinners as lightning bolts from heaven. It does not refer to the future Day of Judgment that the Scriptures foretell, because Paul makes it clear that this wrath is going on right now (see Romans 1:18). The wrath of God, as Paul speaks of it here, refers to the consequences that naturally arise when we misuse God's gift of sexuality: broken and distorted relationships, broken families, emotional pain, anxiety, depression, jealousy, violence, and sexually transmitted diseases. These consequences are not caused by God's deliberately smashing sinners beneath his thumb; they proceed in simple cause-and-effect fashion from the choices we make.

Reason Number 5: A Christian cannot preach against immorality while indulging in it. In verses 11–14 Paul gives us the fifth of his five reasons why Christianity and immorality are mutually exclusive:

> Have nothing to do with the fruitless deeds of darkness, but rather expose them. For it is shameful even to mention what the disobedient do in secret. But everything exposed by the light becomes visible, for it is light that makes everything visible. This is why it is said:
> "Wake up, O sleeper,
> Rise from the dead,
> And Christ will shine on you."

Sexual immorality is incompatible with the Christian faith because the Christian is commanded to expose the true character of sexual sin. How can you expose what you are engaging in? That is not just inconsistent, it's hypocrisy! The church of Jesus Christ is directed by the Holy Spirit to be a source of biblical truth on matters of sex.

In 1 Timothy 3:15, Paul calls the church "the pillar and ground of the truth" (KJV). Only the church is qualified to teach the world the true nature of sex. We are commanded to unmask the false sexual values of this age and reveal God's truth about how sex is to be expressed within marriage. We are not just to shun immorality—what

Paul calls "the fruitless deeds of darkness," but we are also to expose those deeds for what they are.

How do we expose sexual sin? Not by denouncing it—the world is unimpressed by people who go around denouncing sin. What makes an impression on the world? People who live the truth and exemplify God's wholesome, beautiful plan for marriage and human sexuality. We expose error not by screaming about the error but by illuminating truth with the brilliant example of our lives, lived in healthy, holy obedience to God.

Paul concludes with a wake-up call: "This is why it is said: 'Wake up, O sleeper, rise from the dead, and Christ will shine on you.'" Keep your minds and hearts alert. Hold fast to the Word of God, to the truth as it really is, and Christ will give you light. Then let your light shine! Live the truth and speak the truth. Speak it boldly. Yes, talk about sex—the kind of sex life that God designed and intended for each of us. Expose the darkness by shining God's truth out into this morally dark world.

God does not call us to retreat to a monastery or a convent somewhere. He calls us to live out a Christian code of morality and sexuality in a pagan and perverse world. As Paul tells us in Philippians 2:14, God calls us to live "blameless and pure, children of God without fault in a crooked and depraved generation, in which you shine like stars in the universe." Or, as the Amplified Version puts it, we are to live "in the midst of a generation of crooks and perverts." What a challenge! What a clarion-call to holy living in a world of deceit and sin!

Friend in Christ, this is an important subject and we must regard it with all seriousness. We are being engulfed on all sides by a tidal wave of sexual propaganda designed to undermine the foundations of morality and Christian faith. Christians must take a bold stand in obedience to God's moral law, both in their words and in their lifestyle before the world.

History shows that when the gospel of God's grace penetrates a society, even in the midst of the most depraved sexual practices, islands of purity and Christlike love have formed and spread, touching entire cities, and ultimately transforming the sexual practices of empires. This is where the power of the church lies—in the willingness of its people to obey the Word of the living God.

CHAPTER TWENTY-FOUR

Watch How You Walk

Ephesians 5:15–20

Aman walking a tightrope has no concern as to *where* he should walk. A rope stretched across an abyss is a very narrow and well-defined path! But a tightrope walker must give a great deal of attention to *how* he should walk. And that is the situation that confronts you and me as we come to Ephesians 5:15–20.

We have been looking together at the great passage in Ephesians where the apostle Paul deals with our preparation as Christians for living in a sin-sick and corrupt society. We have seen that the problems first-century Christians faced were essentially the same problems we face today. Now we come to Paul's summary of this subject in Ephesians 5:15–20:

> Be very careful, then, how you live—not as unwise but as wise, making the most of every opportunity, because the days are evil. Therefore do not be foolish, but understand what the Lord's will is. Do not get drunk on wine, which leads to debauchery. Instead, be filled with the Spirit. Speak to one another with psalms, hymns, and spiritual

songs. Sing and make music in your heart to the Lord, always giving thanks to God the Father for everything, in the name of our Lord Jesus Christ.

We are to be careful, Paul says, how we walk—that is, how we live. We are to live not as unwise but as wise. This passage is a review of all that the apostle has been teaching us up to this point—that we are no longer to live as the Gentiles do, that we are to put off the old nature and put on the new. That simple process of putting off and putting on is what the apostle means by our "walk." Everyone knows that a walk consists of two steps repeated over and over again—right, left, right, left. This is an apt simile for how to live the Christian life. We are to continually put off the old and put on the new. That is what Christian living is all about.

Paul has also talked about practical Christianity, the practical application of the daily Christian walk to the situations of everyday life. He has come to grips with some of the great issues of his day—and ours—including the issue of sexual morality.

Now, in Ephesians 5:15–20, Paul summarizes his message with one statement that says it all: "Look carefully then how you walk." That is the supreme issue we face: not *where* to walk, but *how* to walk. Where we walk is a relatively easy problem, but it's a lot more difficult to know how we should apply Christian principles to every moment of our lives.

When you are driving down a road, there is no problem knowing where to drive. The road is paved, marked with lines and signs, so there is little danger of getting off the road. But knowing how to drive is a different matter, because conditions and situations change. How do you drive if a car stops suddenly in front of you, or if a truck pulls onto the road from a side street and cuts you off? How do you drive if a child dashes out into the street? How do you drive if you suddenly experience a blowout or a loss of steering power? So we must not only know where to drive. More importantly, we must know how to relate the principles of good driving to every changing situation along the road.

This is the exhortation of the apostle Paul: "Look carefully how you walk." Then he goes on to give us the two characteristics of walking rightly: 1. Walk with understanding; 2. Walk in the Spirit. Let's look at the first of these characteristics. Paul writes, verses 15–17: "Be very careful, then, how you live—not as unwise but as wise, making the most of every opportunity, because the days are evil. Therefore do not be foolish, but understand what the Lord's will is."

1. WALK WITH UNDERSTANDING

Paul says we must walk wisely, understanding the nature of life ("the days are evil"), the nature of our opportunities, and the nature of God's will. He is pointing out to us that evil times create opportunities for good. We must make the most of those opportunities created by evil days. The phrase "making the most" is one Greek word in the original text that is used in the New Testament for "redeeming." It means to buy up commodities in order to turn a later profit. If you buy stocks at a low price to sell later at a high price for a profit, you are "making the most of every opportunity." You are snatching up bargains. Whenever "the days are evil" in the stock market, when stock prices fall and investors panic, there are always a few shrewd investors who know how to make the most of the opportunity in evil days, buying up bargain-priced stocks that someday will return a handsome reward. That is the analogy suggested by Paul's statement in these verses.

That's a far cry from the outlook many Christians have toward evil days! Most of us see evil days as obstacles, as times of withdrawal and defeat. The wise Christian knows how to take advantage of evil times in order to advance the agenda of God's kingdom. If you are under pressure, make the most of that time by manifesting the overcoming grace of God. Walk with understanding and buy up the opportunities.

Paul also tells us that we need to understand the will of God. We need to be aware of what God wants out of every situation. Some people would understand the term "the Lord's will" to mean specific guidance on what to do next, where to live, what job to have, whom to marry, and so forth. But that is not what Paul means when he talks about understanding the will of the Lord. God is not nearly so interested in what you *do* as in what you *are*.

Earlier in Ephesians 5, Paul said, "Live as children of light . . . and find out what pleases the Lord" (Ephesians 5:8, 10). Understanding what pleases the Lord is the same thing as understanding the will of the Lord. What pleases the Lord? One thing: *Faith!* "Without faith it is impossible to please God," says Hebrews 11:6. Faith is believing God, believing what He says about life, believing what He says about people, believing what He says about ourselves. This is what the apostle is referring to: Not trying to get specific guidance about this or that decision, but remembering that in every situation of our lives we are to act in reliance upon the Word of God.

Acting in faith means to adopt God's evaluation of what the great values of life are. Acting in faith means to reject the success image that the world is constantly holding before us, and to seek the riches of Christ rather than the riches of this world. Acting in faith means that we live the same way on Monday through Saturday as we live on Sundays. We apply Christian principles to our business relationships, our family relationships, and all the other relationships of our lives.

Paul is telling us not to be foolish and unwise, not to live as the Gentiles (nonChristians) live. We are not to blindly swallow the immoral propaganda that has infected our society. We are not to go along with the world in which we live; we are to stand against it. We are to live by faith and walk wisely, understanding the evil nature of the world, and understanding the will of God for our lives.

2. WALK IN THE SPIRIT

The next word Paul gives us in this passage has to do with our resources in the Spirit. We are to live life in the overflowing power and presence of the Holy Spirit. He writes in verse 18, "Do not get drunk on wine, which leads to debauchery. Instead, be filled with the Spirit." Paul contrasts two opposing kinds of influence on our lives: being drunk with wine versus being filled with the Spirit. It is interesting to note the parallels as well as the contrasts between being drunk with wine and being filled with the Spirit. The same pressures in life, the same troubles and demands, will drive some people to drink, but will drive others deeper into the embrace of the Spirit. Under the influence of wine, people lose their inhibitions and gain confidence—but lose control. Under the influence of the Spirit, people gain boldness under God's control.

The word here translated "debauchery" is the Greek word *asotia*, which means "without limits, with reckless abandon." It refers to escapism and the tendency to throw all restraints overboard and live out of control. By contrast, Paul tells us that when we feel we need strength to face life with its troubles, we should not seek the reckless escapism of alcohol, but the strength and power of the Holy Spirit.

Here is the great secret of real Christianity—the reality of being filled with the Spirit. When you become a Christian, when you believed in Jesus Christ and received him as your Lord, the Holy Spirit came to live in you. You are sealed by the Spirit and you are indwelt by the Spirit—but the paradox is that we still need to be constantly, repeatedly *filled* with the Holy Spirit. The filling of the Holy Spirit is the momentary access of the resources of the Spirit for individual situations. It has nothing to do with a "religious experience" or with feelings. It is a quiet drinking from an inner supply of strength.

Jesus put it beautifully when he spoke with the Samaritan woman at the well. The story is recorded John 4:7–14:

> When a Samaritan woman came to draw water, Jesus said to her, "Will you give me a drink?" (His disciples had gone into the town to buy food.)
>
> The Samaritan woman said to him, "You are a Jew and I am a Samaritan woman. How can you ask me for a drink?" (For Jews do not associate with Samaritans.)
>
> Jesus answered her, "If you knew the gift of God and who it is that asks you for a drink, you would have asked him and he would have given you living water."
>
> "Sir," the woman said, "you have nothing to draw with and the well is deep. Where can you get this living water? Are you greater than our father Jacob, who gave us the well and drank from it himself, as did also his sons and his flocks and herds?"
>
> Jesus answered, "Everyone who drinks this water will be thirsty again, but whoever drinks the water I give him will never thirst. Indeed, the water I give him will become *in him* a spring of water welling up to eternal life."

Notice those two key words I have italicized in verse 14: "in him." The well, Jesus says, is no longer going to be outside of us, so that you have to go somewhere else, but it will be *in us*. That well is the Holy Spirit, and we can drink from it at any time. The Spirit is our adequate and ever-present resource for any demand that is made upon us.

Paul says that life is to be lived constantly with the recognition that demands and pressures come all the time. We are not to meet them with artificial means, with alcohol or tranquilizers or any of the more modern substitutes. We are to meet them by being filled with the Spirit. We are to drink from the Spirit within us, not from a bottle of wine.

THREE RESULTS

Paul goes on to tell us of three results that we can expect as we walk in understanding and walk in the Spirit. He writes in verses 19–20:

> Speak to one another with psalms, hymns and spiritual songs. Sing and make music in your heart to the Lord, always giving thanks to God the Father for everything, in the name of our Lord Jesus Christ.

Notice the three verbs in these verses: *speaking*, and *singing*, and *giving thanks*. These are the marks of one who is drawing every moment upon the well of the Spirit within.

The first mark of the Spirit-filled life is that you will talk about what you have read in the Scriptures, about what the Lord has taught you from His Word. The more deeply you drink from the well of the Spirit, the more a love for the Bible will be manifested in you.

The second mark of the Spirit-filled life is singing, making melody to the Lord with all your heart. Now, I'm sure Paul includes actual singing with the voice, but I am so grateful he talked about making music "in your heart," singing from the heart.

I have a great deal of trouble singing with the voice. I used to sing in a choir until I missed one day and someone thought the organ had been fixed! But I can sing beautifully in my heart. I know well that inner bubbling of a melody to my Lord and Savior. I know the inner joy of knowing that God is in control and He is working things out, even in times of trouble.

The third mark of the Spirit-filled life is giving thanks. Notice how Paul puts it: "always giving thanks to God the Father for everything, in the name of our Lord Jesus Christ." That statement eliminates all complaining and murmuring.

I remember when I was in the Navy, we took our meals in the mess hall. If you ever saw a Navy food tray with Navy food plopped on it, you'd know why they call it a mess hall. I recall sitting with a Christian friend across the table from a big, burly quartermaster who was a foul-mouthed pagan. As we always did, my Christian friend and I bowed our heads and gave thanks for the food. Then, my Christian friend looked at the food and began to complain about it. Suddenly, the pagan fellow across the table said, "Look, didn't you just give thanks for that slop? Then shut up and eat it!"

The pagan was right. You cannot give thanks and complain at the same time.

Notice that Paul enjoins us to give thanks "for everything." Why does Paul say that? Surely he doesn't mean *everything*? Oh, but he does!

The will of the Lord is that we be put in difficult situations and have unpleasant circumstances in order that we might have opportunity to manifest the life of Jesus Christ. So don't complain—give thanks! Because these circumstances will do something to you that nothing else could do. This is what Paul tells us in 2 Corinthians 4:17–18:

> For our light and momentary troubles are achieving for us an eternal glory that far outweighs them all. So we fix our eyes not on what is seen, but on what is unseen. For what is seen is temporary, but what is unseen is eternal.

And the writer to the Hebrews agrees:

> No discipline seems pleasant at the time, but painful. Later on, however, it produces a harvest of righteousness and peace for those who have been trained by it (12:11).

God has a purpose in all that happens in our lives. Therefore, we should give thanks in all things.

That is the way the Lord Jesus, our example, conducted His life. He gave thanks even in the most disastrous circumstances. His earthly ministry was, by human standards, a total failure by the time He arrived at the cross. In Matthew 11, he is faced with the disbelief and questioning of John the Baptist. He remarks that wherever He preaches, He is rejected and the children of Israel refuse to give Him credence. He chastises the cities where most of His mighty works were done and warns those cities that they are in danger of judgment. Then, in Matthew 11:25, He says, "I praise you, Father, Lord of heaven and earth, because you have hidden these things from the wise and learned, and revealed them to little children." Yes, Father, for this was your good pleasure.

In spite of all the failure and the opposition Jesus faced, He could say, "I thank you and praise you, Father, because no one can see what you are doing. You have hidden your real workings from the educated minds, and you have revealed them to those of childlike faith." That is what it means to understand the will of God and to give thanks in all circumstances.

So we walk in understanding of God's will, and we walk in the power of the Spirit. As we do so, the result of our lives will be singing and thanksgiving—the music of praise.

CHAPTER TWENTY-FIVE

The Cure for Conflict

Ephesians 5:21

One of the most frequently heard complaints about the church today is that it is only interested in preserving the status quo. The church's slogan, say the critics, is "Come weal or come woe, our status is quo." As someone once observed, status quo is Latin for "the mess we're in."

Let's be honest and admit that this is all too often true in the church today. Many churches are all too interested in the status quo—a regular Sunday rigmarole of hymns and religious ceremonies and moral platitudes, without really affecting lives or engaging the burning issues of our world. Let's admit that, all too often, the church really is irrelevant to the problems people face and it does not meet people where they live.

And let us further stipulate that wherever that is true, it is invariably because the church has veered away from the wisdom and authority of Scripture. Some churches have treated God's Word as a collection of tales suited for Sunday school children but completely unworthy of a modern man or woman's intelligence. Others rigorously revere the Sacred Word, but keep it enshrined under glass, never really attempting to apply it to the gritty realities of life. In either case, the Bible is relegated to irrelevance—despite the fact that this is the most relevant, timeless, practical Book ever written! It is the Book that contains the radical secret of Christianity—that Jesus Christ is alive and ready to take up residence in your life and mine, and wants to express His life through ours.

In Ephesians 5:21, the apostle Paul takes up the issue of Christian relationships. In a single sentence, he spells out the solution to all the conflicts that ever take place among Christians. That sentence is this:

Submit to one another out of reverence for Christ.

The statement is the overture, the summary statement, of everything he will say from this point through Ephesians 6:9. He will apply this theme to situation after situation in the church and in the Christian family: Submit to one another out of reverence for Christ. That is the remedy for all the conflicts we encounter as Christians.

AN INDIVIDUAL SOLUTION

Mutual submission is not the way the world solves social issues and conflicts. The world's way of solving problems is to assert power. We engage in political conspiracies, or we stage a protest or a riot, or we call out the National Guard, or we call a press conference to get public opinion on our side, or we picket and boycott and strike. I'm not condemning these approaches. I'm just saying they are the approaches of the world, the application of force or pressure or persuasion.

Paul says, in effect, "As a Christian, you are not to use the world's approach to solving problems. You are not to seek power and leverage over one another. Instead of creating a power bloc, start on an individual level. Instead of trying to win the war, submit. Instead of seeking power, seek to give way.

This is always the way God says to solve problems. As you read through the New Testament, you notice that God never calls for corporate action in solving the basic problems of society. His solution is always addressed to individuals. Start where you are by doing one simple thing: "Be subject to one another out of reverence for Christ."

In applying this, Paul will discuss the relationship of husbands to wives, which brings in the whole realm of marriage and the problems that arise there. Then he will take up the matter of children and parents, which brings in the whole issue of juvenile delinquency—its causes and what can be done about it. Then he will take up the issue of management and labor, masters and servants, employers and employees. In each case, the remedy is always the same: "Submit to one another out of reverence for Christ."

If we are going to understand the world in which we live and the reasons for the strife, conflict, and violence in the world, we have to go back to the basic cause of all human strife. It always begins at the level of the individual.

Every individual seeks fulfillment. God has placed the drive for fulfillment within each of us. It is not wrong to want happiness and satisfaction in life. The problem comes when two people, both in search of fulfillment and satisfaction in life, both set on the same goal, come together on a collision course. Perhaps it is two people who want the same promotion or position in a company. Or two church leaders who feel their approach to ministry should be adopted by the church (a story as old as Paul and Barnabas). Or two siblings who contend for the love and attention of a parent (as Jacob and Esau did in the Old Testament).

Sooner or later, one person begins to suspect the other of sabotaging his efforts. What may have begun as a cordial competition becomes a cold war or intrigue, back-stabbing, and gossip. He insists on his rights, she insists on hers. The cold war breaks out into an open conflict. Each side gathers allies and supporters, and what began as a competition between two individuals becomes a civil war between factions—now we have a divided company, a divided team, a divided family, or a divided church. People who were once friends are now enemies, unable to find any common ground for compromise, because the emotions and personal relationships have become poisoned with bitterness.

It's a tragic pattern that is played out again and again, day after day. But the apostle Paul cuts across the grain of this pattern like a rip-saw as he introduces two radical and powerful factors that drastically alter the equation of conflict:

First, Paul reminds us that the path to true fulfillment doesn't lie in pursuing our own wants and needs, but in seeking the fulfillment and happiness of others: "Submit to one another . . . ."

Second, Paul reminds us of the presence of a third party who is present in all our relationships: "Submit to one another *out of reverence for Christ.*"

Let's examine each of these factors in Paul's equation for conflict resolution.

1. "SUBMIT TO ONE ANOTHER . . . ."

The great paradox of the Christian life is that the more we focus on fulfilling ourselves, the emptier we become. That is a fundamental (but widely ignored!) law of life. That is why so many people in our society are asking the wrong question: "How can I get what I want so I can be fulfilled?" People who get what they want usually find that it doesn't fulfill as they thought it would. It is only when we forget ourselves and devote ourselves to the fulfillment of others that we find our own hearts brimming with grace, peace, and satisfaction.

A billionaire was once asked how much money it takes to be happy. His answer: "Just a little bit more." That's the deception of self-fulfillment—even more than enough is never enough. We cannot fulfill ourselves by seeking our own happiness. We only attain happiness by giving happiness away to others. Our Lord put it this way: "Whoever wants to save his life will lose it, but whoever loses his life for me will find it" (Matthew 16:25). And "Seek first his kingdom and his righteousness, and all these things will be given to you as well" (Matthew 6:33).

It becomes, then, a question of priority. What is the right way to find fulfillment? If we are Christians, we must face honestly and thoughtfully this pronouncement of our Lord that life is so constructed that if we try to find it we will never do so. You cannot have your rights by insisting upon them. You can have them only when you seek to give another person his rights. The person who loves and does not think of himself finds himself. The one who is constantly seeking is always cheated.

Do we dare to test the truth of our Lord's paradoxical pronouncement? Do we dare to test the validity of this radical, revolutionary principle right where we live?

The problem is not that we have not known it, but that we do not act on it. We acknowledge it as true. We nod our heads when we hear these words of Christ. But when it comes to a specific situation where someone is cutting across our pathway and we find ourselves in the direct, head-on collision—our wants, our needs, our ego, our goals, our rights—we revert to the old basis by which the world lives: "I demand my rights!" The result is bitterness and division.

But Paul gives us the solution: "Submit to one another out of reverence for Christ." Do we dare to try it? Do we dare to apply this solution in the laboratory of life?

A true story: A Christian couple moved into their dream house. They had not been in their house more than a day when the new homeowner was confronted by his next-door neighbor in the yard. The neighbor screamed and threatened him because of some minor inconvenience. He threatened to take the Christian family to court if he was ever inconvenienced again.

Too shocked and disheartened to make any response, the Christian man trudged back inside and told his wife what all the yelling was about. "It seems our dream house came with one little drawback," she glumly reflected, "a very cantankerous neighbor."

"Honey, what are we going to do?" asked the man. "We wanted to live here the rest of our lives—but how can we live next to a man like that?"

His first (and completely natural) response was to want nothing to do with the cantankerous neighbor. Don't antagonize him, don't even speak to him—just cut him off. "Well," said his wife, "why don't we pray about it?" So they prayed.

A day or so later, the wife was baking a pie, and it occurred to her to make an extra pie for her neighbor. She baked it and, at lunch time, she took it over to the neighbor's house. She rang the doorbell with fear and trembling. The door opened, and it was the wife of the cantankerous neighbor—and she looked even less friendly than her husband! Her face was set in hard, unyielding lines, and she said, "What do you want?"

The Christian woman tried to put a perky, joyful note in her voice as she said, "I was baking pies today, and I thought of you—so I baked you this pie." The neighbor lady took it, mumbled a thank-you, and went back inside.

About an hour later the phone rang. It was the wife of the cantankerous neighbor. Her voice sounded animated and pleased. "How did you know that was my husband's favorite pie? He loves lemon meringue!"

And the Christian lady had an inspiration. "Well, that's wonderful!" she said. "Why don't you both come over to dinner tomorrow night?"

The neighbor lady seemed shocked. "Well—I'll ask my husband." She soon called back and said, "Yes, we'd love to come over."

Over the next few weeks, these two couples became good friends— and the once-cantankerous neighbor and his wife began coming to church with the Christian couple. That is what God wants to do with our conflicts. That is what He can do when we submit to one another out of reverence for Christ.

2. "... OUT OF REVERENCE FOR CHRIST."

That brings us to our motivation for mutual submission in our relationships. As Christians, we must never forget that, in every relationship of life, another Person is present. Our conflicts are never just a matter of husband versus wife, parent versus child, boss versus employee, pastor versus parishioner, church member versus church member, neighbor versus neighbor. There is always a third Person present: the Lord Jesus Christ. To a worldling who does not recognize the universal presence of Christ, the primary concern is "what I want versus what you want." To the Christian, the primary concern is the lordship of Jesus Christ.

So here is the second half of the solution. The great issue for the Christian must never be "what I want versus what you want," but, "What does Christ want me to do?"

Notice that, in the verses that follow Ephesians 5:21, Paul will place Christ at the center of every relationship and every conflict, again and again:

> Ephesians 5:22: "Wives, submit to your husbands *as to the Lord.*"

> Ephesians 5:25: "Husbands, love your wives, *just as Christ loved the church and gave himself up for her.*"

> Ephesians 6:1: Children, obey your parents *in the Lord,* for this is right."

> Ephesians 6:4: "Fathers, do not exasperate your children; instead, bring them up in the training and instruction *of the Lord.*"

> Ephesians 6:5: "Slaves, obey your earthly masters with respect and fear, and with sincerity of heart, *just as you would obey Christ.*"

> Ephesians 6:9: "And masters, treat your slaves in the same way. Do not threaten them, since you know that *he who is both their Master and yours is in heaven,* and there is no favoritism with him."

In each of these relationships, the apostle reminds us that we do not face those relationships alone. Christ is in the midst of all our relationships—and all our conflicts. If we do not recognize His presence, then we cannot submit ourselves to one another. If we do not see Christ alongside us in our conflicts, we see only the adversarial relationship, me versus you. Pride immediately gets in the way, blocking communication and compromise, stiffening our stubborn determination to win at all costs.

"Let him back down first!" demands one. "Let her apologize first!" insists the other. When neither side moves off-center, the stage is set for war.

But when we see Christ, the One who gave His life to end the conflict between humanity and God, the One who reconciled us to God when we were sinners, then we realize that we owe everything to Him—including our submission and humility. Then we can step aside, we can back down—if not for the sake of the other person, then at least for the sake of Jesus, in response to the love and forgiveness He had given us.

When we insist on satisfying the urges within ourselves for self-justification or vindication, then those urges become our god. We have idolized the self. But if we obey Christ, we prove that He is our God. So our responsibility is to obey Him—our Lord and our God. We become willing to mutually submit ourselves because, as Paul wrote in 2 Corinthians 5:14, "Christ's love compels us."

THE WORLD IS WATCHING

If the world could see Christians living by the truth of Ephesians 5:21, I believe our nation would be radically changed. Our political institutions would change. Our race relations would change. Our neighborhoods would change. Family relationships would change. The world settles conflicts by force and manipulation because it has never had a better example to go by. We in the church have never set a better example, because all too often we have operated by the rules of the world instead of the guidelines of the Lord.

Paul tells us that the key to resolving conflict in the body of Jesus

Christ is to "submit to one another out of reverence for Christ." The world is watching and waiting to see a demonstration of this key truth. Worldlings cannot grasp the reality of this principle until they see it in action among Christians.

We have the answer to conflict in our grasp. It is simple yet powerful. The only question is: Will we put it to use?

CHAPTER TWENTY-SIX

Husbands and Wives

Ephesians 5:22–33

We have just seen that the key to resolving conflict between Christians is to "submit to one another out of reverence for Christ." Now, in the remaining verses of Ephesians 5, Paul applies this key principle to the specific relationship between husbands and wives. There is probably no relationship in life that carries a greater potential for conflict than the marriage relationship. The oldest battle of all time is the battle of the sexes.

Paul begins with counsel for wives, Ephesians 5:22–24:

> Wives, submit to your husbands as to the Lord. For the husband is the head of the wife as Christ is the head of the church, his body, of which he is the Savior. Now as the church submits to Christ, so also wives should submit to their husbands in everything.

It is important to remember that this is an application of the general principle in Ephesians 5:21. Submission is mutual. The husband is to subject himself to the wife as much as the wife is to the husband.

There are different ways we subject ourselves to each other in marriage, because the roles of husband and wife are different. The apostle will now go on to spell out for us what this means for husbands and wives in specific terms.

TO WIVES

Addressing wives, Paul uses the same word he used in 5:21: *Submit.* This is a word that raises the hackles of many in our times, especially in this era of feminist politics. It sounds to the modern ear as if Paul is telling women, "Stay in your subservient place. Accept your inferiority. You must be resolved to role as slave to your master-husband." That is not at all the thought that Paul has in mind. A more accurate sense of the word *submit* would be "voluntarily place yourself under the authority of" or "willingly adapt and adjust yourself to the authority of." The apostle is saying to the wife, in effect, "Adapt yourself to your own husband, adjust to him."

This is the fulfillment of the initial word of the Creator to the woman when He said that she was to be "a helper suitable for him" (Genesis 2:18). She is not to be his rival. She is not to be his slave. She is to be his partner, equal but loyal, and they are to work together to accomplish the aims and goals he sets for their life together. The husband has a leadership role, but that in no way diminishes the worth of the wife. He is incomplete without her, and it is in this partnership role with the husband that she finds fulfillment and completion.

The apostle Paul immediately links his practical command for submission to a biblical rationale for that command: "Wives, submit to your husbands as to the Lord. For the husband is the head of the wife as Christ is the head of the church, his body, of which he is the Savior." The key phrase here is "as to the Lord." The wife is subject to her husband not because her husband is such a wonderful human being, but because she has a prior and primary relationship to her Lord. The phrase "as to the Lord" does not mean that the wife is to worship her husband as though he were the Lord (despite the fact that many a young bride has set a burnt offering before her husband!). It means she is to yield to her husband in order to please her Lord, Jesus Christ.

A Christian woman once asked me, "Does Ephesians 5:22–23 mean that my submission to my husband is a gauge of the degree to which I am submitted to Christ?" Yes, I told her, it is exactly that. The submission of a wife to her husband in the proper areas of his authority is precisely the gauge of her submission to Christ.

"Well, then," she replied, "that means that my submission to my husband is not some sort of gift I give my husband, that he should feel indebted to me for. Nor should I use my 'submission' to him as a form of manipulation or blackmail. I can't say to my husband, 'I've submitted myself to you, now you have to do such-and-such for me.' Nor can I say to God, 'I've submitted myself to my husband, so You have to produce certain results in my life.' No, if I submit to my husband as unto the Lord, I shouldn't care what the results are—that's up to my husband and God."

She got it! That's the full intent of Paul's word to wives in this section of Ephesians. He wants wives to understand that a woman is never more free to be herself than when she is joyfully, willingly submissive to her husband's authority. It is all a matter of headship, and headship means authority and leadership. That is why Paul writes in 1 Corinthians 11:3, "Now I want you to realize that the head of every man is Christ, and the head of the woman is man, and the head of Christ is God."

THE ELEMENTS OF HEADSHIP

If you search the Scriptures that describe the Lord Jesus in relationship to His Father, you discover four elements that make up the headship of the Father:

1. Identity. Jesus said, "I and the Father are one" (John 10:30). The Scriptures say that the same is true of a husband and wife. When they are married, they become one (see Genesis 2:24; Matthew 19:5–6; Mark 10:7–8). There is an identity of persons, one with the other, that takes place in this matter of headship.

2. Mutual cooperation. The Lord Jesus, on another occasion, said, "My Father is always at his work to this very day, and I, too, am working" (John 5:17). In other words, they cooperate together. Headship involves mutual cooperation. So the husband and wife are to cooperate.

3. Shared honor. The Lord Jesus says of His relationship with the Father, "I honor my Father" (John 8:49) and "My Father . . . glorifies me" (John 8:54). There is a mutual sharing of honor that indicates again what headship means.

4. A difference in authority. Finally, the Lord says, "The Father is greater than I" (John 14:28b). In words full of mystery, Jesus suggests that even though He and the Father are identified with each other, cooperate with each other, and honor each other, there is a difference of authority. "I always do what pleases him," says Jesus in John 8:29.

So the four elements of headship are interpreted for us by Christ: (1) identity as to nature; (2) cooperation as to work; (3) honor as to person, and (4) subservience as to final decisions. That is headship. That is what it should mean to a wife to be subject to her husband.

No doubt, some wives reading this would protest, "But you don't know the kind of brute I live with! How far am I supposed to take this 'submission' business?" Paul answers that in verse 24: "Now as the church submits to Christ, so also wives should submit to their husbands *in everything.*" That's the answer: wives are to submit to their husbands *in everything.*

But this is not to say that there aren't exceptions to this rule. There are husbands who abuse drugs or alcohol, and thus pose a danger to their wife and children. There are husbands who commit violence against their wife and children. There are husbands who demand that their wife do things that are morally wrong, such as telling lies, filing false returns with the IRS, or cutting corners in business. There have even been cases where an evil husband, in order to make a business deal, has told his wife to go to bed with a client. Obviously, a wife should not submit to the immoral demands of a husband in any such circumstances.

Remember, the wife's prior and primary duty is to Christ, even before her husband. She is to submit to Christ first, and if submission to her husband ever comes in conflict with submission to Christ, then obedience to Christ and His moral leadership takes precedence. Barring such extreme situations, however, the wife is to allow the husband to make final decisions, and she is to respect those decisions. That is what Paul means when he says, "in everything."

TO HUSBANDS

Husbands reading to this point may be thinking, "Well, I've got it made in the shade! I hope my wife is getting all of this!" But Paul isn't through. Beginning with verse 25, Paul takes aim at husbands:

Husbands, love your wives, just as Christ loved the church and gave himself up for her to make her holy, cleansing her by the washing with water through the word, and to present her to himself as a radiant church, without stain or wrinkle or any other blemish, but holy and blameless. In this same way, husbands ought to love their wives as their own bodies. He who loves his wife loves himself. After all, no one ever hated his own body, but he feeds and cares for it, just as Christ does the church—for we are members of his body. "For this reason a man will leave his father and mother and be united to his wife, and the two will become one flesh." This is a profound mystery—but I am talking about Christ and the church. However, each one of you also must love his wife as he loves himself, and the wife must respect her husband.

The key phrase here is, "Husbands, love your wives, just as Christ loved the church." Everything beyond that phrase is clarification.

To fully understand Paul's meaning, we have to define our terms. There is probably no word in our modern language more misused and misunderstood than this word *love*. It is used to describe everything from lustful passion to patriotic emotion. Certainly there is great room for confusion when the same word can be used to say, "I love God," "I love my wife," and, "I love pizza."

But Paul defines this word unambiguously with the statement that husbands should love their wives as Christ loved the church *"and gave himself up for her."* This is an illuminating phrase! Here, Paul calls husbands to an all-encompassing, self-sacrificing love. A husband is not the slave-master of the wife. He is not the cruel, demeaning overlord of the wife. He is the self-sacrificing *servant* of the wife! That is what love is!

What Paul is describing once again is mutual submission—the wife submits herself to the husband in accordance with her role, and the husband submits himself to the wife in accordance with his role. The form of submission is different because the role is different, but the principle is the same: mutual submission, just as Paul expressed in 5:21: "Submit to one another out of reverence for Christ."

The wife is to give in. The husband is to give up. She gives in to his leadership role. He gives himself up for her. No husband is fulfilling his proper role in marriage until he learns to give himself up to his wife. How does he do that? In every way and at all times. He gives himself up by opening his heart to her, by sharing his emotions and dreams with her, by disclosing his joys and disappointments to her. There is nothing that makes a woman happier than knowing she fully enters into her husband's life. That fulfills her, and it fulfills him. That is how she is the helper God designed her to be to her husband.

The example of Christ is our model as Christian husbands. So, as we examine the model He gave us, we see that He gave himself up for the church in a deliberate and purposeful way, with certain objectives in mind. In fact, His purposes were threefold, as we see in this passage. The apostle says that Jesus gave himself up for the church so that:

(1) He might sanctify her (verse 26);

(2) He might present the church to himself in splendor (verse 27); and

(3) He might fulfill the mystery of His own being (verse 30).

These same goals apply to the husband and wife relationship:

1. The husband is to give himself up for his wife in order that he might sanctify her, "to make her holy, cleansing her." To sanctify something means to put it to its proper use. *Sanctify* is not a religious word—it can apply to anything. You sanctify a chair when you sit on it and you sanctify a pair of reading glasses when you put them on your nose and read a book. The Lord Jesus gave himself up on the cross so that we could be sanctified for the original use and function God created us to have. And this should be the husband's goal: To give himself up for his wife so that she might fulfill her womanhood, her purpose.

The purpose of a wife is to be a helper for her husband. But it is impossible for someone to help you unless you let that person into your life. If a husband excludes his wife from the world of his thoughts, feelings, goals, and dreams, she cannot be his partner and helper. She is on the outside looking in. She will know that she is being deprived of that for which she was made. Her purpose is being thwarted.

It is also the purpose of a wife to contribute beauty to his life. That is why women are more beautiful than men! They are intended to contribute beauty at every level—not only beauty of form, but of spirit as well. As Peter says in 1 Peter 3:4, a wife's beauty "should be that of your inner self, the unfading beauty of a gentle and quiet spirit, which is of great worth in God's sight." That is what a woman can uniquely contribute to life. But it is the husband who opens the door of opportunity for a woman to do this by sharing himself with her.

2. The husband is to give himself up for his wife in order that he might present her to himself perfect and radiant. Paul writes, verse 27, "and to present her to himself as a radiant church, without stain or wrinkle or any other blemish, but holy and blameless." The husband should continually seek ways to honor, glorify, and exalt his wife in his own thinking, in the family circle, and in their circle of friends and acquaintances. This is his role in marriage.

A wife was once filling out a form, and in the space marked "occupation" she wrote "housewife." Her husband saw this and sweetly said to her, "You're not a *house*wife, dear. You're *my* wife!" That sincere statement of his exalted view of her went a long way to cementing their relationship.

Look at the face of a woman who is loved and exalted by her husband and you will see a glory that cannot be duplicated. An honored wife fulfills womanhood. It means that there must be no sarcasm, contemptuous language, rudeness, or degrading criticism in the relationship. Moreover, it means he must make a positive, assertive effort to find ways to build her up, to praise her, to make her feel valued, esteemed, prized, respected, and loved.

3. The husband is to give himself up for his wife in order that he might fulfill the mystery of his own being. The apostle Paul says, "In this same way, husbands ought to love their wives as their own bodies. He who loves his wife loves himself. After all, no one ever hated his own body, but he feeds and cares for it, just as Christ does the church—for we are members of his body." Again, Paul raises the example of Christ. He loves us and continually gives himself up for us because we are part of Him, and we belong to Him. We who are Christians are part of His body in this amazing mystery. To substantiate his point, the apostle quotes from Genesis 2:24: "For this reason a man will leave his father and mother and be united to his wife, and the two will become one flesh."

That is not simply beautiful language. There is a profound reality behind this: A husband and wife are not just two people rooming together. Their lives actually do blend into one another. They actually become one. It is profoundly true that what hurts the wife hurts the husband. It cannot help but do so. That is why, if you have had a squabble with your wife, you may find yourself unable to do your work properly that day—and it works both ways. The husband and the wife are one flesh.

This truly is, as Paul says in verse 32, "a profound mystery."

UNILATERAL OBEDIENCE

The final point the apostle makes here is given in verse 33: "However, each one of you also must love his wife as he loves himself, and the wife must respect her husband." Notice that he puts this on the basis of each person in the marriage relationship fulfilling his or her responsibility to Christ, regardless of what the other does. That is the key. We are not to withhold our obedience until the other obeys. We are to obey these principles, just as Christ was obedient to the Father, giving himself up for the church even while we were still estranged from Him.

I have seen Christlike unilateral obedience work wonders in marriage relationships. Husbands and wives have been brought together, harmony has been restored in bitterly divided homes, grace and peace has been brought to homes that were once ugly, pain-wracked battlegrounds.

So this is the key to Christian marriage: Husbands, love your wife as yourself, and let the wife see that she respects her husband. This is the pattern that was given to us by our Lord Jesus Christ.

CHAPTER TWENTY-SEVEN

Parents and Children

Ephesians 6:1–4

We come now to the second of Paul's elaborations on the theme he expressed in Ephesians 5:21: "Submit to one another out of reverence for Christ." In Ephesians 5:22–33, he applied this principle to the realm of the marriage relationship. Now, in Ephesians 6:1–4, we come to the issue of the parent-child relationship. Paul's first word is addressed to children:

> Children, obey your parents in the Lord, for this is right. "Honor your father and mother"—which is the first commandment with a promise—"that it may go well with you and that you may enjoy long life on the earth."

Notice, this is not a simple exhortation for children to obey their parents. It goes a step further: "Children, obey your parents *in the Lord.*" The key to the command is "in the Lord." Just as wives are to submit to husbands as unto the Lord, and just as husbands are to love their wives after the example of the Lord, so it is with children: They are to obey their parents for Jesus' sake.

This word *obey* is, literally, a Greek word meaning "to stand under." It means to be under another's authority, and it is used in many places in the Scriptures as a military term. It is the same word that would apply to a solider in obeying his orders. To put it very practically and plainly, Paul says, "Children, do what your parents say."

TO CHILDREN

This is a crucially important matter. All through the Word of God you find exhortations to parents to teach their children to be obedient, and exhortations for children to be responsive to that teaching and to obey their parents. A child must learn the most important lesson of all: to be an obedient, respectful child. This is much more important than simply accomplishing the immediate wish to the parent, whatever it may be. Developing the character trait of obedience is the real issue.

I know one family in which obedience is taught to children in a very thoughtful, deliberate fashion. An order or request is given, and if the child procrastinates or refuses, the parent does not nag or repeat the command. Instead, Mom or Dad says, "Do what Mother (or Father) told you to do." That may seem like a subtle distinction, but it is really very important. The second command is different from the first. It is no longer focused on carrying out a chore or request. It is focused on teaching the importance of *obedience* and *respect* toward the parent. The first command had to do with getting the child to perform a task; the second command has to do with building Christlike, obedient character in that child.

It is significant that Paul gives a reason why children should obey their parents: "for this is right." Do not take this statement lightly. There is a natural human tendency to read those words and shrug them off without giving them much thought. But Paul is saying, quite significantly, that obedience to parents is realistic, it accords with fundamental reality, it is one of the basic laws of life. In other words, Paul says that if children obey their parents, everything will turn out right. If they refuse to do so, everything will go wrong, because disobedience to parents violates one of the fundamental laws of living.

THE MEANING OF HONOR

In verses 2 and 3, the apostle Paul presses deeper into this subject. He goes behind the actions to the attitudes. He says it is not only important to obey, but to obey in such a way as to *honor* your father and your mother. The *attitude* of obedience is exceedingly important. We know, of course, that it is possible to obey with a disobedient heart—a heart of icy rebellion and coldness. The actions are outwardly correct, but the heart is wrong. Inwardly, the child is just waiting for an opportunity to rebel and revolt.

This attitude is exemplified by the story of the little boy whose mother wanted him to sit down but he wouldn't sit down. Finally she took hold of him and sat him down in the chair. He looked up at her with defiant eyes and said, "You may make me sit down outside, but I'm still standing up inside!"

That kind of obedience is not true obedience at all because, as the apostle points out, it is dishonoring to the father or mother. It dishonors the parent by treating the parent as a thing, an obstacle, not as a human being who gives love, nurture, and care to that child. It ignores every generous gift of parental love. That is why the first commandment with a promise, as the apostle reminds us, is the commandment, "Honor your father and your mother, so that you may live long in the land the LORD your God is giving you" (Exodus 20:12).

What does this promise mean: "that you may live long in the land the LORD your God is giving you"? Does that sound like mere shallow superstition? No. God's Word is never shallow. It is always solidly substantial. This statement means that glad obedience, with an attitude of honor and respect, creates the conditions that tend to produce a long, healthy, happy life. Obedient children live constructively and productively, and they are less likely to fall prey to self-destructive temptations and snares—alcoholism, drug abuse, juvenile crime, laziness, poverty, and other forms of foolishness and rebellion.

Every day, our newspapers are filled with stories of young people who have gone astray, who have been killed in a drinking spree or by a drug overdose or in gang violence. So is obedience important? Absolutely. It can be a matter of life and death.

The issue of honor does not end with graduation or moving out of the house. Learning to obey and honor parents is necessary preparation for learning to obey and respect authority later in life. Adults are as much under authority as children. Everyone is accountable to some authority. Even the president of the United States must answer to the Constitution, the Congress, and the Supreme Court. No one is above authority. The sooner a child learns this lesson, the better his life will be.

TO PARENTS

But Paul doesn't stop with children.

This passage is, of course, an amplification of Ephesians 5:21: "Submit to one another out of reverence for Christ." Submission, as we have seen, is always a two-way street. The Word of God never says to one party only, "Submit." Submission is always mutual.

So if children are to submit themselves in obedience to parents, it is equally true that parents are to submit themselves to their children.

Paul explains in verse 4:

> Fathers, do not exasperate your children; instead, bring
> them up in the training and instruction of the Lord.

The word translated *Fathers* could just as well be translated *Parents*,
because it includes both the father and the mother. The emphasis is
laid largely upon the father, however, for it is his responsibility as
to what the children become. That is a sobering issue for fathers to
consider. Mothers may enforce policy, but it is the father's task to set
it, and to see that his children are raised properly.

How, then, does a father submit himself to his children? By avoiding the actions that make a child rebel—by not exasperating the
child. Obviously, there will be times when children become angry,
and when they rebel. There will be times, of course, when even the
best, most well-deserved, and most appropriate discipline will make a
child angry. These times of anger are momentary and to be expected.
That is not what Paul refers to here.

Paul is warning parents, and particularly fathers, to avoid the kind
of actions that, over time, tend to produce an overwhelmingly ex-
asperated, frustrated, sullen, rebellious nature in a child. The word
translated *exasperate* comes from a Greek word from which we get
our English word *paroxysm*. It means "anger that results in rebellion."
Paul is saying, in effect, "Fathers, do not provoke your children to the
place where they completely lose control and rebel against authority."

There are two styles of parenting that tend to produce rebellion in
children: indulgence and harshness. Both make a child feel unwanted
and insecure.

An over-indulgent parenting style leads a child to wonder, "Don't
my parents care about me enough to set boundaries and give me

discipline?" The child grows up into a spoiled and immature adult, expecting always to get his own way, and never caring about the needs or feelings of others.

An overly harsh parenting style makes a child think, "My parents always hurt me, they're unfair. I'm going to harden my emotions so that they can't hurt me anymore. When I escape my parents' control, I won't be anyone's victim anymore. I'll do all the shouting and bullying and hurting!"

In a previous time, the father was often a tyrant in his family. Children had to toe the mark and often had very little loving contact with their parents. Consequently, there was a great cultural swing away from this style of parenting.

But in our own day, we have seen the pendulum swing too far to the opposite extreme, toward indulgence. Today, all too often, we give our children everything and let them have their own way. We entrust to our children the power to make decisions they are not capable of making, including decisions about how late to stay out at night, what movies and music they should expose themselves to, their choice of friends, and so forth.

I remember being in the home of a Christian family with a three-year-old daughter. The little girl was watching television, and a show came on that was obviously unsuitable for a child of three. The father noticed the show and he said to the child, "Now, dear, you don't want to watch this, do you?" She said, "Sure, I do!" He pleaded rather weakly, "But I don't think this is good for you. Don't you think you'd better turn it off?" "No." "Well," he said, "you really shouldn't be watching this." She ignored him. Finally, the father shrugged and left the child to watch a completely inappropriate program.

I submit that a three-year-old child is totally incapable of making that kind of moral decision. The father should have acted without harshness, but firmly and decisively. That is exercising appropriate, godly parental responsibility. It is no wonder I observed this child behaving disrespectfully and disobediently—she had no boundaries and no sense of security. A lack of proper discipline, more than anything else, will create insecurity in a child, a sense of being unloved.

The limits of godly discipline are like walls. Walls can sometimes feel frustrating and confining. But walls serve a beneficial purpose. They symbolize safety and protection. Walls make us feel secure when night falls, when dogs howl outside and the wind blows. A child who momentarily rebels against walls during a time of discipline will one day be thankful for the safety and security and sense of love those walls supplied on a consistent basis, year after year, through childhood and adolescence.

Paul contrasts these two exasperating parenting styles with the right way to raise children: "instead, bring them up in the training and instruction of the Lord." Notice the two terms Paul uses: *training* and *instruction of the Lord*. The word *training* means discipline—a balance of love and limits. *Instruction of the Lord* means exhortation and teaching, or as the original Greek suggests, "putting in mind the things of the Lord."

As the child grows older, training (which involves forms of discipline ranging from spanking to taking away privileges) is to be replaced by teaching and helping the child to understand the principles that underlie rules and restrictions. As we train and instruct our children, we continually seek to show them that we are concerned for them and we love them. As training gives way to instruction, it does not mean we relax the limits. It means we enforce them in different ways, and gradually give children more responsibility and trust as they prove they are capable of handling it.

Dr. Howard Hendricks has summarized the principles for godly parenting with his *Seven Pointers For Parents.* They are:

1. Provide an atmosphere in the home that builds warm, close, personal relationships. Make sure the home is a place of belonging and acceptance. That means spending time with your children, so that they know you and you know them.

2. Be a good example to your children. Your faith and values will be more likely *caught* by your kids than *taught* to your kids. Don't be afraid to admit mistakes. Kids need to see that you are human, and big enough to accept grace and forgiveness. Then they will grow up into adults who can forgive and accept forgiveness as well.

3. Allow gradual emancipation from the apron strings of parental authority. Begin early to feed them responsibility, a little at a time. Evaluate the results and adjust their freedom according to their ability to handle it.

4. When children need guidance and counsel, provide a relaxed, informal setting. Spend time building a warm relationship with your child so that he or she will be more willing to accept your counsel.

5. Set limits. Children want and need the security of boundaries and restrictions. But discipline your children only in a context of love. Your children will not accept your limits unless they know they are loved, and you tell them you love them not only with words, but more importantly with your time, attention, and genuine interest.

6. Apply the law of natural consequences as they grow up. As your children grow in their ability to make decisions, let them decide—but also let them live with the results of their

decisions. If we make all their decisions for them, they will lose confidence in their own ability to make decisions. If we bail them out and shield them from the consequences of their decisions, they will grow up with an irresponsible attitude, expecting never to have to deal with consequences. In some cases, it's healthy for children to make mistakes and accept the consequences—as long as they are not consequences that cause serious or lifelong harm.

7. Most importantly, surround your children with a fortress of prayer. Trust the Spirit of God to care for them, cover for your inevitable occasional mistakes, and bring your children to a place of faith and maturity.

These are seven principles for raising children in a relationship of mutual submission. Our task as parents is to submit ourselves to our children by devoting ourselves to the process of loving, guiding, training, teaching, and praying for them, as they submit themselves, in attitude and deed, to our firm but gentle authority.

CHAPTER TWENTY-EIGHT

Employers and Employees

Ephesians 6:5–9

The apostle begins the next section of Ephesians 6 with counsel to slaves. You might think, "There are no slaves in my neighborhood or my church—this section of Ephesians doesn't apply to me or anyone I know!" Yet, if you're like a lot of people in today's workforce, you may feel more like a slave than an employee!

At the time Paul wrote the letter to the Ephesians, it is estimated that one-half of the population of the Roman Empire consisted of slaves, and many of these slaves were Christians. The Christian message did not come first to the upper classes, but to the working classes and the slaves. Many of the first century slaves were highly educated people who had been captured in the war and brought to other parts of the empire to be sold into bondage. It was among these people that the Christian message was first received.

There were also many slave-masters who had been changed by the Christian gospel. As these Christians, both slave and free, came together in worship, they learned that in Christ there is neither slave nor free. There are no distinctions in Christ over class or race or gender. The ground is level at the foot of the cross.

After church, of course, both slave and slave-master returned to their homes and their work, and the question naturally arose: "Well, what now? Are we only brothers on Sunday? What should our relationship be on Monday through Saturday?" This question had to be settled, and that is what the apostle does here in Ephesians 6:5–9. In the process, he sets forth principles that apply not only to slave and slave-master, but to the relationship between employee and employer.

CAPITAL AND LABOR IN MUTUAL SUBMISSION

It's true that Abraham Lincoln freed the slaves, but it is equally true that, when we work for an employer, we voluntarily sell our time and our labor to another person for a certain period of months or years. We work out a mutually agreeable relationship, and within the limits of that agreement, we are slaves to those to whom we sell our time and labor. So the issues Paul addresses are exactly the same today as they were in the first century: "How should we conduct ourselves toward those who work under us, or toward those for whom we labor?"

This implicit question underlying Paul's text points up the terrible failure of labor-management relations in our own time. From time to time, our entire nation experiences the paralyzing effects of the conflicts between capital and labor. These conflicts, which begin as wars of words in bargaining sessions and on picket lines, frequently escalate into wars of violence and even murder. The solution to all these problems is to be found once again in that single, simple sentence of the apostle Paul in Ephesians 5:21: "Submit to one another out of reverence for Christ." That is the key.

In Ephesians 6:5–9, Paul amplifies on the theme of that verse, applying it to the world of capital and labor. He begins by addressing labor—the first century slaves:

Slaves, obey your earthly masters with respect and fear, and with sincerity of heart, just as you would obey Christ. Obey them not only to win their favor when their eye is on you, but like slaves of Christ, doing the will of God from your heart. Serve wholeheartedly, as if you were serving the Lord, not men, because you know that the Lord will reward everyone for whatever good he does, whether he is slave or free.

In this illuminating passage, the apostle deals with two aspects of the employee's response to his employer: 1. The work or activity of an employee; 2. The attitude of the employee. Later, in verse 9, the apostle will deal with the employer's responsibility to the employee. If these Christian principles which govern the employer-employee relationship were observed in the world, the great conflicts between labor and management would be easily resolved. Let's look at each of these aspects of the employer-employee relationship.

COUNSEL FOR EMPLOYEES

1. Activity

First, there is an activity required on the part of employees, and it is put in one word—*obedience*. In verse 5, Paul says, "Slaves, obey your earthly masters with respect and fear, and with sincerity of heart, just as you would obey Christ." This word *obey* is the same Greek word that occurs in 6:1—"Children, obey your parents." It is a military term meaning "to follow orders." Christian employees are under the same obligation of obedience as a soldier under the authority of a superior officer or a child under the authority of a parent. His obligation is very simply: Do what the boss says.

It is interesting that there is not one word said about unfair conditions or collective bargaining or strikes or picket lines. Someone reading Paul's words today might think, "Well, this is obviously inadequate advice. It doesn't cover the kind of unfair situations that labor faces today." Really? What kind of a labor situation is slavery? It is without question the epitome of unfairness! There is nothing more degrading you can do to a man than deprive him of his freedom!

Yet nowhere in the New Testament is there a word that says slaves should rise up, revolt against their masters, organize into unions, or bring political pressure to bear upon society. Despite this fact, history shows that Christianity has been a liberating force in the world. The Christian faith produced liberation and the end of slavery not by direct assault upon the institution of slavery, but by slowly undermining the cultural foundation of slavery with Christian grace and love, with the principle that in Christ there is no slave or slavemaster, that all are brothers and sisters, members of the body of Christ.

It is significant that one section of Edward Gibbon's classic work of history, *The Decline and Fall of the Roman Empire,* begins with these words:

> While that great body [the Roman Empire] was invaded by open violence or undermined by slow decay, a pure and humble religion gently insinuated itself into the minds of men, grew up in silence and obscurity, derived new vigor from opposition, and finally erected the triumphant banner of the cross on the ruins of the capital.

That is how Christianity threw slavery out of the Roman Empire— not by a siege of violence, but by the spread of Christlike love and acts of humble mutual submission.

2. Attitude

After activity, Paul addresses the *attitude* of the Christian employee. Paul has two things to say about the Christian employee's attitude. The first thing is this: Live out your obedience "with respect and fear." Respect and fear of the boss? No! He may be an ogre and an unjust man, but no Christian is ever exhorted to be a trembling, spineless, chinless individual in the presence of any other human being. Paul is not suggesting you should be "a mouse studying to be a rat."

The respect and fear Paul mentions is to be directed toward our own human frailty. Paul is talking here about a healthy recognition of the danger of a Christian getting sucked into the power struggles that characterize labor-management relations. He is warning the Christian worker not to play the rebellious power games of this world, which would destroy the possibility of God working through him. God wants to release His power through us in the situations of our daily lives, but He can't work through us if we are planning a slave revolt against the boss!

Whenever we see this phrase "respect and fear" (or, as some translations render it, "fear and trembling") in Paul's writings, the context makes it clear that this respect and fear is directed inward. He wants us to respect and fear the fact that we are capable of acting in our human flesh and missing out on what God wants to do through us. In 1 Corinthians 2:3–5, Paul writes,

> I came to you in weakness and fear, and with much trembling. My message and my preaching were not with wise and persuasive words, but with a demonstration of the Spirit's power, so that your faith might not rest on men's wisdom, but on God's power.

Here, Paul uses the term "fear and trembling" in reference to his own human weakness. His fear and trembling was not directed at other men, nor at God. He feared lest he came to the Corinthians reflecting his own fallible thoughts or wise, persuasive words of some worldly philosophy. He wanted only to come in God's power, because if he came in his own power, he would rob those people of the power of Jesus Christ.

In Philippians 2:12, Paul again uses the term "fear and trembling" when he writes, "continue to work out your salvation with fear and trembling." Why with fear and trembling? Because, as he says in the next verse, "it is God who works in you to will and to act according to his good purpose." We should be afraid of trying to do God's work in our own fleshly strength. His purpose is to work through us in His own limitless strength—and we should have fear of falling short of that.

In verse 6 and 7, Paul goes on to talk about an employee's attitude of *integrity*. Paul writes, "Obey them not only to win their favor when their eye is on you, but like slaves of Christ, doing the will of God from your heart. Serve wholeheartedly, as if you were serving the Lord, not men." In other words, we should work with the same intensity and care whether we are being observed or not. We shouldn't need to have the boss standing over us with a stick, making sure we get the job done.

The word *integrity* comes from the same root word as *integrated*. When we have integrity, our outer self is integrated and consistent with our inner self, our public side matches our private side, what the boss doesn't see matches what the boss does see. We are the same person doing the same job with the same attention and intensity, whether anyone is watching or not. Why? Because we are not merely pleasing the boss, we are pleasing the Lord—and He is *always* watching. When you do your work as unto Christ, your supreme concern is your loyalty to Him. When He is the one you are trying to please, you can do your job joyfully and well—even if your boss is a cantankerous old slave-driver.

We work for Christ! What a glory this gives to every task. If you approach your work with this attitude, you will never have another dull day. You will never grow bored with the routine of the day as long as you recognize that you are doing everything under the watchful eye of the Lord, looking only for His approval.

You may ask, "But in my job, I am never rewarded or even commended for the work I do—and that's very discouraging and demoralizing to me as an employee. How can I stay motivated to do my job when I never receive any positive feedback or incentive?" To that question, Paul replies in verse 8 that you should be motivated by the knowledge "that the Lord will reward everyone for whatever good he does, whether he is slave or free." It doesn't matter what your status on the job is, whether you work in the corner office or the basement, God will reward you for a job well done. He doesn't promise to change your conditions of employment, He doesn't promise that your boss is going to be nice to you—but He does promise to reward you for everything you are going through in obedience to the gospel.

COUNSEL FOR BOSSES

In verse 9 we see that Paul again carries out the consistent reciprocity of Ephesians 5:21: "Submit to one another out of reverence for Christ." Employees must submit to their bosses for the sake of Christ—but bosses must also submit to employees for the same reason. Paul writes:

> And masters, treat your slaves in the same way. Do not threaten them, since you know that he who is both their

Master and yours is in heaven, and there is no favoritism with him.

This is an amazing thing Paul has said to bosses. He has just told employees to obey their bosses—and now he turns around and commands bosses to treat their employees "in the same way." Does Paul mean that bosses should *obey* their employees? Yes! But not by doing their work for them or taking orders from them, because that would be a reversal of their roles. What the apostle means is that bosses should be sensitive to the needs and feelings of their employees. Employers need to hear their workers' suggestions, complaints, and ideas. They should submit to their workers in the sense of really listening and noticing when a situation needs correcting.

In the parallel passage in Colossians, Paul puts it this way: "Masters, provide your slaves with what is right and fair, because you know that you also have a Master in heaven" (Colossians 4:1). Christian boss, remember that you also have a Master, and He shows no favoritism toward a boss. Before the Lord, masters and slaves are on an equal footing. He will demand an accounting from you as to how you have treated those He has entrusted to your care and stewardship. So listen to them and value them. Honor the image of God that is reflected in each one.

Paul also warns bosses not to threaten employees. Why? Because the primary cause of employee unhappiness is to constantly have a sword of Damocles over their heads. Threats of dismissal or other kinds of retribution and punishment serve to knot the stomachs and poison the minds of employees, filling them with resentment and bitterness. It creates more problems than it solves. That is not the way our Master treats us, and you, as a boss, should not treat your employees that way, either. Yes, if someone is not qualified to do the job, then follow correct procedures and dismiss him—but don't constantly threaten and intimidate him on the job. That is wrong in the eyes of God. The godly way of management is based on mutual respect and submission, not on fear and intimidation.

Paul's counsel in this passage completely cancels out the comments so often heard today: "I don't mix business and religion." Or, "The church is one thing, but business is business." Or, "These days, you have to do these things to stay on top." Nonsense, Jesus is the Master of your workweek, just as He is the master of your worship. If you shut Him out of your business on Monday through Friday, then how dare you call Him "Lord" on Sunday?

Ephesians 6:5–9 calls all of us—master and slave, boss and worker, capital and labor—to a single focus: mutual submission under the authority of Jesus Christ. Whatever our status, whatever our title, whether we call the shots or do the grunt work, we serve the same Master—

And the ground is level at the foot of the cross.

PART FOUR

Spiritual Warfare

Ephesians 6:10–20

CHAPTER TWENTY-NINE

Facing the Battle

Ephesians 6:10–13

Os Guinness, the Christian author of *The Dust of Death*, once went to England to give a lecture series at Essex University. As he was being introduced to the audience, moments before he was about to speak, he noticed a young woman sitting in the front row. What caught his attention was that the young woman had the most peculiar expression on her face—a look of fierce anguish. Recalling a warning he had received that antichristian protesters might attempt to disrupt his lecture series, Guinness paused to pray that God would bless the meeting and restrain Satan so that God's own message would go forth with power.

Then Guinness stepped to the lectern and proceeded to give his talk. The lecture proceeded without interruption and was enthusiastically received. After his talk, the young woman with the strange expression came up to him. She was angry—and baffled. "How did you do that?" she demanded.

"How did I do what?" asked Guinness.

"What sort of spell did you cast on me to keep me in my seat?" the woman asked. "You knew I had been sent here by the witches' coven to protest your talk, didn't you? And you put some kind of spell on me to keep me silent!"

"The only 'spell' I used," Guinness gently replied, "was to pray in the name of the Lord Jesus Christ."

A few weeks later, Os Guinness was back in America. A Christian lady asked how his Essex lecture series had gone. "The reason I ask," she explained, "is that at the same time you were about to begin your lecture in England, I was suddenly overcome by an impression of you standing on a platform and a woman seated in the audience in front of you. I had a sense that a battle was going on between you—a spiritual battle between the power of God and the power of Satan. And I immediately went to my knees and prayed for you and for the woman in the audience."

The apostle Paul would have told Os Guinness and his praying friend the same thing he now tells us in Ephesians 6: There *is* a battle raging—a battle between unseen forces in our own visible world. It is *spiritual warfare*, and you and I are on the front lines of that battle.

FACING REALITY, FACING THE BATTLE

We can only truly understand life when we see it as the Bible sees it. That is why the Word of God was given: to introduce us to real reality. All that we think of as reality—the world of human society, the events that parade across our TV screens and newspaper headlines, the world of politics, commerce, society, and entertainment—is mere illusion compared to the deep reality God has presented to us in His Word. When we come to the Bible, we learn the truth. Here the world is set before us as it really is.

One of the most fundamental truths the Bible presents to us is that, behind the façade of this world, there is an invisible battle raging. This battle takes many casualties, and there are no innocent bystanders, no noncombatants. Every human being on this planet, whether he or she is aware of it or not, is forced to take one side or the other in this great cosmic war. There is no room for neutrality.

So it is critically important that you and I know how to defend ourselves and arm ourselves for battle. Satan is locked and loaded, and his bullets have our names on them. If we don't want to end up on the casualty list, we need to train ourselves for the battle and arm ourselves with the armor God has provided.

In Ephesians 6:10–13, Paul writes:

> Finally, be strong in the Lord and in his mighty power. Put on the full armor of God so that you can take your stand against the devil's schemes. For our struggle is not against flesh and blood, but against the rulers, against the authorities, against the powers of this dark world and against the spiritual forces of evil in the heavenly realms. Therefore put on the full armor of God, so that when the day of evil comes, you may be able to stand your ground, and after you have done everything, to stand.

In this passage we see that Paul's view of life can be summed up in a single word: *struggle*. Life, he says, is a conflict. The reality of Paul's words is confirmed constantly by our experience.

We don't like to hear this. We would rather think of life as an idealized, peaceful journey, drifting from birth until the moment God calls us home to be with Him. We would rather think of the world as a wonderland of images from the pages of *National Geographic*. It is disturbing and troubling to think of life as a struggle and the world as a battleground.

But Paul won't let us duck reality. He wants us to understand the struggle we face so that we can withstand the onslaught and emerge victorious. He doesn't want us to end up as victims but as victors in this heroic struggle. And the only way we can hope to survive is by understanding the nature of the battle and the enemy we face. He is trying to jar us out of our materialistic stupor, make us look beyond the paper-thin walls of this fading world, and confront us with the bedrock realities that encircle us.

"Therefore put on the full armor of God," he tells us, "so that when the day of evil comes, you may be able to stand your ground." That sounds ominous, doesn't it? What "day of evil" is Paul foreshadowing in this passage? Clearly, Paul implies that all days are not the same. Some times are more evil than others. There are seasons in life when pressures are more intense, when problems are more insoluble, when everything seems to come upon us at once. Sometimes it is an actual day, sometimes it is a week, sometimes months. But thank God, all of life is not that way. There are good days, and there are evil days.

Tragically, most of us take the times of refreshment, blessing, and glory for granted, never returning a word of thanksgiving to God for the good times in our lives. We see the good times in life as our due, and see the evil days as unfair intrusions into our perfectly ordered lives. The fact is, evil is our due as sinners, and all the good we receive is a gift of God's grace, for which we should be continually grateful. Instead of complaining about the evil days, we should recognize— with the realism of the apostle Paul—that life is a constant struggle, varying in intensity over time, but extending from the cradle to the grave. That is reality. That is the message of Ephesians 6.

OUR ENEMY

In verse 12 Paul tells us, "For our struggle is not against flesh and blood, but against the rulers, against the authorities, against the powers of this dark world and against the spiritual forces of evil in the heavenly realms." This is a crucially important point: our conflict is not against flesh and blood. The invisible war involves human beings, it is waged within and around human beings, and there are human beings on both sides of the battle lines—but human beings are not the enemy. Those human beings who appear to be against us are really nothing more than pawns of the *real* enemy. Our struggle is not man against man. Our enemy is an *inhuman* enemy.

We look around us and see the great conflicts in the world. We see warring philosophies—East versus West, communism versus capitalism, totalitarianism versus democracy. The evil empire of Soviet communism has fallen—but has the cold war ended? No, the balance of power has shifted, and China is emerging as a new superpower, seeking world domination. But is communism our enemy in the great invisible struggle that Paul talks about? No. Communism, despite its godless, atheistic underpinnings, is a mere momentary blip on the radar screen of this long, invisible struggle. Our struggle is not against flesh and blood communists, but against an invisible—and even more frightening—enemy.

Our battle is not against Democrats or Republicans, nor against Libertarians or Socialists. The political parties keep society stirred up with their speeches and political intrigues and stubborn attempts to paint themselves as the saviors of the nation and their opponents as the worst evil this side of Adolph Hitler. But the flesh and blood political ideologues of the left and the right are not our enemies. I'm not saying that political issues are inconsequential, nor that voting and participating in politics is meaningless. But let's be clear about this: The political battle between left and right is not the battle Paul calls us to in Ephesians 6.

Our battle is not against any nation or race. Our battle is not against the upper classes or the lower classes. Our battle is not against the press or the business establishment. Our battle is not even against the Internal Revenue Service—though the wiles and schemes of the IRS certainly seem diabolical at times!

Our battle, in short, is not against other people. That's hard for us to get through our heads—but that's what Paul wants us to understand. As long as we look only for human enemies, we are in danger of being blindsided by the *real* enemy. Arrayed against you and me and the entire human race are forces beyond our comprehension— rulers, authorities, powers of this dark world, and spiritual forces of evil in the heavenly realms. The nature of our battle, and the reality of our enemy, can only be understood by Christians.

The world ridicules and rejects the biblical analysis of reality, including Paul's warnings about our spiritual enemy. The rulers and powers Paul alerts us to in Ephesians 6 have been reduced to a silly pantheon of mythical refugees from a Halloween costume party— goblins, vampires, witches, spooks, and ghouls. No wonder the modern mind rejects the supernatural, since the unseen world is generally represented (or misrepresented) in this way.

I am well aware of the disdain and contempt that so often greets the concept of a real, personal devil these days. "Are you going to insult our intelligence by talking about the devil?" people ask. "Surely you don't expect us to believe in that ridiculous creature in red tights, with horns and a pitchfork and cloven hoofs!" No, I don't expect you to believe in any such laughable caricature. Instead, I ask you to examine with me the spiritual reality that Paul presents—which is not laughable in any way whatsoever.

It is not only atheists and agnostics who scoff at the idea of a real and personal devil. I once spent an evening in Berlin with a number of very learned and intelligent pastors and theologians. Though we never once opened a Bible, we spent the whole evening together discussing various passages from the Bible—these men knew the Bible so well, they could quote entire passages from memory. Yet they all rejected the idea of a personal devil. By the end of the evening, they admitted that, in their rejection of the devil, they also had no answer to the problems and puzzles of life—the existence of every sort of evil from such random acts of madness as the Manson cult murders to the deliberate, methodical stockpiling of weapons of mass destruction.

The question I kept posing to them was, "If there is no devil, then how do you explain what is going on in the world? How do you explain the horrible entrenched evil in human history and in our newspapers every day?" They had no answer.

It is clear that we cannot understand life unless we begin with Paul's revelation of the hidden war that rages behind the scenes of human history. Once we accept the proposition of a spiritual battle and a personal devil, then so many events in history become clear: the repeated persecutions against Christians and attempts to destroy the church; the relentless attempts through history to ban, burn, and eradicate the Bible; the pogroms against the Jews and the genocidal Holocaust of World War II; the repeated attempts by various nations to scour the nation of Israel off the map. Clearly, there is a vast demonic conspiracy seeking to upset God's program, but His plan is sure, His ultimate victory will take place in the fullness of time.

RULERS, AUTHORITIES, POWERS, AND FORCES

Paul goes on to tell us that our real battle is "against the rulers, against the authorities, against the powers of this dark world and against the spiritual forces of evil in the heavenly realms." The world, Paul tells us, is in the grip of invisible world rulers! The world rulers of this present darkness are headed by the devil, whom Scripture says is a fallen angel of malevolent power and cunning. That is not the claim of an isolated passage of the Bible. That is the consistent teaching of the Bible from beginning to end, from Genesis to Revelation—*especially* in Genesis and Revelation, in fact!

Jesus himself put his finger on the whole problem when He said to certain men of His day, "You belong to your father, the devil, and you want to carry out your father's desire. He was a murderer from the beginning, not holding to the truth, for there is no truth in him. When he lies, he speaks his native language, for he is a liar and the father of lies" (John 8:44). In that analysis, the Lord stripped the devil of his disguises and revealed his true character—a liar and a murderer. What the devil does is because of who he is, just as what we do is due to what we are. Because he is a liar and a murderer, the devil's work is to deceive and to destroy. There you have the explanation for all that is going on in human history.

The devil has the ear of the human race. Scripture calls him "the god of this age" who "has blinded the minds of unbelievers, so that they cannot see the light of the gospel of the glory of Christ, who is the image of God" (2 Corinthians 4:4). The world listens to everything he says, and he spins a beautiful, attractive lie that makes the world drool with desire. But the end of his lie is destruction, murder, and death—death in all its forms, not only the cessation of life, but also in the form of defeat, despair, meaninglessness, and emptiness. Whom the devil cannot deceive he tries to destroy, and whom he cannot destroy he attempts to deceive.

"Well," you say, "this is all very depressing. I would rather not think about it." I would rather not think about it either—but I have discovered that you cannot get away from it. There is only one way to handle this struggle and that is to "be strong in the Lord and in his mighty power" (Ephesians 6:10). That is the only way of escape. There is no other.

This is a call to intelligent combat. It is a call to fight the good fight, to stand fast in the faith, to be strong in the Lord in the midst of battle. Don't you hear the trumpet call in these words of Paul's? We must take this seriously and learn what life is all about. We must learn to recognize these dark systems and how they work.

More than that, we must learn how to overcome the rulers, authorities, powers, and forces arrayed against us. They cannot be fought by weapons of the flesh. The weapons of our warfare are not of the body, but of God. Our weapons are mighty, capable of pulling down satanic strongholds and bringing into captivity every thought. That is our arena—the realm of thought, of ideas, of soul, of spirit, or will, of obedience. That is our challenge—to answer the trumpet call and submit ourselves to the military leadership of our Lord and Commander, Jesus Christ, as He leads us into the greatest battle of all time, of all eternity. That is our battle cry—"Be strong in the Lord and in his mighty power!"

THE STRONG MAN—AND THE STRONGER MAN

Notice that Paul suggests that the only ones who can successfully battle against these dark forces are Christians: "For *our* struggle is not against flesh and blood . . . ." The phrase "our struggle" refers to the struggle of Christians. This is a uniquely Christian battle. No one but Christians are capable of being victors in this war; all others are victims.

Jesus makes this point clear in Luke 11. There He is challenged by the religious leaders because He goes about casting out demons. His opponents say that He is able to cast out demons because He has a relationship with Beelzebub, the prince of demons—another name for Satan. The name Beelzebub means "lord of the garbage." The Jews regarded hell as a cosmic garbage dump, and in a real sense they were right, for that is exactly what hell is—the awful repository of wasted lives. The god who reigned over this garbage heap was the devil, and because a garbage pile always attracts flies, they called Beelzebub the lord of the flies.

When these religious leaders accuse Jesus of casting out demons by the authority of Beelzebub, Jesus replies, "If Satan is divided against himself, how can his kingdom stand? I say this because you claim that I drive out demons by Beelzebub" (Luke 11:18). His argument is simply this: Satan never fights against himself. Satan is too cunning to divide his forces in that way. If he did, his kingdom would fall. Therefore, Jesus suggests that any man under the control of Satan has no possibility of deliverance apart from an outside, intervening force.

He elaborates in Luke 11:21, "When a strong man, fully armed, guards his own house, his possessions are safe." Who is the strong man? Satan. What is the house of the strong man? The world. What are the strong man's possessions? People. Apart from the intervention of God, we as human beings belong to Satan. We are powerless and hopeless in our own strength. As 1 John 5:19 tells us, "We know that we [Christians] are children of God, and that the whole world is under the control of the evil one." That is the position of the Bible—the world has fallen under the control of Satan. Not the world of trees and mountains and lakes and seas; that is God's world. But the world of organized human society has fallen under the control of Satan, and there is no possibility of escape apart from outside intervention.

Here, our Lord puts His finger on the reason for the continual failure of human efforts to correct evils and wrongs. They fail because they do not come to grips with the essential problem. All our methods of correcting the evils of our society—legislation, education, social programs—are merely rearranging the deck chairs on the Titanic. The real problem we face is below the water line of human awareness, in the invisible realm. Human efforts can never solve the central problem of evil because they do not come to grips with the power of Satan.

The obvious failure of human efforts to correct human evil has led many of our leading activists and philosophers into despair. The atheistic philosopher, Bertrand Russell, sums up the conclusion of all who have tried to end human evil through such efforts as increased legislation, education, and social engineering:

> The life of man is a long march through the night, surrounded by invisible foes, tortured by weariness and pain, toward a goal that few can hope to reach and where none can tarry long. One by one as they march our comrades vanish from our sight, seized by the silent orders of omnipotent death. Brief and powerless is man's life. On him and all his race the slow, sure doom falls, pitiless and dark. Blind to good and evil, reckless of destruction, omnipotent matter rolls on its relentless way.

Those words express the despair of our age, the feeling of utter human hopelessness and helplessness in the face of towering human evil. What the lawmakers, educators, and social tinkerers fail to understand is that they are contending against rulers, authorities, powers of this dark world, and spiritual forces of evil in the heavenly realms. In short, they are hopelessly outmatched and don't even know it! They think they are wrestling against flesh and blood—then they are baffled and bewildered when the evil they confront is so monstrous and cosmic in scope!

THE CRISIS OF HISTORY

In Luke 11:22, our Lord introduces us to the solution to the problem of human evil: "But when someone stronger attacks and overpowers him, he takes away the armor in which the man trusted and divides up the spoils."

Who is this stronger one? It is Jesus. He is speaking of himself. He says that when a strong man (Satan), fully armed, guards his house (the world), his possessions (human beings) are securely kept within his grasp. But when One who is stronger comes (Jesus), He breaks the power of that strong man, and frees the possessions (human beings) from the evil strong man's grasp.

This is the good news of the gospel: Jesus is the stronger man who breaks the power of Satan and sets us free, as in the words of the hymn:

> He breaks the power of canceled sin,
> He sets the prisoner free;
> His blood can make the foulest clean,
> His blood availed for me.

In the mystery of the cross of Jesus, in the power of His resurrection, we who have been born into a world under the dominion of satanic forces are now set free. The power of Satan and sin has been canceled and broken. There is no other power that can do that but the power of the "stronger man," Jesus. That is why the Christian gospel is unique. It offers the solutions to the problems of the human race—solutions that our best and brightest human minds have despaired of finding in their own human strength and wisdom.

Jesus came into the world "to destroy the devil's work" (1 John 3:8). There is no adequate explanation of His coming apart from that explanation. Paul says that God, through Christ, "has rescued us from the dominion of darkness and brought us into the kingdom of the Son he loves" (Colossians 1:13). This is what the gospel is for; it has no other purpose. If we try to channel it first into smaller areas of life, such as applying it to social concerns, we only reveal how far we have mistaken its purpose. The gospel ultimately finds its way there, certainly, but it must first and foremost make its impact upon this basic problem of human life—the problem of sin and enslavement under the dominion of Satan.

Our Lord reveals one other crucial principle in Luke 11:23: "He who is not with me is against me, and he who does not gather with me, scatters." Jesus is saying that no neutral ground is possible. If you are not on the Lord's side, you have sided with the enemy. There are always those who say, "I understand something of the gospel, and I see a lot of valuable principles in the Christian faith. I wouldn't call myself a 'born-again Christian,' and I have never gone so far as to personally receive Christ as my Lord and Savior, but I am a friend of Christianity." Jesus says that such a position is impossible. There is no neutrality. If Jesus has not delivered you from sin by grace through faith, then you are still under the bondage and control of the dark powers of Satan. There are no exceptions.

This is why Jesus Christ is the crisis of history. He spoke of himself that way—as the divider of men. He divides nations, societies, communities, families, and even church congregations into two groups—those who are with Him and those who are against Him. Either you have received Him or you have rejected Him. Either you are a child of God—or you are a child of wrath. There is no middle ground.

Jesus has come to destroy the devil's work. That is the nature of the real but invisible war that rages within us and around us.

You must decide today. You must choose one side of the battle line or the other. Whose side are you on?

CHAPTER THIRTY

The Satanic Strategy

Ephesians 6:10–13

In 1862, at the height of the Civil War, General Ulysses S. Grant had surrounded Fort Donelson, Tennessee, and was undecided whether or not to attack. As Grant's forces waited, a Confederate deserter was caught escaping from the fort. He was searched in General Grant's presence and found to have six days' rations in his kit. Grant instantly made up his mind to attack. When his men asked why, the general replied, "You don't give six days' rations to soldiers in a fort unless you intend to retreat. The men in that fort mean to retreat, not stand and fight. Prepare to attack."

And Grant captured Fort Donelson.

When you know the enemy's plans, you have the key to victory in your hands. In Ephesians 6:10–13, Paul gives us the key to victory in our spiritual warfare by placing the devil's plans—the satanic strategy—in our hands. The apostle writes:

Finally, be strong in the Lord and in his mighty power. Put on the full armor of God so that you can take your stand against the devil's schemes. For our struggle is not against flesh and blood, but against the rulers, against the authorities, against the powers of this dark world and against the spiritual forces of evil in the heavenly realms. Therefore put on the full armor of God, so that when the day of evil comes, you may be able to stand your ground, and after you have done everything, to stand.

We have already examined this passage in the previous chapter of our study. Now we will give closer attention to Satan's strategy—and our Lord's counterstrategy—for the actual conduct of this battle.

THE DEVIL'S SCHEMES

The first step for any soldier in training is to study the strategy and weapons the enemy will use against him. The devil is a cunning and wily strategist. As Martin Luther wrote in the hymn "A Mighty Fortress Is Our God":

> For still our ancient foe
> Doth seek to work us woe;
> His craft and power are great,
> And, armed with cruel hate,
> On earth is not his equal.

Read the Old Testament and you will see that every saint, every prophet, every patriarch, every one of the great and glorious kings of Israel was defeated at one time or another by the devil. The wisest and greatest of men are absolutely helpless to outwit the devil by their own human power.

Yet we are not without hope. The Bible tells us that we can be victorious over Satan. "Resist the devil, and he will flee from you," says James 4:7. Think of it! This diabolically brilliant strategist who has held the world in chains for centuries will flee when you are alert to his schemes.

What, then, is the satanic strategy?

The only human being who ever consistently defeated the devil, not only in life but in death, is the Lord Jesus Christ. He put His finger squarely on the strategy and the tactics of Satan when He said, ". . . the devil . . . was a murderer from the beginning, not holding to the truth, for there is no truth in him. When he lies, he speaks his native language, for he is a liar and the father of lies" (John 8:44). The strategy of the devil is to murder. The tactic by which he accomplishes this is to lie. If we consider these phrases carefully, we will see how accurate they are.

How does the devil plan to oppose the work of God in the world? By murdering and destroying. One of the names given to the devil in the book of the Revelation is "Apollyon," which means "the Destroyer." To destroy is to create chaos, to lay waste, to ruin, to make desolate. There you have the explanation for the whole tragic story of human history: a Destroyer is at work among men. Our God is a God of creativity, beauty, harmony, order, and perfection. There is enough evidence left in the world of nature, and in the world of ideas, to see this marvelous symmetry, beauty, and perfection of God. The world was created as orderly and beautiful.

Then came the Destroyer.

It is his delight to smash, mangle, twist, mutilate, disfigure, and blast in every way he can. It does not make any difference whether it is bodies or souls, flesh or ideas, matter or spirit—the aim of the devil is exactly the same in every case. That is why the devil can never offer anything positive to human beings. He can make nothing. He is not creative. All he can do is destroy what God has made. His power is totally negative, completely destructive in every way.

The devil carries out his tactics by lying, distorting, counterfeiting, and masquerading. He uses illusion and fantasy to lure human beings to their destruction. This is what Paul calls "the devil's schemes." Read through the Bible, and you will see how many times the work of the devil is referred to this way—as snares, traps, illusions, wiles, and schemes.

The tactics of the devil fall into two major divisions. He attacks the human race both directly and indirectly. And through these two avenues he maintains his worldwide control over the human race. The Bible tells us there are hosts of fallen, rebellious angels called "demons," whom Paul calls here rulers, authorities, powers of this dark world, and spiritual forces of evil in the heavenly realms.

The term "heavenly realms," of course, does not refer to heaven, the dwelling place of God. It refers to the realm of the invisible, the unseen, spiritual realities of life. The devil and his hosts are not visible. The devil's activity is carried out in the heavenly places, where God works, as well as the devil.

The Bible tells us very little of the origin of the devil and his angels, these authorities and invisible powers. There is enough to suggest that Satan was created originally as an angel of light and strength and beauty. There is a brief reference to the fall of this great angel, whose name was Lucifer, due to the sin of pride. The mark of the devil is arrogant, rebellious pride. Lifted up by pride, he set out to rival God and, in doing so, he fell from his exalted place, taking a third of the angels with him. They became the devil and his organized kingdom of darkness, set in opposition to the kingdom of God. It is through these hosts of wicked spirits that Satan is able to make a direct assault upon human life.

DIRECT ASSAULT

This demonic direct assault is what the Bible refers to as "demon possession," the outright control of a human personality by the power of a wicked spirit. It also extends to such activities as soothsaying, occultism, spiritism (or spiritualism), and related black magic arts such as astrology, fortune-telling, voodoo, and so forth. While there are many charlatans and frauds who practice in these areas, deceiving people for dishonest gain. I believe there are also genuine practitioners of black magic—and such people are in league with demonic spirits.

The Bible consistently warns against dabbling in these matters. Under the Old Testament law, the people of Israel were strictly forbidden to have anything to do with wizards and those who make contact with the dead. This prohibition was because any investigation into this realm immediately lays one open to powers beyond people's understanding. This is dangerous ground. It opens the way, oftentimes, to outright demon possession.

Some people confuse demon possession with mental illness. The Bible, however, makes a distinction between mental illness and demon possession. The writers of the Scriptures were certainly aware of this distinction. One of them, Luke, was a physician himself and was acquainted with the distinction between diseases, mental illnesses, and demon possession (see Luke 4:40–41). In Matthew 4:24 a careful distinction is made between those who were afflicted by diseases, those who were demon possessed, and those who were mentally ill.

It is important to note that biblical cases of demon possession do not conform to the clinical pattern of mental disease. There are diseases of the body and there are diseases of the mind. Diseases of the mind, like those of the body, present standard clinical patterns which can be recognized. But when you examine the biblical accounts of demon possession you find that they do not fit the standard patterns of mental diseases.

In the first place, there is always a debasing element in biblical cases of demon possession—an uncleanness, a moral defilement. Also in the biblical accounts of demon possession there is an immediate recognition by the demon of the Lord Jesus Christ. When Christ approached these demons who had taken possession of an individual, the demon would often call out, "What do you want with me, Jesus, Son of the Most High God?" (see Matthew 8:29; Luke 8:28). They called Him by name and used titles for Him that the possessed victims would not be acquainted with.

Further, there is always the presence of a totally distinct and different personality involved. In some cases many personalities were involved, as in the incident when Jesus asked the name of the demon and the reply was, "My name is Legion, for we are many" (Mark 5:9).

Finally, we see that Jesus was able to command demons from an individual to animals, as when He sent the demons into the pigs in Matthew 8. If demon possession is merely mental illness, how do we explain the demons leaving the man and entering the pigs, causing them to rush down the hillside and drown themselves in the sea? These cases simply do not conform to any clinical pattern of known mental disease.

Jesus himself described these cases as demon possession, and He treated them that way. He dealt with such manifestations on a regular basis. He also sent out His disciples and gave them authority to cast out demons, "Well," you might say, "I can explain that. Jesus was accommodating himself to the superstitious thought of the people of His day. They believed in demons, and He simply spoke their language." But it is impossible to take that position and be consistent with the rest of the account of Christ's ministry, for we see him constantly correcting misconceptions of that sort. On one occasion He told His disciples concerning another matter, "If it were not so, I would have told you" (John 14:2). He came to reveal the truth, not leave people in ignorance and superstition.

Throughout the Christian centuries, there have been outbreaks of demon possession described by missionaries in many lands. Wherever Christian teaching spreads, the direct assault of evil powers is held in check. Even secular teaching based on the Bible and Christian values has an ability to keep these manifestations under control.

But when education becomes purely secular and denies the reality of God and the validity of the Bible, then even though men and women reject superstition and profess a degree of sophistication about such matters, they invite direct satanic attack. As our world grows more godless and secularized, we are finding a rise of demonic manifestation sweeping over our culture. Today, witchcraft and the occult are widely considered alternative religions, right alongside Christianity and Judaism.

We are in desperate need of revival, of a revived and revitalized church that will stand against the demonic onslaught against our society. When the gospel goes out into a society with prayer and power, demons are held in check.

When Christians are confronted with what they suspect is demon possession, the one thing we are told to do in order to help such people is to pray. Cases of demon possession, Jesus said, yield themselves to concerted and persistent prayer. Prayer is the recommended therapy in any case of this type, and we should give ourselves to prayer and nothing more.

I believe there is altogether too much concern among Christians about this matter of demon possession. That sounds almost as though I am contradicting what I have said before, but I am merely trying to balance it. I know certain Christians who feel they must "bind" Satan before they do anything of a spiritual nature. When they go into a room to have a meeting, they pray to bind the powers of darkness before they open the meeting. I know others who ascribe every problem of human life to some manifestation of demonic activity.

There are no grounds in the New Testament for such an approach. The apostles very seldom mention the direct attack of Satan against human beings. There are a few instances of it in the gospel accounts, but after our Lord physically left the world, there seems to be a lessening of the evidences of demonic activity. These dark powers were no doubt stirred up by His presence on earth, but to a degree this activity faded after He ascended, so that in the epistles you do not get the same concern for demonic activity as you do in the gospels. There is much about Satan in the letters of Paul, but little about the direct attack of satanic forces. Nowhere do you read that Christians are instructed to go around binding the powers of darkness before entering a room, nor are we instructed to view common problems as the result of demonic activities.

INDIRECT ASSAULT—THE WORLD

By far the majority of the satanic attacks against Christians are not direct but indirect. That is why they are called the schemes of the devil. Scheming suggests deviousness, deception, and subterfuge. A direct attack of the devil upon a human life is an obvious thing, but much more common is the crafty, deceptive, almost undetectable assault—those subtle satanic suggestions and misdirections that come to us through the natural, commonplace channels of life.

The indirect attack comes to us primarily through two channels the Bible calls "the world" and "the flesh." You may have heard it said that the enemies of the Christian are the world, the flesh, and the devil. But there are not three enemies, just one: the devil. And the devil will use the world and the flesh as a way to get his hooks into us. In Ephesians 2:1–3, Paul writes:

> As for you, you were dead in your transgressions and sins,
> in which you used to live when you followed the ways of
> this world [here is the first channel, the world] and of the
> ruler of the kingdom of the air, the spirit who is now at
> work in those who are disobedient.

Paul is saying, "Don't forget that, as Christians, you once followed
the course of this world, under the grip and in the control of the
devil." Then he goes on to add:

> All of us also lived among them at one time, gratifying the
> cravings of our sinful nature [that is the second channel,
> the flesh] and following its desires and thoughts. Like the
> rest, we were by nature objects of wrath.

The Bible presents a consistent picture of these two channels—the
world and the flesh—that Satan effectively uses to undermine us as
Christians.

"The world" is the corporate expression of all human individuals
and human institutions. It is comprised of all human philosophies,
ideas, attitudes, goals, values, media, and so forth. When you read
a book that expresses an atheistic philosophy, or see a movie that
presents an immoral view of life, or see an advertisement that appeals
to the sensual and lustful side of you, these are all expressions of the
world. The world bombards you with anti-Christian messages, and
Satan uses these messages to get a foothold in your brain, your attitudes, your emotions, and ultimately your will.

One example of the many ideas and belief systems that comprise
what the Bible calls, "the world" is the commonly held belief in
"moral relativism," the notion that there are no absolute values, no

absolute right or wrong. Moral relativists say, "You have your morality and I have mine. You have no right to judge my morality or the way I live my life, and I do not judge you." This is the state of moral anarchy that has produced abortion on demand and the plague of AIDS. And there is something even deeper and more sinister lurking in the belief in moral relativism.

Because it is part of God's plan, as revealed throughout Scripture and particularly in the book of Revelation, to use the nation of Israel as the centerpiece and staging ground of all the great events of the Great Tribulation and the Millennium, it is a key part of Satan's plan to *destroy* Israel. One of the most grisly and horrifying of Satan's efforts against the children of Israel came during World War II, when the Nazi Holocaust killed over 6 million Jews. The world recoiled in horror at the scenes of Auschwitz and other Nazi death camps and a cry rang out around the planet: "Never again!"

Decades later, however, Satan is using moral relativism—part of the thought system that the Bible calls "the world"—to undermine humanity's determination to prevent future holocausts. Robert Simon, professor of philosophy at Hamilton College, says he has noticed a major shift in the thinking of students about the Holocaust in recent years as a result of moral relativism. Many of today's students say that, even though they acknowledge that the Nazis murdered millions of innocent people, they cannot bring themselves to condemn mass murder as wrong! One of Simon's students told him, "Of course I dislike the Nazis, but who is to say they were morally wrong?" As more and more people with such deceived thinking move into decision-making roles on the world scene, the stage is set for Satan to engineer yet another Holocaust in the world—without any moral opposition!

The combined expression of all such destructive ideas and messages that surround us constitutes what the Bible calls "the world," and determines the philosophy and morality of the society. The world exerts enormous pressure on each of us to conform, adjust, and keep in step. That is why the Bible tells us as Christians, "Do not conform any longer to the pattern of this world, but be transformed by the renewing of your mind" (Romans 12:2). In other words, don't let the world squeeze you into its mold. Why? Because the world is corrupt, and it is the first channel Satan uses to gain access to our minds and hearts. The world is dominated by the mind of Satan, the ruler of this dark world.

The best antidote to the poisonous influence of the world, of course, is to immerse our minds in God's Word. We need to continually baptize our intellect, our imagination, our attitudes, and our beliefs by the washing of the Word. Instead of "zoning out" in front of the TV for two or three hours every night (and absorbing the world's dying values and belief system in the process), we should spend time in the Word, both in individual study and in discussion and prayer with other believers. The mindset of the world is an opportunistic virus that seeks to take over our minds and emotions. The Bible is God's inoculation against the virus of the world.

INDIRECT ASSAULT—THE FLESH

The second channel is that which the Bible calls, symbolically, "the flesh." This term does not refer literally to our bodies—the meat and blood and bones of our physical life. It is a term that describes the human urge to self-centeredness, the distortion of human nature that makes us want to be our own god. The flesh is the proud human ego, the uncrucified self, the seat of willful defiance and rebellion against God's authority.

We are all born with this channel, the flesh, built into us. We never had to be taught or trained to be rebellious or selfish—it came naturally. It is a sin-distortion of the beauty God intended and created us to have. It is the part of us described by Romans 3:23, which says in the Phillips translation, "Everyone has sinned, everyone falls short of the beauty of God's plan." The flesh is that inner urge toward total independence, toward being our own little gods. It is our inner core of self-centeredness. The devil can gain access to us through our sin nature, the flesh, and attack us indirectly—and with devastating effectiveness.

You can immediately see how universal this is. We all have what the Bible calls "the flesh" within us, and it is a battlefield. This is not something remote from us, nor something that only a chosen few Christians must face. This is universal. All of us, without exception, are on the front lines of this war, every moment of our lives. We cannot escape it, we cannot run from it, we cannot leave it behind. We must learn how to be victorious soldiers in this war.

IS DEFEAT POSSIBLE?

I often hear Christians say, "I thought that when I became a Christian, Christ would set me free from the kingdom of Satan, and the devil could not longer touch me." Is that your concept of the Christian life? You couldn't be more mistaken. When you become a Christian, the battle is just beginning!

It is true that the devil can never totally defeat a Christian. Those who are genuinely the Lord's, who are born again, who have come into a saving relationship with Jesus Christ, are delivered from total defeat. The devil can never get us back into the position of unconscious control that he once exercised over us, as he does over the rest of the world.

But the devil can demoralize the Christian. He can frighten us, he can make us miserable, he can defeat us in many ways. He can make us weak and ineffectual as instruments of God's eternal purpose. It is quite possible to be more unhappy and miserable as a Christian than you ever were before you became a Christian, at least for a period of time.

The devil is especially interested in defeating Christians. After all, the unredeemed worldling is not a problem to the devil. All the sincere but pathetic efforts of worldlings to solve the problems of their lives through legislation, education, and social policy do not bother the devil in the least. He is quite content to let them go on rearranging the pieces of the puzzle without ever solving it.

But the presence of every Christian in this world bothers the devil greatly. Why? Because each of us, as members of the body of Christ, sealed and empowered by the Holy Spirit, is a threat to the solidarity of the devil's kingdom, to his rule over the rest of humanity.

If the devil lets the Spirit of God have His way, any individual Christian would be a powerful force to destroy the devil's kingdom of darkness. Every Christian is a witness, a source of truth, a door of escape that worldlings may find to escape the domination of the world rulers of this present darkness. The devil cannot let that happen! So he attacks us.

Understand this: Satan is marshaling all his forces against you, sometimes attacking as a "roaring lion" (see 1 Peter 5:8), and sometimes alluring with stealth and deception, appearing as an "angel of light" (see 2 Corinthians 11:14). The devil comes charging in, ripping, slashing, and dominating like a lion whenever he can—which is why history is replete with names like Nero, Hitler, and Saddam Hussein, demonic men motivated by strange and murderous passions. Sometimes the devil assails us through the world, with its monstrous pressure to keep in line, to conform. But most often the devil comes in disguise, through the channel of the flesh—our inner selves—with silken, subtle, suggestive wiles. That is why I want to focus very intently on this avenue of satanic attack—the avenue of the flesh.

UNDERSTANDING THE FLESH

According to the Bible, the flesh is identified with the mortal body. In Romans 8 the apostle says, "But if Christ is in you, your body is dead because of sin, yet your spirit is alive because of righteousness" (Romans 8:10). We would say, "The body is dying because of sin," but the apostle looks on to the end and says that it is as good as dead already. We all agree with this. We all must die, we say. In this temporary state before the resurrection, the body is the seat of sin or the flesh—this evil principle of self-centeredness in each of us. So the flesh is with us for life. We shall never escape it until that wonderful day of the resurrection from the dead.

But the body, soul, and spirit of a human being are inextricably tied together. No one can understand this. Where does your soul live in your body? You don't know—but you know that you have a soul, though no one can locate it in the body. The relationship between the body, soul, and spirit is beyond our comprehension. But because they are so inextricably tied together, the flesh, linked to the body, touches the whole human being in all dimensions. This means that the devil can influence us—body, soul, and spirit—through the channel of the flesh.

We need to understand how this works: Through the channel of the mind, the devil makes his appeal to our human pride. We regard our reason as the greatest gift God has given to man—and not without justification. Obviously it is our ability to reason that makes us superior to the animals and separates us from the rest of the lower creation. We take pride in this ability to reason—and our pride gives the devil access to the channel of the mind.

Through our emotions, he works on our fears. Emotion is really our most human characteristic. It is a mistake to think of ourselves as primarily beings of reason. We are governed much more by emotion and feelings than we are by logic and reason. The realm of emotions includes our urges, desires, instincts, loves, hates, fears, and even our subconscious drives. The devil makes his appeal to us by playing on our fears, especially our fear that if we obey God, we will miss out on some delicious, desirable aspect of life.

The devil appeals to our desire for pleasure, because our fleshly body was designed by God as a sensory instrument, responsive to sensory stimuli. We learn early in life that there are certain stimuli that are very pleasurable, while others are unpleasant. We learn to seek the pleasant and avoid the unpleasant. So the body constantly seeks that which thrills or excites while avoiding that which hurts or merely bores. The devil is able to appeal to us through the realm of our senses.

The story of Eve's temptation in the Garden of Eden presents all the elements of this kind of satanic attack. We read in Genesis 3:6 that she saw that the fruit was good for food—it offered the pleasant sensation of taste, an appeal to the senses. It was a delight to the eyes—yet another appeal to the senses, as well as an appeal to the emotions. She also saw that it was able to make one wise—an appeal to the pride of mind. Satan's attack through the channel of the flesh was successful. Eve took and ate the fruit.

At the same time, it is important to notice that God also reaches out to us through the channel of our flesh—through our mind, emotions, and senses. Through the mind we read and understand His Word. Through our emotions, we reach out to Him in prayer. Through our senses, we experience His goodness and love in nature and in His provision for us.

If both God and the devil reach us through these channels of our flesh, then how does God's approach differ from Satan's? The difference is simply this: God moves to create balance, harmony, and beauty. The devil moves to create an imbalance, an extreme. God reaches us through our senses and enables us to enjoy the good and beautiful things in life in harmonious balance: a good meal, a good film, a good book, and good sex with our spouse in a protective enclosure of the marriage commitment. Satan reaches us through our senses and drives us toward obsessive and addictive behavior with these good things: we become gluttons, alcoholics, drug addicts, pornography addicts, violence addicts, and promiscuous sex addicts.

It is the same in the realm of our human minds. God reaches us through our intellect, enabling us to understand and appreciate His truth. Satan reaches us through our intellectual pride, turning us into cold, extreme rationalists, agnostics, and atheists. Satan's ploy is to take our natural desire for the good things of God and to push us toward extremes of thought, emotional obsession, and behavioral imbalance.

The example of our Lord Jesus Christ is an example of perfect poise and balance. He was balanced in His intellect. With His mind, sharper than that of the keenest attorney alive today, He challenged the greatest lawyers and religious thinkers of His time. They were continually astonished by His words, His insight, and His ability to escape the verbal traps they continually set for Him.

But Jesus was not only a supremely balanced intellectual. He was also warmly human. He continually expressed human compassion and kindness. He was easy and inviting to be with. He readily expressed emotion, from love to grief to anger, whenever the situation called for it. What an amazing sanity of balance in this Man!

We see this same sanity of balance in the Bible. It ministers to the whole human being—body, soul, and spirit, in delicate equilibrium. When God gets hold of us, He takes us as whole human beings, and He touches every part of our lives.

But what does the devil do? He tries to create imbalance—to build up one element of our nature at the expense of the others. He tries to make us into gross and grotesque caricatures of humanity. He tries to push us to the extreme of coldly rational intellects without any warmth or emotion; or he tries to push us to become walking, sloshing puddles of emotion, without the ability to make informed, rational decisions and choices; or he tries to make us become obsessed with only the emotional aspect of Christianity, such as miracles or speaking in tongues; or he tries to harden us into rigid, unfeeling Pharisees who care only about religious rules and regulations, leaving no room for feeling, caring, or the moving of the Holy Spirit; or he tries to focus our minds on rationalism and scientism, so that we are constantly doubting and never coming to a settled faith regarding any aspect of the Christian gospel; or he will push us into taking some perfectly valid aspect of biblical truth and blowing it up out of proportion, so that one doctrine or principle (say, Bible prophecy or the meaning of numbers in the Bible) becomes our entire belief system to the exclusion of all other truth, with the result that we become cultic, hysterical, and heretical.

Extremism is always the devil's scheme, his favorite way of undermining us and neutralizing our effectiveness for God. He even promotes extremism in regard to his own person. He seeks to make people (including Christians) either extremely obsessed with the devil, so that they are continually looking under their beds and in closets for demonic manifestations—or he seeks to make people so rationalistic and skeptical that they simply pooh-pooh the idea of a personal devil without ever investigating the biblical and contemporary facts about the devil.

The devil always appeals to our fears. God always appeals to our faith. From faith comes hope and love—but the devil continually pushes toward the opposite extreme. Again and again, Jesus' word to His followers was, "Do not be afraid. Do not be troubled. Do not be anxious." Why? "Because I am with you." Faith produces courage and hope. Fear produces discouragement and despair. That's why Satan works so hard at producing fear in our lives—he wants to undermine our effectiveness for God. He wants us to feel defeated. He wants to destroy God's work in us.

In dependence upon God, we must not allow that to happen. As Christians we are salt and light. Salt is a preservative. Light is illumination. Our presence in the world preserves society against destruction and illuminates the world with the light of God's truth. We are here on this battlefield called Planet Earth in order to do battle with Satan and satanic forces—not in our strength but in the strength of the Lord. If we were not here, holding back the darkness, human society would be a planet-wide hell. By telling the Christian story, teaching Christian values, and living out Christian character, we make possible—despite the horrors and evils of this world—those moments of goodness and joy in life that even nonChristians are able to experience.

Now, as we are moving closer than ever to the last days, as the darkness of the demon-dominated systems of this world closes in around us, Paul's trumpet call sounds louder than ever: "Be strong in the Lord and in his mighty power. Put on the full armor of God so that you can take your stand against the devil's schemes" (Ephesians 6:10–11).

God has made a provision for us to defeat the schemes of the devil—and the power to defeat him begins with a humble recognition of our own weakness and God's great strength. That is why Paul does not say, "Be strong in your own willpower," or, "Be strong in your own emotions and intellect." He says, "Be strong in the Lord and in *His* mighty power."

It is when we recognize our own weakness that God is able to unleash His power through us. God has provided the means by which we can stand in the fiery battle that rages not only around us but within us. We can live in victory. And the means of victory is something Paul calls, "the full armor of God."

What is that armor? We will explore that question in the next chapter.

CHAPTER THIRTY-ONE

The Armor of God

Ephesians 6:10–17

In the Battle of Jutland during World War I, the British fleet went up against the German fleet in an intense sea battle. Both sides traded heavy artillery shells. The British gunners quickly sighted in their targets and began pounding the German battleships, but with little effect. The shells exploded on the decks and superstructures of the Kaiser's fleet, but none of the hits appeared fatal.

Meanwhile, however, the German ships began raining heavy artillery shells on the British fleet—and the effects were devastating. The H.M.S. *Lion* was hit first, and a massive explosion erupted. The ship quickly listed and began to sink. Then the H.M.S. *Indefatigable* was hit in the powder magazine and blown to bits. Minutes later, the H.M.S. *Queen Mary* was hit. It went down before lifeboats could be lowered, taking a crew of 1,200 to a watery grave.

The British were forced to retreat. British naval engineers later discovered the reason for the horrible losses. The British ships had been constructed with heavy armor on the sides of the ships—but the designers had not reckoned with the way long-range artillery shells hit their targets. The shells do not come in from the side. They arc high into the air, lose momentum, then drop almost straight down from above. Unlike the heavily top-armored German ships, the British ships were topped by thin wooden decks and were completely vulnerable to German artillery.

In any war, victory and defeat is often determined by how well armored we are. If we leave any part of ourselves exposed, we give the enemy an advantage in battle. That is why Paul tells us in Ephesians 6, "put on the *full* armor of God." We dare not armor and equip ourselves for battle in any partial or slipshod manner. Our enemy is too crafty and too fierce for half-hearted measures. If we give him any edge at all, he will use it to destroy us. Our armor must be full, impenetrable, and without chinks that the enemy can exploit.

TWO CLASSIFICATIONS OF ARMOR

Paul warns us of the severity and intensity of the battle before us in Ephesians 6:10–13. In verses 14–17, Paul goes on to describe the full armor of God in detail, so that we can be fully armored on every side, leaving no part of our soul or spirit exposed to the enemy:

> Stand firm then, with the belt of truth buckled around your waist, with the breastplate of righteousness in place, and with your feet fitted with the readiness that comes from the gospel of peace. In addition to all this, take up the shield of faith, with which you can extinguish all the flaming arrows of the evil one. Take the helmet of salvation and the sword of the Spirit, which is the word of God.

This is highly figurative language—a series of symbols suggesting a deep and tangible spiritual reality. The various pieces of armor

Paul details for us here are the specific ways we carry out his call to be strong in the Lord. The armor is nothing more than a symbolic description of various facets of the Lord himself. The armor is the life of Christ, lived out in your life and mine.

There are two general classifications of the Christian's armor, indicated by the tenses of the verbs used. The first division, verses 14 and 15, covers the first three pieces of armor:

"with the belt of truth buckled around your waist";
"with the breastplate of righteousness in place";
"with your feet fitted with the readiness that comes from
     the gospel of peace."

These three pieces of armor refer to something that has already been done if we are Christians. These are pieces of armor we only have to put on once and for all. We need never put them on again—but we must be aware of them and continually remind ourselves of what they mean in our lives.

The second division, verses 16 and 17, includes those things that are to be put on or taken up at the present moment:

"take up the shield of faith";
"take the helmet of salvation";
"take . . . the sword of the Spirit."

These three pieces of armor are aspects of Christ that we must deliberately take up again and again whenever we are under attack.

The order in which these pieces are given to us is very important. You cannot reverse them or mix them up. The reason many Christians fail to properly exercise the sword of the Spirit, for example, is that they have never buckled the belt of truth around their waist. You cannot do it in reverse order. Scripture is very precise in this.

THE BELT OF TRUTH

The first classification of our armor begins with the belt of truth. That's the place to start whenever you are under attack, whenever you feel discouraged, defeated, or depressed. The officers in the Roman army wore short skirts, like Scottish kilts. Over them they had a cloak or tunic secured at the waist with a belt. When they were about to enter battle, they tucked the tunic under the belt to leave their legs free and ready for action. Being belted in this way—what is called "girding the loins"—symbolizes one's readiness to fight. You cannot do battle until you have surrounded yourself with the belt of truth.

In practical terms, this means you remind yourself that, in Jesus Christ, you have found the truth behind all things. You have found the key to life, the secret of reality, the One who is himself the truth. He is the One "in whom are hidden all the treasures of wisdom and knowledge" (Colossians 2:3). We know that Jesus is the truth by the things He said; the temple guards who heard Him speak at His trial, shortly before the crucifixion, said, "No one ever spoke the way this man does" (John 7:46). No one ever expressed such insight into the human condition nor spoke with so much authority as Jesus did.

He also demonstrated the truth by what He did. The New Testament record is filled with His amazing works and miracles—those spectacular intrusions from the invisible realm into the visible. Most important of all, He demonstrated the solution to the most insoluble problem of all—the problem of death. He raised people from the dead—and He arose from the dead himself. We know Jesus Christ is the truth, because He solved the problem of death.

Truth is reality. It explains all things. You know you have found the truth when you find something wide enough and deep enough and high enough to encompass all things. The truth of Jesus Christ does that.

Because truth is reality, truth never changes. It does not need to be updated, revised, or modernized. If something was true ten thousand years ago, it is true today, and it will be true tomorrow.

I love the story of the man who went to visit his old friend, a music teacher, and casually asked, "What's the good news today?"

Without saying a word, the elderly music teacher walked across the room, picked up a hammer, and struck a tuning fork. As the note sounded, the old man said, "That note is A. It is A today, it was A five thousand years ago, and it will be A ten thousand years from now. The soprano upstairs sings off-key, the tenor across the hall flats his high notes, and the piano downstairs is out of tune. But this—" He struck the note again. "This is A, my friend, and that's the good news for today!"

That is the good news of Jesus Christ—He is the truth, the same yesterday, today, and forever (see Hebrews 13:8). That is how you know you have the truth. He is the one to whom we can tune our lives. Remember that fact when you are under attack and when doubts come into your mind. And remember that doubt is always an attack on faith, so the fact that you have doubts proves that you have faith. Go cling to the ground of your faith. Surround yourself with the belt of truth.

THE BREASTPLATE OF RIGHTEOUSNESS

The second piece of armor is the breastplate of righteousness. What is the breastplate of righteousness? A breastplate fits over the heart and symbolizes God's protection of our emotional wellbeing. The breastplate of righteousness is Christ, the source of your righteous standing before God. If you wear the breastplate of righteousness, you can rest secure that your heart is securely guarded and adequately protected against attack.

The heart—our emotional core—is perhaps the most frequent avenue of attack against a Christian's faith. We often feel a lack of assurance. We feel unworthy of God. We feel we are a failure in the Christian life and that God, therefore, is no longer interested in us. When we feel that emotional sense of guilt and misery, we need to recognize it as a satanic attack, an attempt to destroy what God intends to do in us.

How do you answer an attack like this? You remember that you have put on the breastplate of righteousness. In other words, you do not stand on your own merits. You stand on the merits of Christ. You quit trying to be good enough to please God. You rest on the infinite merits of Christ.

This is why Paul begins his great eighth chapter to the Romans with the words, "Therefore, there is now no condemnation for those who are in Christ Jesus" (Romans 8:1). *No condemnation!* You are believing a lie when you believe that God rejects you. Remember, you stand on Christ's merits. It is God who justifies. Christ, who died for us, is the only One who has the right to accuse us—and He will never accuse us because He loves us.

This is not to say that unrighteous living means nothing to God. He wants us to live righteous lives and make righteous choices—but He does not judge us once we have come to Him for salvation. He deals with us as a Father, in love and discipline—but not as a judge.

The apostle Paul wore the breastplate of righteousness when he was under pressure or feeling discouraged. He had tremendous inner struggles because of his past as a brutal persecutor of the church. No doubt, he frequently encountered families of people he had put to death before Christ called him dramatically. He was often reminded by many people that he was not one of the original twelve apostles, that his calling was suspect, that perhaps he really was not an apostle at all. Writing in 1 Corinthians 15:9, he called himself "the least of the apostles," unfit "to be called an apostle, because I persecuted the church of God." No wonder Paul often felt discouraged!

But Paul goes on to say, "But by the grace of God I am what I am, and his grace to me was not without effect" (1 Corinthians 15:10). Here, Paul uses the breastplate of righteousness. "I don't defend what I am," he says, in effect. "I simply say to you, by the grace of God, I am what I am. What I am is what Christ has made me. I'm not standing on my righteousness, I'm standing on His. I am accepted by His grace, and covered by His righteousness."

The breastplate of righteousness protects the emotions. You do not need to be discouraged. Of course you have failed. Paul failed, you fail, I fail, but failure is simply part of our learning curve. It is part of the process of discovering how to overcome. Jesus knows we will fail, we will struggle. Our lives will be an up-and-down experience, and we will lose a battle now and then. But Jesus has won the war, and we do not need to be discouraged or defeated, because we know we will win in the end.

FEET SHOD WITH THE GOSPEL OF PEACE

In verse 15, Paul introduces the third piece of armor: "and with your feet fitted with the readiness that comes from the gospel of peace." Shoes are absolutely essential to fighting. Imagine a soldier clad in armor from head to ankle—but completely barefoot! Imagine how quickly the rough ground would tear and bruise his feet. His aching feet would render him unfit to fight. But with a stout pair of shoes he would be ready and equipped to fight.

Note that word *readiness*: "with your feet fitted with the *readiness that comes from the gospel of peace.*" It is peace in the heart that makes you ready to fight. Christ, our peace, gives us the calm courage to face the battle without flinching. He keeps our morale high, so we are ready for anything. No ground can be too rough for us, because Christ guards our steps.

These, then, are the first three components of our armor—the belt of truth, the breastplate of righteousness, and the shoes of the gospel of peace. These three components comprise the first of two classifications of the Christian's armor, as listed in Ephesians 6:14–15. The three pieces of armor in this first division are pieces we only have to put on once and for all—yet it is important that we remind ourselves frequently that they are there, ready for our use in time of need.

Now we move to the second division, verses 16 and 17, consisting of three pieces that we must consciously, actively take up and put on—the shield of faith, the helmet of salvation, and the sword of the Spirit.

THE SHIELD OF FAITH

Paul writes in verse 16, "In addition to all this, take up the shield of faith, with which you can extinguish all the flaming arrows of the evil one." What are these flaming arrows that Paul speaks of? The devil's arrows come in many forms, including blue moods of depression, dark nights of fear, gray days of doubt, and more. Sometimes those arrows come in the form of evil thoughts—and they occasionally come at the most unwelcome, incongruous times. We may be reading the Bible or on our knees, in prayer or thinking about something else entirely when suddenly a filthy, lewd, or blasphemous thought comes to mind. *Where did* that *come from?* we wonder. But we don't need to wonder at all. It is a fiery arrow of the devil—and we should recognize it as such.

Sometimes the idea comes to our imagination that Christianity is nothing but a hoax. Maybe the miracles of the Bible can be explained as psychological manifestations. Maybe Jesus was just a victim of grandiose delusions. All Christians have had such feelings from time to time, mingled with a sense of queasy anxiety. Where do such thoughts and feelings come from? Again, these are nothing more than the fiery arrows of the evil one. The devil's fiery arrows can be recognized by two characteristics:

1. The flaming arrows of Satan seem to arise out of our own thoughts. They seem to come from within us. We think, "What a shocking thought! How could such a thing even cross my mind?" But it is really the devil whispering to us, trying to influence us. In our ignorance and innocence, we blame ourselves for a horrible thought that really has its source in the deceiver. That, of course, is exactly why the devil sent that thought your way. He sends us doubts to make us think we have already lost our faith. He sends us horrid thoughts to make us feel dirty and unworthy. He sends us blue moods to make us feel hopeless and defeated.

The arrows of the devil take their toll on us in the form of mental anguish, emotional strain, confusion, and tension. It is important that we recognize the source of such thoughts. It's important that we recognize the lies of the devil for what they are. We are not the source of such thoughts. Satan is.

2. The flaming arrows of Satan always seem to attack our position in Christ. They always insinuate doubt about the reality or reliability of our relationship with God. This is

always the way of the devil. Read the Bible from beginning to end and you see this satanic strategy all the way through, beginning with Satan's subtle attack on Eve in the garden: "Did God really say . . . ?" (Genesis 3:1). Here is a subtle insinuation of doubt—not a blatant attack, but a sneaky undermining. The same devil was at it again—not in a garden this time, but in a barren wilderness—when he tempted Jesus with these words, "If you are the Son of God, tell these stones to become bread" (Matthew 4:3; Luke 4:3). If?! The devil knew well who Jesus was, but that word *if* is subtly inserted to insinuate that Jesus' sonship was somehow in question.

So what can we do? How can we combat the devil's arrows of fire? The apostle replies, "Take up the shield of faith!"

Notice that Paul does not say "the shield of belief." Faith is more than a belief system. To have faith means to *act* on what we believe. Faith is a decision, resolution, action. Faith is working out the implications of belief. That is the shield of faith.

Have you learned to take up the shield of faith when doubts come? It means saying to yourself, "Christ is the truth. He is reality. I have been convinced of His reality many times over. I have committed myself to Christ because I have been persuaded that He is the way, the truth, and the life. So I reject this thought that Christianity is a hoax. I will continue to act in faith despite my feelings of doubt."

Have you learned to take up the shield of faith when feelings of unworthiness come? It means saying to yourself, "Yes, I've failed God—but His promise to me is that He always accepts me. All of the great men and women of the Bible have failed God from time to time, yet God still used them, and I know He will use me. Christ is my righteousness—I am one with Him and His righteousness covers me. Nothing can separate me from the love of Christ."

Have you learned to take up the shield of faith when depression and anxiety come? It means saying to yourself, "Feelings are not facts. Feelings come and go, but the truth of God is forever. I refuse to believe the lie of Satan. With the Lord Jesus Christ as my shield, I am going to cling to my faith despite my feelings."

Have you learned to take up the shield of faith when evil thoughts arise? It means saying to yourself, "These evil thoughts are not my thoughts. They came into my mind as fiery arrows from the devil. I do not want these thoughts. I reject them. Lord Jesus, fill my mind with Your thoughts. Drive everything out of my mind but what You want me to think!"

This is what the Bible calls resisting the devil (see James 4:7). This is the shield of faith. Refuse to believe the lie of the devil. Take refuge in the truth of God. When you resist the devil, says James, he will flee from you. Resist those thoughts whenever they come your way, refuse to yield your position, and sooner or later, those thoughts will clear up. Your feelings will change. The attacks will cease.

THE HELMET OF SALVATION

In Ephesians 6:17, Paul tells us, "Take the helmet of salvation and the sword of the Spirit, which is the word of God." The figure of a helmet immediately suggests to us something designed to protect the mind, the intelligence, the ability to think and reason. This helmet can keep our thinking straight and preserve us from mental confusion as we make our way through this dark and evil-infested world.

We live in confused times. The demon-dominated world system bombards us with conflicting philosophies and antichristian belief systems, all designed to undermine the faith of Christians and prevent nonChristians from ever discovering the truth. But the Christian is not defenseless. We have the helmet of salvation.

What is this helmet that keeps our thinking straight in the midst of a confused world? Paul answers in one word—salvation. Understand, Paul is not talking here about the salvation of the soul. He is not referring to salvation as regeneration or conversion. In other words, he is not looking back to the moment where he invited Christ into his life as Lord and Savior. He is looking to the *future*. He is talking about a salvation which is a future event. This is what he means when he says elsewhere in the New Testament, "Our salvation is nearer now than when we first believed" (Romans 13:11).

The helmet of salvation is further defined for us in Paul's first letter to the Thessalonians: "But since we belong to the day, let us be self-controlled, putting on faith and love as a breastplate, and the hope of salvation as a helmet" (1 Thessalonians 5:8). This future tense of salvation can be found in a number of passages, especially Romans 8:18–25:

> I consider that our present sufferings are not worth comparing with the glory that will be revealed in us. The creation waits in eager expectation for the sons of God to be revealed. For the creation was subjected to frustration, not by its own choice, but by the will of the one who subjected it, in hope that the creation itself will be liberated from its bondage to decay and brought into the glorious freedom of the children of God.
>
> We know that the whole creation has been groaning as in the pains of childbirth right up to the present time. Not only so, but we ourselves, who have the firstfruits of the Spirit, groan inwardly as we wait eagerly for our adoption

as sons, the redemption of our bodies. For in this hope we were saved. But hope that is seen is no hope at all. Who hopes for what he already has? But if we hope for what we do not yet have, we wait for it patiently.

Paul is talking about the day of resurrection, when creation will be delivered from its bondage, when Christ will return to establish His kingdom. This helmet, therefore, is the recognition that all human schemes to obtain world peace and harmony are doomed to fail. But Jesus Christ is working out His own plan, which will culminate in His appearing again and the establishment of His own reign in righteousness on the earth. That is the helmet of salvation which will keep our thinking straight, even in unsettled times, when the systems of the world collapse around us, when society is torn by wars and rumors of wars. No matter how terrible and chaotic this world becomes, we trust in God and patiently await our ultimate salvation.

History is not a meaningless jumble but a controlled pattern, and the Lord Jesus Christ himself is directing these events. He is the Lord of history. Not only do we know that everything will work out right in the end, but we actually know that, despite all appearances, the end of history is being worked out right now!

One of the great reasons the church says so little to the world of true significance today is that we have neglected the helmet of salvation, we have neglected the hope of the coming of the Lord. There are very few sermons preached on it, and very little is said about it. There is no time given to a consideration of what it means and why it is set forth so frequently and clearly in the Scriptures. Great sections of the Scriptures deal with this matter, yet they are simply ignored among Christians. As a result, our thinking is muddled and confused. So the church sounds an uncertain trumpet in the battle, and few hearts are encouraged. This is one of the great tragedies of the church today.

We are to remind ourselves frequently of the coming of the Lord. Jesus continually told us to watch and be ready for that hour (see Matthew 24:42 and 25:13). We must live daily in that hope and anticipation. The battle is not ours. This battle we have been examining in Ephesians 6 is an epic struggle against the devil and his angels, against the principalities and powers—yet it is being fought right where we live, in our homes, our offices, our churches, and the inner core of our hearts. Yet we must never forget that this battle is not ours, but the Lord's. We are individual fighting units in a great army. The ultimate cause is sure and the end is certain. In this struggle between Jesus Christ and Satan, we already know the outcome.

With our minds securely protected by the helmet of the ultimate salvation of God, we can face the evil days ahead with our thoughts ordered, our hearts calm, and our souls undisturbed by the trumpets of war. The battle is coming, and we are almost ready to meet it. We only need one more implement to make our armor complete: a sword.

THE SWORD OF THE SPIRIT

Finally, Paul tells us, "Take . . . the sword of the Spirit, which is the word of God." What is the word of God? It is Christ. The Lord Jesus Christ is our life—but in this instance, Paul means that Christ is made available to us in practical ways through the writings in His Word. I think it is important to stress this. It is easy to have a vague sense of following Christ, but to not know exactly what this means. That is why the Word of God has been given to us: to acquaint us with the nuts and bolts of our faith, so that we can live it in daily practice.

Christian truth as a whole is more than we can handle. It has to be broken down into manageable pieces. This is what the Word of God does.

In writing to the Colossians, Paul says, "Let the word of Christ dwell in you richly as you teach and admonish one another with all wisdom, and as you sing psalms, hymns and spiritual songs with gratitude in your hearts of God" (Colossians 3:16). By this he is indicating that the authority of Jesus Christ and the authority of the Scriptures are one and the same.

There are many voices which tell us that as Christians we must follow Christ and accept the authority of Christ, but we need not accept the authority of the Bible. But Paul answers that one by calling the Scriptures "the word of Christ." You cannot separate the two.

I once attended a meeting of ministers in Palo Alto where a Christian professor from Stanford presented an excellent talk on science and the Christian faith. After he had finished, he was questioned by members of the audience. One man said, "I can accept the Bible as the witness of certain men as to what they thought of Jesus Christ. But you seem to go further. You have used the word 'inspired' on several occasions in your paper, and this seems to suggest that in your opinion the Bible is more than the views of men, that it has divine authority. Is this true?"

The Christian professor replied, "My answer may sound to you like Sunday school propaganda, but I can only put it this way: The center of my life is Jesus Christ. I have found Him to be the key to everything I desire in life. And yet I could know nothing about Christ if I did not learn it from the Bible. The Bible presents Christ, and Christ defines the Bible. How can I make a distinction?"

The questioner could do nothing but throw up his hands and change the subject.

The authority of Scripture is the authority of Jesus Christ. They are indivisible. To attempt to distinguish the two is like asking which blade of a pair of scissors is more important, or which leg of a pair of pants is more necessary. We know Christ through the Bible, and we understand the Bible through the knowledge of Christ. The two cannot be separated. That is why Paul calls it "the word of Christ."

The apostle chooses his words carefully when he says, "Take . . . the sword of the Spirit, which is the word of God." It is important to understand that it is not the complete Bible that is referred to by the phrase, "the word of God." There are two words used in Scripture for *word*. There is the familiar Greek word *logos* that is used in the opening verse of John's gospel: "In the beginning was the Word [*logos*], and the Word [*logos*] was with God, and the Word [*logos*] was God" (John 1:1).

But there is another Greek word translated "word" in English, but which is used less frequently in Scripture: *rhema*. This Greek word has a somewhat different meaning. *Logos* refers to the total utterance of God, the complete revelation of what God has said. *Rhema* means a specific saying of God, a passage or a verse that has special application to an immediate situation. In modern terms, *rhema* is the Word of God applied to our practical experience.

When Paul says, "Take . . . the sword of the Spirit, which is the *word* of God," he uses the word *rhema*, not *logos*. So the "sword of the Spirit" is the saying of God applied to a specific situation. This is a powerful weapon in the hands of a believer. If you are a Christian, you have almost certainly experienced the power of God's *rhema* many times in your life. Have you ever read a passage of Scripture and felt that the words suddenly seemed to come alive and leap off the page at you? Have you ever felt a passage of Scripture grip your soul and resonate in your ears so that you could not escape its power? Have you ever heard or read a Scripture passage and thought, "That is God speaking directly to me!"? That is God's *rhema*, His word applied specifically to your life and your situation.

Or perhaps someone has asked a question or shared a problem with you, and you were caught off guard, without an answer for that person. Then, in the next moment, you felt a glimmer of illumination and a word of Scripture came to mind—and suddenly you had the answer your friend was seeking. That's God's *rhema*, spoken in your thoughts so that you can minister God's word to that person.

These are examples of God's *rhema*, God's word that slices through all the extraneous clutter of our scattered thoughts, cutting right to the heart of the matter. That is why God's *rhema* is called "the sword of the Spirit," because it is not only originated by Him as the author of the Word, but it is also recalled to mind by the Spirit and made powerful by Him in our lives. It is the Spirit's answer to the attack of the devil, who comes to discourage us, deceive us, and defeat us. This is the sword of the Spirit.

As a sword, it is useful both for defense and for offense. This, by the way, is the only part of our armor that has an offensive capability. It both defends and protects us, but it also pierces other hearts and destroys the lies of the devil in others besides ourselves. This is its great effect. As Christians we are to wield this sword in the battle against the lies of Satan. We are to go on the offensive, proclaiming the word of God. We do not need to defend it. We are simply to declare it. As Hebrews 4:12 tells us, "For the word of God is living and active. Sharper than any double-edged sword, it penetrates even to dividing soul and spirit, joints and marrow; it judges the thoughts and attitudes of the heart."

The sword of the Spirit pierces the rationales and prejudices of unbelievers, shatters excuses and objections, penetrates stubborn pride and sinful rebellion, striking home to the human heart. It is this offensive quality of God's Word that explains why the Bible is so continuously under attack. For centuries, the devil-dominated enemies of the gospel have tried to destroy the Bible or diminish its significance. With clever words and subtle arguments, the devil speaks through people of prominence and intelligence to undermine the testimony of the Scriptures. This does not mean that these people are hypocrites or that they are deliberately and knowingly destructive. Many of them are sincere but deceived. The evidence that they are pawns in a satanic attack upon the Bible, and that their thinking has a satanic bias, is seen in the specific target of these attacks.

The critics of the Bible always attack the historic genuineness of the biblical record. They attempt to reject the supernatural character of the biblical accounts—the intrusion of the invisible realm of God's kingdom into our commonplace space-time realm. The critics of the Bible demonstrate an almost visceral disgust and distaste for the miraculous, and they hasten to use the miracles of the Bible as "proof" that the Bible is incredible or unreliable, so that no one will bother to read it. That is the satanic strategy: to keep human beings from taking God's Word seriously.

Many of the worst critics of the Bible are actually professors and doctors of theology—those who profess to be Bible experts yet who betray the Scriptures with the kiss of Judas and mislead many. Yet all that is needed to put their pretentious claims to rest is to simply read the Bible—and particularly the account of the nativity, life, death, and resurrection of Christ—has done more to change the course of history than anything else in history.

The sword of the Spirit has certainly altered my life. Looking back, I recall many times when God's *rhema* saved me from error and delusion:

As a young Christian, I was stopped many times at the edge of disobedience when some temptation seemed so logical, so reasonable, so widely practiced that I was strongly lured by it. I was often stopped by a word of Scripture I had memorized, and which has come to me many times since: "Trust in the LORD with all your heart and lean not on your own understanding" (Proverbs 3:5). This *rhema* from God has often come to me, reminding me that I am not the rational being I like to think myself to be. There is much illusion in our world and I'm not intelligent enough to see through the *phantasmata* or lies of the devil. This word from the Lord reminds me to lean on God's truth, not my own faulty understanding of reality.

Sometimes God's *rhema* has come to me after I had made a painful mistake—too late, perhaps, to save me from defeat in that situation, but at just the right time to teach me a valuable lesson and prevent me from making that mistake again. For example, I remember one embarrassing episode where I lost my temper and made a fool of myself in the process. Immediately afterwards, the words of James 1:20 came to my mind: "for man's anger does not bring about the righteous life that God desires." That verse pulled me up short at that moment, and it has been a helpful reminder against repeating that sin ever since.

I remember when my heart was once pierced by these words of God's wisdom: "Pride only breeds quarrels" (Proverbs 13:10). When we get involved in contentions and strife with one another, it is so easy to blame the other fellow: "He started it!" One day, I observed a quarrel between my daughter and my nephew. "Who started this?" I asked, and the boy said, "She did! She hit me back!" That is a typically human response, isn't it? But the Word says that quarrels are bred by pride. Where there is strife and conflict, there is pride at work and both parties are usually guilty.

I remember experiencing, as a young Christian, the lure and temptation of sexual sin. The world tells us that promiscuous behavior is right and healthy, and that godliness and chastity are "unhealthy repression." When I was tempted by such worldly rationalizations, God would bring to mind His *rhema* for my situation: "Let no one deceive you with empty words, for because of such things God's wrath comes on those who are disobedient" (Ephesians 5:6). Those words stopped me short as a young man. Later, when I came to understand more fully what the wrath of God means—that it is not a lightning bolt from heaven, but rather the dehumanizing disintegration of life that comes when one gives way to these kinds of things—this *rhema* from God took on even more power in my life.

Obviously, the more you expose yourself to the Scriptures, the more the Spirit can use this mighty sword in your life. If you never read or study your Bible, you are terribly exposed to defeat and despair. So read your Bible regularly—read it all, for each section has a special purpose. The Lord Jesus said, "You diligently study the Scriptures because you think that by them you possess eternal life. These are the Scriptures that testify about me" (John 5:39). This is the way you come to know Christ. There is no way to come into full maturity as a Christian apart from the Scriptures.

A word of caution is needed here, however, for we must always be careful to compare Scripture with Scripture. The fact that a particular verse of Scripture comes to our mind at a particular moment does not automatically mean that we have received a *rhema* from the Lord. Remember, the devil can quote Scripture as well—as he did when he tempted Jesus in the wilderness. But the quotation of the Scripture by the devil is never balanced. Whenever the devil attempts to wield the sword of the Spirit, it becomes an uncouth weapon, eccentric and out of balance.

When Jesus was tempted by Satan (see Matthew 4 and Luke 4), He always countered by quoting Scripture or by comparing Scripture with Scripture. Satan said to Jesus, "If you are the Son of God, tell this stone to become bread." Jesus immediately met him with the sword of the Spirit: "It is written: 'Man does not live on bread alone, but on every word that comes from the mouth of God.'" So the devil said, in effect, "Well, if you are going to quote Scripture, I can quote it too." And he took Jesus to the top of the Temple, urged Him to cast Himself down, and quoted from the Psalms: "He will command his angels concerning you, and they will lift you up in their hands, so that you will not strike your foot against a stone." But Jesus knew how to handle the devil; comparing Scripture with Scripture, Jesus said, "It is also written: 'Do not put the Lord your God to the test.'"

Finally, the devil took him up and showed him all the kingdoms of the world and said, "All this I will give you if you will bow down and worship me." And again our Lord answered the devil with the sword of the Spirit: "Away from me, Satan! For it is written: 'Worship the Lord your God, and serve him only.'" Then the devil left him. This is always what happens. Resist the devil and he will flee from you. He is put to rout by the sword of the Spirit, the greatest weapon against evil in all the world.

Do not act on the strength of a single verse yanked out of context. It is not enough to have someone quote a verse of Scripture to you, or to hear a verse come flashing into your mind. Compare it with other Scripture. Is it in balance? Or has that verse's meaning been distorted by isolating it from the rest of God's Word? The sword of the Spirit is a powerful weapon. Use it wisely, carefully, and prayerfully.

MAKE YOUR STAND

What good is armor if it is allowed to rust away in a closet?

If you are a Christian, you have the full armor of God available to you. Are you using it? Have you put it on? Have you flexed it and tested it in battle? When you find yourself growing cold or luke-warm, when you are under attack by the schemes of the devil, when you are anxious or depressed, when you are beset by doubts or fears, when you feel the lure of lusts—do you take refuge in the armor and mighty strength of the Lord?

Remember, these components of our armor are given to us in this order for a good reason. They are steps to take in times of satanic at-tack. We need to familiarize ourselves with this armor, learn its use, practice its use, and put it to the test in real-life situations. When we are under attack, we need to systematically and repeatedly go through these steps. We need to remember the armor we already have, that God put on us at the moment we came to Christ.

I urge you to put on your armor daily. Read through this passage of Ephesians 6 again and again, and familiarize yourself with the armor God has given you to prepare you for the greatest battle ever fought. If you do, God's promise is sure: No matter how fierce the battle that rages around you and within you, victory will be yours.

Finally, remember why you have been given the full armor of God. As Paul writes in Ephesians 6:13, "Therefore put on the full armor of God, so that when the day of evil comes, you may be able to stand your ground, and after you have done everything, to stand." The point of this spiritual armor is to make sure that we will be able to stand in the day of evil.

What does that mean, "to stand"? Picture a football team defend-ing its goal line. Its back against its own end zone, the defense lines up on the scrimmage line and digs in, standing tough, refusing to be moved. This is called a "goal-line stand." This is exactly what Paul's word picture suggests to us. We are to refuse to move from the ground of faith we have taken. We will yield no ground. We will not surrender even an inch.

Why does Paul want us to stand? Shouldn't we fight, advance, charge against the enemy? Why doesn't he use a military term that speaks of moving out against the enemy and taking new ground? Paul always chooses his words with precision, so we know that if he says "stand," he means stand. It is the only word which describes the attitude we must have to insure absolute victory.

Paul wants us to think soberly about what spiritual warfare really means. He encourages us to stand because he knows there will be times when that is all we can hope to do. There are times in battle when the fight is so furious that a soldier can do no more than defend his position and stand his ground. Paul knows that the day of evil is coming. He knows that as we draw nearer to the time of our Lord's return, evil days will come with greater frequency and intensity. Most of all, he doesn't want us to be knocked off our feet by the terrors of that day.

We also need to realize that the war we are engaged in is primarily a defensive action. Our Lord and Commander, Jesus Christ, has the might and power to take offensive action—and indeed He accomplished His mission when He was nailed to a cross two thousand years ago, and when He arose in resurrection power. Only He has the power to go face to face and hand to hand with the prince of darkness. Our role in this war is to make a defensive stand, a goal-line stand, a defense against the siege of Satan. Our primary function is not to take new ground, but to repel invasion and defend that which is already ours.

As the apostle Jude writes, "I . . . urge you to contend for the faith that was once for all entrusted to the saints" (Jude 1:3). Or as Paul writes to the Corinthians, "Be on your guard; stand firm in the faith; be men of courage; be strong" (1 Corinthians 16:13). Amazingly, our defensive action is the greatest offense we could mount. The Christian who learns to put on the armor of God and pray and remain immovable becomes an impenetrable barrier to the schemes of Satan. He demonstrates Christlike peace and poise to a troubled and fearful world—and in the process, he draws more and more people to consider the gospel of Jesus Christ.

So, friend in Christ, I urge you along with the apostle Paul: Be strong in the Lord and in his mighty power. Put on the full armor of God so that you can take your stand against the devil's schemes. And when that evil day comes—and make no mistake, it is coming!—you may be able to stand your ground, and after you have done everything, after the smoke and haze of battle clears, the enemy will lie vanquished at your feet. And you will stand, joyful and victorious, beside your Lord and Commander, Jesus Christ.

CHAPTER THIRTY-TWO

Fighting the Battle on Our Knees

Ephesians 6:18–20

Missionary John G. Paton tells of an experience that occurred soon after he and his wife began missionary work in the rain forests of the New Hebrides Islands. One night, hostile tribesmen surrounded the mission headquarters where he and his wife lived. The torch-bearing tribesmen were determined to burn the building down, killing Paton and his wife. Alone in a strange land, far from anyone who could help them, the Patons spent the entire night on their knees in prayer, expecting their house to go up in flames around them at any moment.

The hours passed without an attack. Finally morning came and John Paton got up from his knees and peeked out the window. He was astonished to see that the hostile tribesmen had left. Instantly, John and his wife dropped again to their knees—this time to thank God for their deliverance.

The Patons continued their work among the tribespeople and saw many of them come to know Jesus Christ as Lord and Savior. After about a year of evangelistic effort, even the chief of the tribe became a follower of Christ. Remembering the night of terror when he and his wife thought they were about to be burned alive in the mission station, Paton asked the chief what had prevented him and his men from torching the house.

"We were afraid of the men that protected you," replied the chief.

"What men?" asked Paton. "There were no men protecting us. My wife and I were in the house alone."

"No," the chief insisted, "there were many men around the house—men with shining clothes and swords in their hands. They stood around the building and would not let us harm you."

Then John Paton knew why he and his wife were spared. Their prayers had been answered that night. God had sent His angels to protect the Patons from attack. That is the power that all Christians, including you and me, have access to whenever we go to our knees in prayer.

PRAYING WITH PURPOSE

We are engaged in a spiritual battle, the greatest battle ever fought. And the message of Ephesians 6 is that this is a war that must be fought on our knees. In Ephesians 6:18–20, Paul writes:

> And pray in the Spirit on all occasions with all kinds of prayers and requests. With this in mind, be alert and always keep on praying for all the saints.
>
> Pray also for me, that whenever I open my mouth, words may be given me so that I will fearlessly make known the mystery of the gospel, for which I am an ambassador in chains. Pray that I may declare it fearlessly, as I should.

Immediately after listing for us our spiritual armor, Paul instructs us in the final complement to the full armor of God: prayer. Notice the order in which Paul discusses these issues. He does not reverse the order and say, "First pray, then put on the armor of God." No, we put on the armor first, then pray. We tend to reverse this order, and that is why our prayer life is frequently so feeble and impotent. Our prayer life would be stronger and more effective if we would carefully observe the designated order of Scripture.

I think most Christians would candidly have to confess that they are dissatisfied with their prayer life. They feel it is inadequate and perhaps infrequent. All of us at times struggle to improve our prayer life by disciplining our schedules or maintaining a prayer list or journal. In other words, we begin with the *doing*—but we are starting at the wrong place. We are violating our basic human nature in approaching prayer this way. The place to start is not with *doing*, but with *thinking*.

Whenever we wish to become disciplined and motivated for some task, we must begin with careful reflection on what that task requires. And Paul tells us that, as we approach the all-important task of prayer, we must put prayer in its proper order. Prayer follows putting on the armor of God. In fact, prayer is a natural, normal outgrowth of putting on the armor of God.

Now, I am not suggesting that we do not need to discipline ourselves as Christians. But discipline comes in at the beginning of the process, when we put on the full armor of God. Then prayer takes place as a natural outgrowth of our discipline in putting on that armor. When we follow the process that Paul outlines for us, our prayer life takes on real meaning and significance.

This is the problem with much of our praying now, isn't it? It is shallow and superficial, on a level with such jingle-prayers as,

> Bless me and my wife,
> My son John and his wife,
> Us four—
> And no more.

Or,

> Now I lay me down to sleep,
> I pray the Lord my soul to keep.

Prayer should be an outgrowth of thoughtfulness about the implications of faith. Thoughtful prayer that is an outgrowth of the full armor of God is prayer with depth, meaning, and significance—prayer that is pointed and purposeful.

TWO FORMS OF PRAYER

What is prayer?

Is it a mere superstition as some people think? Is it mumbling, talking to yourself, under the deluded dream that you are addressing a mythical deity?

Or is prayer a form of magic by which we summon God like a mythical genie? Is prayer an Aladdin's lamp that we rub to bend God's will to ours?

Or is prayer a form of "self-talk," a psychological-religious form of navel-gazing in which you plumb the depths of your being, your soul, your conscious and subconscious mind?

None of these notions of prayer accord with the description of prayer we find in Scripture. Paul recognizes two categories of prayer, which in Ephesians 6:18 he calls (1) "all kinds of prayers" and (2) "requests." Let's examine each category of prayer and understand why Paul makes this distinction.

1. "All kinds of prayers." This is the widest classification. If you take the whole range of biblical teaching on prayer, you find that prayer as it is presented in Scripture, is nothing more nor less than conversation with God. That's all. Prayer is simply conversing with God.

A Christian, remember, is a member of the family of God. So prayer is family talk. It is friendly, intimate, frank, unrestricted conversation with God. It is a chat with the Father around the heavenly dinner table. We have been brought into this close, intimate relationship by faith in Jesus Christ. We are no longer strangers—we are children of God, part of the family circle. So prayer is simply carrying on a conversation with God—and that is the first category of prayers Paul talks about.

2. "Requests" or supplications. A request or supplication is a specific plea for God to supply a need. "You do not have, because you do not ask God" says James 4:2. In our conversation with God it is perfectly proper to ask, because we are His children and he is our Father.

In verse 18, Paul commends both of these forms of prayer: "And pray in the Spirit on all occasions with all kinds of prayers and requests. With this in mind, be alert and always keep on praying for all the saints." The apostle is saying, in effect, "After you have put on the armor of God, then talk to God about it. Tell Him your reactions, tell Him how you feel, and ask Him for what you need."

THREE PRINCIPLES OF EFFECTIVE PRAYER

Prayer is often considered to be so high and holy that it has to be carried on in some artificial Elizabethan language or stentorian tone of voice. You hear this so frequently from pulpits. Pastors adopt what has well been called a "stained glass voice," and pray in an artificial manner as though God were far off in some distant corner of the universe. But prayer is simply a conversation with the Father as the apostle describes so beautifully in Philippians 4:6–7:

> Do not be anxious about anything, but in everything, by prayer and petition, with thanksgiving, present your requests to God. And the peace of God, which transcends all understanding, will guard your hearts and your minds in Christ Jesus.

In these few words, Paul gives us three simple principles for effective prayer:

Principle 1: Don't worry about anything. "Do not be anxious about anything," he says. In other words, replace worry with prayer. Many of us try to cure our worries with will-power alone. Some wag has written a poem about this approach to worry:

> I've joined the new "Don't Worry Club,"
> And now I hold my breath;
> I'm so scared I'm going to worry
> That I'm worried half to death.

But Paul presents us with a different solution to the worry problem. God doesn't expect us to banish worry by sheer will-power—He knows that is not humanly possible. That is why God has provided us with the full armor that Paul describes in Ephesians 6. The solution to worry is only possible when you have put on the armor of God. Worry cannot be defeated on any other basis. Worry comes from fear, and the only way to dissolve fear is with facts. To put on the armor of God is to face the facts of reality. It means that we acknowledge the fact that:

> Our belt of truth is buckled securely about our waist; we know we have found the truth of all things, the key to life, Jesus, the living Lord;

> Our breastplate of righteousness is in place, protecting our heart, our emotional well-being, enabling us to feel secure in God's care;

> Our feet are shod with the readiness that comes from the gospel of peace, and God's peace calms our anxieties and steadies us for the great spiritual battle;

> Our faith is our shield against the flaming arrows of the devil—against the fiery satanic attacks of doubt, fear, temptation, and worry;

> Our minds are protected by the helmet of our approaching salvation, our sure hope that God is at work right now to bring about a victorious conclusion to human history;

> Our hands wield the most powerful defensive and offensive weapon of all—the sword of the Spirit, the rhema-word of God.

Once we have examined and tested the reliability of our armor, then anxiety has to vanish, to be replaced by courageous faith. Once we have faced the facts of our faith, we have nothing to worry about.

We serve our Lord and Commander, Jesus Christ, and the battle is His, not ours. He will be victorious.

That is Principle 1: Don't worry about anything.

Principle 2: Pray about everything. Everything? Yes, everything! "In everything," says Paul, "by prayer and petition, with thanksgiving, present your requests to God." You might ask, "You mean God is interested in little things, as well as big things?" Absolutely. All things matter to God. He is interested in the things that interest us. The Scriptures even tell us that the hairs on our head are numbered by Him. God is involved in the most minute details of our life—everything from cancer to lost car keys. So take everything to Him to prayer. Whatever is on your mind, talk it over with Him.

Principle 3: Prayer brings amazing peace. What is the result when you pray? Paul says, "And the peace of God, which transcends all understanding, will guard your hearts and your minds in Christ Jesus." No one can explain this peace. It does not arise out of altered circumstances—in fact, it is available to us in even the worst, most hopeless circumstances. It is inexplicable. There is nothing we need more in this troubled, anxious, fretful, weary, disturbed world than God's amazing, unexplainable peace.

When we pray we recognize the existence of the invisible kingdom of God. We would never pray if we didn't believe Someone is listening, that the invisible realm is the realm of reality. It surrounds us on every side. Though we do not see it, we recognize it and we have confidence that an invisible God directly affects our lives in the visible realm. We know that if we want to change the visibilities, we must start with the invisibilities.

Satan hates it when we pray, because he knows that God answers prayer. Our prayers play a direct and essential part in bringing God's invisible power to bear on visible life. Prayer is purposeful and powerful. It is not the pitiful, pathetic, last-ditch pleading that many people think it to be. No, prayer is powerful, because it links you and me, mere mortal human beings, with the ultimate, infinite power of the universe. God intervenes in human affairs as His people pray.

OUR PRAYERS AND GOD'S PROMISE

We must immediately add that God answers prayer according to His promises—not necessarily according to our wishes and our timetable. This is so necessary to say today, because there are people who take a "name it and claim it" approach to prayer, which says that if we have "enough faith," God gives us whatever we ask for. First, this kind of thinking reduces God to a mere genie in a bottle, doing human bidding, granting human wishes. Second, this false idea of prayer often results in disappointment and gives rise to the widespread belief that prayer is ineffectual. The truth is, God answers every prayer that is based upon a promise.

Prayer does not start with us; it starts with God. God must say He will do something before we are free to ask him to do it. That, of course, is how the father-child relationship is supposed to work. No parent commits himself to give his children everything they want and anything they ask for. He makes it clear that he will do certain things and not do other things. In the realm of those limits, the father commits himself to answer his children's requests. So it is with God. God has given promises and they form the only proper basis for our requests in prayer.

This is what Paul means by his reminder in verse 18 that we are to pray at all times in the Spirit. Here again is a point of great misunderstanding about prayer. Many take Paul's phrase, "in the Spirit," as though it were descriptive of the emotions we should have when we pray. They think it is necessary to be emotionally moved before prayer can be effectual. Certainly, prayer often does engage our emotions at a deep level, but emotionalism is not the key to effective prayer—and it is certainly not what is meant by this phrase, "in the Spirit."

To pray in the Spirit means to pray according to the promises that the Spirit has given and according to the character of God which the Spirit has made known. God has never promised to answer just any prayer, but He does promise to answer prayer in a way that He has carefully outlined for us. He does so invariably and without partiality. He is no respecter of persons in this matter of prayer. In the realm of our personal needs (those needs that call forth most of our prayers), the need for wisdom, power, patience, grace, or strength, God promises to answer our prayers immediately.

It is important to remember that prayer is not just something we do for ourselves. We must remember to support others in the spiritual battle. We are not alone on this battleground of doubt, fear, confusion, anxiety, and temptation. There are others around us who are weaker and younger in Christ than we are, and still others who are stronger than we are. Thus we must fight this battle together on our knees. We cannot put on the armor of God for another person, but we can pray for that other person. We can call in reinforcements when our brother or sister is overwhelmed by the enemy.

Praying for others is called *intercession*, and Paul lays out the principle of intercessory prayer in a very personal way in verses 19 and 20: "Pray also for me, that whenever I open my mouth, words may be given me so that I will fearlessly make known the mystery of the gospel, for which I am an ambassador in chains. Pray that I may declare it fearlessly, as I should." A parallel passage where Paul asks fellow Christians for prayer is Romans 15:30–32:

> I urge you, brothers, by our Lord Jesus Christ and by the love of the Spirit, to join me in my struggle by praying to God for me. Pray that I may be rescued from the unbelievers in Judea and that my service in Jerusalem may be acceptable to the saints there, so that by God's will I may come to you with joy and together with you be refreshed.

In this passage, Paul asks his fellow Christians to pray for three things on his behalf: (1) Paul's physical safety when he visits Jerusalem; (2) a sensitive, tactful spirit when he speaks to the Christians there; and (3) an opportunity to visit the believers in the city of Rome. Here are three specific requests—and the record of Scripture is that each of them was answered exactly as Paul had asked.

At the same time, we have to acknowledge that God's answers to prayer don't always come in the form or at the time that we expect. Someone has wisely said, "God is never late—but He's never early, either." It's true. God is always right on time. He may not *seem* to be on time by your watch and mine, but that's because we are impatient and don't know all the facts, not because God is late. Time is a factor that God alone controls.

God constantly calls us to a ministry of prayer, both for ourselves and for one another. When we learn to pray as God teaches us to pray, we release in our own lives and in the lives of others the immense resources of God—resources to strengthen the spirit and embolden the soul to meet the pressures and problems of life.

LOOKING TO THE END

Paul closes his letter with a few personal notes to his beloved friends in Ephesus:

> Tychicus, the dear brother and faithful servant in the Lord, will tell you everything, so that you also may know how I am and what I am doing. I am sending him to you for this very purpose, that you may know how we are, and that he may encourage you.
>
> Peace to the brothers, and love with faith from God the Father and the Lord Jesus Christ. Grace to all who love our Lord Jesus Christ with an undying love.

Paul has given the Ephesian believers a powerful, practical message on Christian living, concluding with a call to arms and a challenge to prepare for the greatest battle in history. He concludes by commending to them his friend Tychicus—the man to whom Paul dictated this letter, and the one who hand-delivered it to the Ephesian church. Along with Tychicus, Paul sent his encouragement and prayers for peace, love, faith, and grace from God the Father and His Son, Jesus Christ.

Picture Paul, confined by the Roman Caesar, yet considering himself a prisoner of Jesus Christ himself. What can he do for his Ephesian friends from that rented room? He is living under house arrest, chained day and night to a soldier. He is reduced from a globe-trotting missionary to a mere writer of letters. Yet Paul still has a profound ministry for Christ. He is still on the front lines of the great war between Christ and the prince of darkness.

All Paul could do was write letters—but *what* letters! The letter to the Ephesians was circulated around Asia Minor and beyond. It was copied and recopied, read in church after church. Ultimately, it was handed down to you and me. For generations, Christians have read the stirring, life-changing words of this letter and have armed themselves for battle with the full armor of God. Through Ephesians and other letters he wrote, the ministry of Paul radiated out from that stuffy little room in Rome, and it resounded around the world and down through the ages.

Paul was a good soldier of Jesus Christ. He put on his armor. He made his stand. He fought the good fight in the strength of Christ. He helped bring the devil a little closer to his ultimate defeat.

Satan probably thought he finally bottled Paul up in that little room. He figured he had finally gotten Paul out of the way. But Satan was wrong about Paul, just as he's been wrong about so many things. When Satan tried to shut Paul up, he over-reached himself.

That is the devil's fatal flaw. Whenever Christians stand on the ground of faith, the devil always over-reaches himself and goes too far. He commits himself to extremes—and therein lie the seeds of his defeat. Sooner or later, the truth becomes apparent. Because God is truth and God never changes, truth must finally prevail. The devil will ultimately be defeated if Christians simply stand on God's truth.

The devil over-reached himself when he thought he had destroyed Jesus on the cross. For a few hours, that bloody wooden cross looked like Satan's supreme achievement. All the powers of darkness howled with glee as they saw the Son of God lifeless and broken upon the crude instrument of torture. Satan, it seemed, had won.

Yet that was, in fact, the very moment when the devil lost everything. On the cross, the fate of Satan was forever sealed, his power destroyed. This is what God does in every aspect of life. Whenever the devil sends sickness, death, darkness, suffering, and defeat, whenever it appears that Satan has won—that is when God is working to engineer His marvelous victory. God takes the worst that Satan can throw at us, and He uses it to strengthen and bless us, to teach and enlarge us. Again and again, Satan does his worst, thinking he has finally managed to destroy us—but when the dust clears, we are still standing.

One of these days, the Bible says, the struggle will end. The Lord will come, and the events recorded in the book of Revelation will finally bring history to a close, with all its war and struggle and suffering. The struggle will end for the devil in the lake of fire—but it will end for you and me in unimaginable glory, joy, and peace. We who have endured the battle wearing the helmet of our hoped-for salvation will finally see that salvation in all its glory, and a loud voice in heaven will say, "Now have come the salvation and the power and the kingdom of our God, and the authority of his Christ. For the accuser of our brothers, who accuses them before our God day and night, has been hurled down. They overcame him by the blood of the Lamb and by the word of their testimony; they did not love their lives so much as to shrink from death" (Revelation 12:10–11).

For a little while longer, as the day grows more evil, we must endure and fight the battle here on Planet Earth. But we eagerly look toward the end, toward our salvation, toward the triumphant return of our Lord and Commander, Jesus Christ.

As you make your stand for Him, my prayer for you is nothing less than Paul's prayer for his Ephesian brothers and sisters: "Peace to the brothers, and love with faith from God the Father and the Lord Jesus Christ. Grace to all who love our Lord Jesus Christ with an undying love."

Note to the Reader

The publisher invites you to share your response to the message of this book by writing Discovery House Publishers, PO Box 3566, Grand Rapids, MI 49501, USA. For information about other Discovery House books, music, videos, or DVDs, contact us at the same address or call 1–800–653–8333. Find us on the Internet at http://www.dhp. org/ or send e-mail to books@dhp.org.